Freefall

Freefall

The Strange
True Life
Growing Up
Adventures
of

ORAN CANFIELD

EBURY
PRESS

3 5 7 9 10 8 6 4 2

First published in the UK in 2010 by Ebury Press,
an imprint of Ebury Publishing
A Random House Group company
Published in the United States as *Long Past Stopping*

The Random House Group Limited Reg. No. 954009

Addresses for companies within the Random House Group can be found at
www.randomhouse.co.uk

A CIP catalogue record for this book is available from the British Library

The Random House Group Limited supports The Forest Stewardship Council
(FSC), the leading international forest certification organisation. All our titles that
are printed on Greenpeace approved FSC certified paper carry the FSC logo.
Our paper procurement policy can be found at www.rbooks.co.uk/environment

Mixed Sources
Product group from well-managed
forests and other controlled sources
www.fsc.org Cert no. TT-COC-2139
© 1996 Forest Stewardship Council

Printed and bound in Great Britain by Clays Ltd, St Ives PLC

ISBN 9780091924553

To buy books by your favourite authors and register for offers visit
www.rbooks.co.uk

disclaimer

This book is a work of non-fiction based on the life, experiences and recollections of the author. In some limited cases names of people, places, dates, sequences or the detail of events have been changed to protect the privacy of others.

For Kyle and Christopher

contents

Contents

Freefall

prologue

In which our speaker begins to weave his
yarn in a cellar full of strangers

U M . . . MY NAME'S ORAN, and . . ." I begin to say into a micro-
phone, before cringing at the sound of my own voice and then drawing a complete blank. My whole day has been spent obsessing on what
I'm going to say, and even though I've done this a few times, I'm still
deathly afraid of speaking in front of people. My mind is jumping all over
the place from my childhood, to my drug-using period, to the last seven
years in which I've managed to stay clean, and back again.

It's a hell of a lot to think about, and I have no idea where to start,
until someone in the front jars me out of it by whispering, "Start at the
beginning."

one

*In which our protagonist sets foot in this
world, survives a nuclear meltdown,
and learns the secrets of juggling from a
traveling group of hippies*

A S FAR AS I KNEW, life started when I was four. I don't have any
memories from before that. It was as if I had walked into the theater
halfway through the movie and had to pay extraspecial attention to figure out was going on.

There were three of us in a big house somewhere near Philadelphia,
and there was a pool and a kitchen drawer full of sugar. The woman with
the long dark braids wearing Guatemalan clothes was my mom, and
the kid crawling around on all fours in a Guatemalan skirt was my brother,
Kyle. There was another character who hadn't yet made an appearance,
but his name came up almost daily. His name was Jack, and from
everything I'd heard he was the lying, cheating, conniving, manipulative,
inhuman son of a bitch who had left my mom when I was one and she
was six months pregnant with Kyle. I didn't know what kind of clothes
Jack wore, but in my imagination he had red skin and horns.

I watched and I listened, and Mom filled me in on the parts I had
missed.

I WAS BORN AT HOME in a small town in western Massachusetts,
where my parents had recently opened up a holistic health center.
Present at the birth were my mother, my father, a midwife, and ten Bud-

dhist monks from the monastery up the road. The monks were there to chant throughout my delivery.

"Oh, it was so beautiful, Oran. Really just an amazing experience," Mom told me when I was old enough to understand such things. "You were big, though. It took you seventy-two hours to come out and I had to go straight to the hospital afterward. When I got back, we ate the placenta."

"You what?" I asked.

"Of course, honey. That's where all the nutrients are stored for the breast milk. Humans are the only mammals that don't eat the placenta after they give birth."

I took her word for it.

"We've become so detached from nature we're losing our natural instincts. I mean, can you believe that people have their babies in hospitals, under all those fluorescent lights, and the first thing they do is spank you to make you cry? Then they take you away from your mother and they cut off your foreskin? It's barbaric. No way was I going to put you through that. Seriously, the very first thing they do is hit you and then cut off part of your penis." The way she put it, it did sound like a pretty crappy reception.

"Did you cook it?" I asked about the placenta.

"Oh, yeah. We fried it up with some butter. It's kind of like steak."

"Then what?"

"Well, you know, we were extremely busy running this business and taking care of a staff of twenty-five people, so all day you were passed around among the fifty or so people at The Center. Everyone loved you."

In between leading primal or scream therapy sessions, Mom would breast-feed me, or Jack would walk around with me strapped to his chest reading poems he had written. But for the most part, a community of weird therapists, early self-help freaks, and drug-experimenting hippies took care of me.

"It was really an incredible time," she said with a distant look in her eyes.

A YEAR AFTER I WAS BORN, when Mom was pregnant with Kyle, Jack hooked up with the masseuse employed at The Center. He decided that my mom's birthday was as good a day as any to tell her he was in love with someone else and she should probably pack up and leave.

"I didn't know what to do," Mom told me. "After the divorce, we got in the camper and I just started driving. I didn't know where to go, so we just drove around the country."

Kyle was born in a hotel in Mexico, delivered by the town doctor. Mom decided that it might be nice to cook up the placenta with some onions and bell peppers this time. She invited Jack to come down and see his son, but she never got a response. She went back to the States just long enough to take care of Kyle's paperwork and was told by a pediatrician that he was most likely both retarded and a midget, but that it would be a few years before either was noticeable.

Devastated, aimless, and alone with two kids, she decided to continue south to Guatemala, because of a rumor that the Nestlé Corporation was trying to get the Indians to quit breast-feeding and use their scientifically engineered baby formula instead. We moved to an area called Panajachel on a huge lake surrounded by seven villages, each with its own language. With only gutter water to mix with the formula, these Guatemalan babies were dying from all manner of disease. Mom rented a house near a big lake and began her one-woman crusade against Nestlé.

In the beginning, she walked around from village to village wearing a Guatemalan dress and combat boots with Kyle strapped to her chest and me riding on her back. After a catastrophic earthquake that killed twelve thousand people, we were left at home while she went around educating the natives on the benefits of breast-feeding and the evils of American corporations.

"The earthquake was unbelievable," she said. "You were fine, but Kyle almost died. He was only a few months old and his lungs couldn't handle all the dust in the air. When we got to the hospital, they tried to turn us away because they were so full, but when they saw Kyle, they agreed to take him in. We slept in the hall for three days. When we got back home, the house had been taken over by a bunch of Indian families who had lost their huts in the earthquake. It worked out, though, because they were more than happy to take care of you guys while I went out to work."

I loved listening to these adventure stories, and I wished I could remember being there because they sounded like fun.

AFTER TWO YEARS of living in Mexico and Central America, Mom was ready to come back to the States and start her own therapy practice in Philadelphia. For the first few months we lived in a house that belonged to some friends of hers while she looked for a place to start her new therapy center. While we were there I managed to eat an entire drawer full of sugar. Mom thought I liked to climb on top of bookshelves and run around in circles because I was a curious and active kid. The truth was that I was high on the refined sugar that I ate by the handful. I knew it was wrong, but I couldn't help myself. When the high wore off, I'd find a closet or a cupboard to hide in.

We moved from there to an old three-story mansion she bought in the suburbs. In a matter of months her new center was teeming with clients. She liked the house because it was made of stone, and it was a stone house that had saved our lives in Guatemala when the earthquake hit.

The new house had tons of new closets and cupboards to explore. Mom would find me and ask, "Ory, what are you doing under the sink?" or "Hey, Oran, what's going on down there?" I'd poke my head out from under a bed, and she would just kind of laugh at me. If I really didn't want to be found, I would go into a closet and cover my whole body with a pile of clothes, but this would usually instigate some sort of panic and I would have to get out of the closet without being seen and find another hiding place where Mom *could* find me so I wouldn't have to answer any questions about where I'd been. She was confused when she found me in a spot she had already checked.

"Seriously, Oran. Is there something going on in there I should know about?" Mom would ask.

I didn't have an answer for her.

I LIKED MY SPOT ON THE STAIRS, where I could watch Mom's clients come and go. It was right between the first floor and the landing. It faced the front door and gave me a view of the dining room on the right and the entrance to the conference room on the left. I found that I could just hide out inside of my head instead of the closet or cupboard. For the most part none of Mom's clients ever seemed to notice me there; it was almost as good as hiding in a cupboard.

That's where I was sitting when Jack walked in. When Mom told me he would be coming, I expected to see a monster with fangs and horns, but Jack looked just like everyone else who came to the house: khaki pants, tucked-in blue shirt, short hair.

We weren't big huggers around that house, but Jack came up with his arms open and, not knowing what to do, I mimicked him and found myself on the receiving end of his uncomfortably long embrace.

"Oran? I'm Jack, your father."

"Hi" was all I could think of to say.

"You're getting so big I hardly recognized you. What are you, five years old now?"

"Four," I answered.

"Where's Oran?"

"I'm Oran."

"I mean Kyle . . . your brother."

"Outside," I answered.

I was content to stay on the stairs while Jack went out to find Kyle, but Mom's face made it clear that I was to follow them outside.

"Hey, Oran. I hardly recognized you, you're so big," he said to Kyle. Kyle glanced at him for a second before going back to playing with a pile of pinecones he'd collected.

"That's Kyle," Mom said.

"I mean Kyle. Hey, Kyle, how old are you now?" he asked, walking over to him. Kyle wasn't doing too much talking yet and seemed not to hear him.

"He's three," I answered for him.

"How can he be three if you're four?" he asked, visibly confused. Truth be told, I was confused about that, too. Some of the time I was two years older.

"They're eighteen months apart. Remember, Jack, how I wanted them to be close in age so they could be friends?"

Jack nodded, but it didn't look as if he remembered much of anything about us. I was surprised that Mom was being so nice to him considering all the time she spent ranting and raving about what an evil monster he was. "Can you imagine leaving your wife when she's six months pregnant and taking care of a one-year-old?" she often asked me. I always shook my head. "I really thought he was different. What a fool I was. They're all the same. He used to read me these love poems—he wrote wonderful poems, by the way. Then on my birthday he took me to the lake house, and that's when he told me he was sleeping with that blond masseuse, and I cried and told him we could work it out, and he said it was over, that he was in love with her. Can you believe it?" Again I shook my head.

That's about all I knew about this guy, and I was relieved when he left and I got to go back to my stairs.

A MONTH LATER THERE was a meltdown at a nuclear power plant a hundred miles away, and, not knowing the extent of the damage, Mom wanted to get Kyle and me out of the area. Mom alternated between screaming and crying on her office phone. "These are your sons, Jack! Well, of course the government is going to say that, but no one really knows how bad it is. That's why you need to come down and get your kids out of here now!" She was still sniffling when she came out to help me pack up my stuff. "So, Ory, Jack has agreed to take you, and Grandma Ada is coming to get Kyle."

"Why can't I go with Grandma?" I asked.

"Because you and Kyle need to start having a relationship with your father. I just thought maybe I was wrong about him and he would come get you guys, but he's too busy to take care of his own kids," she said, choking up. "I had to plead with him just to get him to take you! Can you believe it?" I shook my head.

O NE OF JACK'S FRIENDS picked me up from the train station, and a few days later Jack came and took me to the therapeutic center in Massachusetts that he and my mom had started. He was the main guy there, but beyond that I didn't have any idea what exactly he did. A bunch of adults would go into a room with him and emerge a few hours later. That part was no different from what my mom did in Philadelphia, and I felt lucky that, with two parents who fixed other people, I would never have any problems of my own.

I got to see the room I was born in, and the lake house where he told Mom it was over, and just as Mom had described it, Jack was so busy that I was passed around to the staff, who watched me for a few days until the experts declared that it was safe to return to Pennsylvania.

W HEN I GOT BACK, MOM was concerned that sitting on the stairs all day wasn't good for me, so she hired a piano teacher, sent me to school, and tried to expose me to the arts, science, and nature. I couldn't understand what the problem was. Everything seemed fine to me, but she thought it was bad that I didn't talk to anyone and claimed that she had never seen me smile. She was right for the most part, but what was so bad about not smiling? Plus it wasn't totally true. Mom was a busy woman, running her new center, appearing on television, doing panel discussions, playing music. She was so busy she had to hire someone to take care of us. I smiled when Laurel, our Jamaican housekeeper, would sneak Kyle and me into her room to let us watch TV and give us ice cream. Laurel would have been fired in a second if Mom found out she had given us something containing processed sugar, not to mention let us watch TV, so we kept it a secret.

Laurel worked her ass off for us, but she did get a couple of nights a week to go spend with her family. This was kind of traumatic for Kyle and me, because it meant no TV and ice cream after Mom left for the night to go play piano at one of her jam sessions. Bob, the psychoanalyst who rented a room upstairs, was always around, but we didn't like him too much. We would make the best of it by going through the stacks of records Mom would bring back from her trips to New York. She called it "rap" music, and Kyle and I could listen to these records for hours. We would memorize the lyrics and make up dance routines.

Like almost everything else that seemed normal to us, such as carob, tofu, macrobiotics, Rolfing, homeopathy, and Gestalt therapy, I didn't know anyone who had ever heard of rap music. Laurel hated it, though, and would go into one of her fits if she heard us listening to it. "Lord have mercy on my soul. Turn off dat racket, boys. I don't know what has become of black folks in dis country. Dey call dat music? And what you white boys listenin' to dis for? Your mother is a crazy woman, going to New York and carrying on the way she do. Lord have mercy on *your* souls is more like it. I'm going to pray for you boys. It's too late for your mother. Prayer won't help dat woman. I don't know what will." We listened to Laurel in the same way we listened to our rap albums. It didn't matter what she was saying, we were mesmerized by the rhythm of her voice, her accent, and her way with words.

Sometimes if we were lucky, Mom would bring us along to her jam sessions in the heart of West Philly. She may not have been able to see me smile from her place behind the piano, but I couldn't help but grin from ear to ear seeing her on the stage. At the bar, she was no longer Dr. Canfield, the accomplished doctor of psychology who was engaged in a one-woman battle against the Man. At the bar they called her the "doctor," and when we walked in everybody knew it. I don't think any white folks had ever set foot in that place; at least I had never seen one, but you couldn't imagine a warmer reception. Everyone seemed to know and like Mom. All the other musicians rotated from song to song, but Mom stayed up there for three hours at a time. She always asked someone, usually whoever was closest to the door, to keep an eye on us, but once the novelty of trying to talk to the two socially retarded white kids wore off, we would never see that person again. It didn't matter much; we just stood on top of the table, watching Mom until we got tired and climbed back down to the booth. At 2:00 A.M. or so she would wake us up and say good-bye to everyone, and we would get in the Peugeot and drive home.

I N AN EFFORT TO EXPOSE Kyle and me to some of the stranger opportunities for American kids, Mom sent us off to a circus-arts camp in New York the summer I turned seven years old. The camp was run by '60s icon Wavy Gravy and his partner.

The circus camp offered classes in tightrope walking, juggling, acrobatics, and magic. Since Wavy didn't really have any skills, circus or otherwise, he played a one-stringed instrument he called a unitar and taught a class called Space Eaters, which could be loosely described as an acting class for the other kids like himself who didn't possess, or have any interest in acquiring, the skills for the more technical circus arts.

I'm not sure what it was that drew me to juggling. I was equally bad at everything I tried to do, but aside from tightrope walking, which was limited in how far you could take it, juggling had less of a performance aspect than most of the other classes. True, you did have to do it front of people, but the clowns had to act goofy, and the magicians had to talk to the audience, and juggling seemed like less work than acrobatics and trapeze. It was kind of like staring into space all day.

Most kids either learned to juggle in a couple of days or just gave up. Three days into it, I could barely throw one ball back and forth, but I had figured out that if I spent the whole day at least trying, no one would talk to me. Occasionally one of the teachers would offer a few words of advice, but for the most part it was the first thing I had found that made *not* talking to anyone socially acceptable. So I kept at it despite not being very good.

By the time my mom came back for the big performance, I had been at it for a week and could keep three balls in the air for a minute or so. I had never performed in front of an audience before, and just the thought of standing in front of a crowd of people made me want to vomit. How the hell could I focus on keeping those balls in the air, when I couldn't even keep my knees from shaking? Unable to think of a way out of it, I walked onto the stage, and for almost one minute I forgot about the audience because it was all I could do to focus on the juggling. And despite myself, I actually smiled.

I DIDN'T KNOW AT THE time that a smile could so drastically change the course of my life. If I had known, I wouldn't have done it, but to judge by my mom's reaction, it was as if Christ himself had come down from the heavens. Actually, Christ coming down would have just pissed her off. It was as if the whole world had just been enlightened by the smile of her seven-year-old son. As a result of this smile, I rather suddenly found myself with an identity, a social network—if you could call it that—and a reason for my existence.

On our return to Philly, Mom lost no time researching the juggling scene, finding out where they met, and who was the best teacher in the city. At that point, I didn't need any outside motivation. As soon as I realized that I could isolate myself in the backyard with my juggling balls, and my new unicycle, without anyone bothering me, I was there. And I stayed there for the next year. Nonetheless, Mom found the best juggler in Philadelphia, and I would go over to his place a couple of times a week for lessons. Fu was a very short Vietnamese immigrant, not much taller than myself, who could juggle seven balls. At the time, there were only four or five people in the world who were capable of that, and all of them seemed to be pretty successful, but Fu didn't use his powers for fame or money. Like me, he just juggled in his backyard. My lessons, however, seemed to have very little to do with juggling. They pretty much consisted of listening to long monologues in his broken English about flow, balance, becoming one with the objects I was juggling, and tuning into the natural order of things. What I actually learned was to tune out and nod my head as if I were listening (which I came to find was also a very useful skill).

Much to my mom's relief, I began talking to people at the juggling meets in Franklin Square, and even made a friend my own age at school. Life was moving along, and aside from the minor things like not being allowed to watch TV or eat anything with sugar, dairy, wheat, chocolate, or meat in it; or having to wait twenty minutes after we ate to drink a glass of water; or not getting our immunizations; or not seeing any Western doctors (even when a car hit me at fifty miles per hour right across the street from the Children's Hospital); or not being allowed to play competitive sports; or finally, being the bastard children of the great white devil himself, who was not a red man with horns like I had thought, but actually a white guy somewhere up in Massachusetts who was posing as a motivational speaker—aside from these small things, there was, in retrospect, a sense of normalcy that we would never experience again.

two

*In which a young man is introduced to the
pleasures of a dark substance, through the
benevolence of a learned professor*

I WAS A TWENTY-THREE-YEAR-OLD art-school dropout living
in a storefront at Sixteenth and Mission streets in San Francisco when
I met Lawrence. He came in to my life like Satan in one of those little
Christian comic books that the Mexican women would hand out on the
street, the ones in which you get in a fight with your parents about not
going to church and suddenly Satan, disguised as a rock star, shows up at
the door with a crack pipe and says, "See, your parents don't understand
you, but I do . . ." Only instead of a crack pipe (that would come later),
Lawrence appeared with a piece of tinfoil, a drinking straw, and a dirty
brown lump of heroin.

My friend Jake, whom I had gone to school with at the San Francisco
Art Institute, had found the storefront about six months earlier, and there
were six of us—mostly artists and musicians—living there. Not knowing
anything about construction, we were still in the process of building our
rooms, learning as we went along. The place was close to six thousand
square feet including the basement, which was filled with two feet of
water when we moved in. Our goal was to eventually create a multipur-
pose space, where we could put on art shows and music events and have
room to work on our own projects as well.

As time passed, my initial excitement about the storefront was diminishing, and depression, which I had experienced in waves for as long as I could remember, was creeping back.

I tried to fight it off by keeping busy. Aside from continuing to work on the space to make it livable, I had taken on an internship with a piano restorer and was playing in my band, Optimist International, plus every Saturday, Eli (my roommate, high school friend, and bandmate) and I ran a music venue out of the large front part of the commercial space we were calling home, featuring experimental music by people who simply had nowhere else to play. We inherited the night from a restaurant in the neighborhood called Radio Valencia, which could no longer justify having three customers on what should have been their busiest night of the week. The owner didn't care so much about losing money, but that he was losing his employees. No one wanted to work a Saturday night shift only to make fifteen bucks in tips. So he donated fifty chairs and gave us his mailing list.

Everyone who lived at the space was encouraged to use it for public events. Jake, having gotten to a point where his art work was Pure Concept and could no longer be expressed through the making of objects, started granting one-month residencies to his ten-by-fifteen-foot studio, having no use for it anymore. His idea was to give artists some space to work for a month and afterward host a public showing of whatever it was they had made.

It was a good idea, considering that the studio wasn't being used. The dot-com boom had driven rents so high that it was getting harder to find both work and exhibition space in the city, but aside from coming in to have a look at the room at the beginning of the month, not one person actually used the space to do any work. Instead, these artists would spend their time talking and thinking about what they were going to do, and then they would talk some more. I couldn't help overhearing some of these conversations, as we still hadn't built our bedroom walls up to the ceiling yet. I'm not sure what was worse, listening to my friends talk about art or listening to them have sex.

"So Jake, listen to this idea," I heard a voice say one morning while I was still lying in bed. It was Erin, Jake's best friend and the visiting artist that month. "I get a suit, and change into it, and then I cut my hair, but I'm smoking cigarettes the whole time. Ha ha . . . What do you think?" Erin loved laughing at his own jokes, 90 percent of which were completely over my head.

"Yeah, that could be good," Jake agreed.

"You don't think it's too much like that piece what's his name did in Nayland Blake's class?" Erin asked.

"Well . . . I hadn't thought about that. I guess it does kind of seem like a similar idea on the surface, but the sweat suit he was wearing has a totally different connotation than the symbolism of a business suit."

"I don't know, heh, heh, it is pretty funny . . . but I'm wondering if it's too didactic?"

Didactic was a word that pissed me off; it was always being thrown around in art school. In fact, you couldn't have a real conversation about art without it, but I could never remember what it meant.

"I guess it depends on what your point is," Jake said. "If what you're trying to say is that we should all give up on art and get jobs, then yeah, I could see how some people might see it as being didactic, but if the statement is that cutting your hair and wearing a suit can be a form of artistic expression, then it could work."

"You don't think people will think I'm making some kind of a state-ment about Jeff Koons?"

"Maybe . . . but is it for or against?"

Then Erin started laughing again. "I know. What if I was telling jokes the whole time?"

Christ, I thought. *If they continue doing shit like this, they're both going to end up wearing a suit and working nine to five, and it's not going to be so funny.* Unable to listen to them anymore, I finally made a move to get out of bed. Erin must have heard my loft creak.

"Oh shit, was Oran asleep?" he whispered to Jake.

"Yeah, but it's one thirty. What am I supposed to do? Not talk in my own room?" He said it loud enough that it was obviously directed at me.

"Hey, go ahead and talk," I yelled back, "but I just want to let you guys know, you sound like total assholes!" I had always hated conceptual art, but since dropping out of school, I had become much more vocal about it. Jake and Erin had heard this from me so many times that they just ignored it.

A month later Erin showed up, cut his hair, put on a suit, smoked a cigarette, and told some jokes. The highlight was when he threw his still-lit cigarette butt into the surprisingly large crowd and it landed in some-one's hair.

The next month our neighbor Izzy, also known as the Sasquatch, got naked and poured champagne all over herself. The month after that, a girl I had never seen before showed up and banged her head against the wall until her forehead was a bloody mess.

I was always judgmental of these projects, but I tried my best to hold my tongue and be supportive if only to offset the fact that every Saturday night my roommates would go straight to their rooms and put on their headphones to avoid the racket coming from our weekly music event in the living room. They were as offended by my musical taste as I was by their art. The truth was that we were both lucky if we got even ten people to show up to one of our functions.

ASIDE FROM JAKE'S "residency program," he was also appealing to other artists in the community to come up with ideas for events. One such idea was from a visiting faculty member at the Art Institute who was also a professor at a neighboring university. Lawrence, while not exactly famous, had managed to make a name for himself in the art world back in the 1980s. I knew who he was because a couple of friends of mine, including Eli, had been in his films, and I had gone along to the shoots a few times in the past. I never saw a final version of any of these films, but the shoots always involved wearing weird colorful costumes, drinking lots of alcohol, and smoking brown lumps of heroin off of tinfoil with a straw. Since the heroin was technically a movie prop and I was not in the movies, I never got to try it.

I wasn't really interested in heroin anyway. I had tried it once when I was eighteen, and again a couple of years later when I was in a very short-lived relationship with a heroin addict. It wasn't bad; it was just that lying around completely immobilized didn't appeal to me. Granted, I was an art-school dropout, not a university professor, but I failed to see the concept or artistic value behind Lawrence's work. In my mind it was nothing more than an excuse to get together with a bunch of people and get fucked up—a theme party with a video camera. Jake, however, was excited that Lawrence wanted to shoot a film there.

He wanted to use the basement, which was flooded again, and still full of rusted, disintegrating metal shelving and other trash from the previous tenants. Because it was built below the water table of the creek that flows through San Francisco's Mission District, it was always wet. The water would drip out of the crumbling brick walls and seep up through the disintegrating foundation. The sump pump was always breaking down, causing six to twelve inches of stagnant water to accumulate, depending on how quickly we noticed it. Our basement was half a block long and sloped down toward the back, where most of the water came from. I would often ignore the flooding until it got within ten feet of my rehearsal studio, at which point I would take off my shoes and wade barefoot out into the darkness, trying to avoid sharp objects and grope around for the hole we had made for the pump, reaching down, sometimes almost to my shoulder, to free the switching mechanism from whatever it was caught on. This was always followed by a mad dash to the shower. Who knows what the fuck was in that water, but afterward any part of my body that had made contact with it was always covered in this light brown, translucent, oily substance.

When we had first moved in, there was also this white fluffy mold that covered almost everything in the basement. We made an attempt to brush it all off with a broom, but it was back the next day and we quickly gave up. Same with the various types of unidentifiable mushrooms growing out of the walls and cracks in the floor. The basement had a dark vibe, to say the least. Maybe that's why Lawrence wanted to use it. So after pumping out the water, consolidating the rusted shelving into a pile, and swapping out the one bare 60-watt lightbulb for a 120-watt one, the place was ready to go.

Lawrence arrived and set up a table underneath the lightbulb. Then he laid out a mirror with a razor blade on it, a piece of tinfoil, some pills that I think might have been Valium, a bottle of tequila, six canisters of nitrous oxide, a bong, a couple tabs of acid, a bottle of aspirin, a conductor's baton, and a colorful pile of little balloons. He began the task of ripping the balloons open, each of which contained a bag of coke and a bag of heroin. After separating the white bags from the brown ones, he emptied a bag of coke onto the mirror and put a lump of brown heroin on the foil. Then he set up his camcorder and waited for people to arrive.

Eventually, maybe twenty people showed up. It was hard to tell because it was so dark. You couldn't really see anyone unless they were within a few feet of the light, and it was so creepy that no one was really speaking above a whisper. At some point, Lawrence broke the awkward hush by standing under the light and telling us about the piece.

"So, this piece is called 'Composition for Mood Swings.' When you feel like it, come up to the table, take the baton, and point to whatever you want."

He then walked over to the camera, turned it on, and walked back to the table. Conductor's baton in hand, he looked straight at the camera and said, "Composition for Mood Swings," waving the baton around as if he were conducting an orchestra. Then he just stood there and waited. The first guy to walk up to the table grabbed the baton and pointed to the bottle of tequila and the aspirin. I'd already decided the piece was total bullshit, but as long as I was there, I was going to try something more interesting than that.

I stood by myself in the back corner, drinking a beer, until almost everyone had gone up and ingested the various drugs. When I finally made my way up there, the cocaine looked yellow and sticky, and the last thing I wanted to do was take acid or smoke pot. The only thing that looked at all intriguing was the heroin. I grabbed the baton and pointed to the tinfoil, but there wasn't much left. Lawrence handed me a straw, set his lighter under the foil, and I inhaled the last of it. Then I headed back to my dark corner and waited for something to happen, but I didn't notice anything different. I was as anxious and judgmental as ever.

Some more people pointed to a few more drugs, and when only the bottle of aspirin remained, everyone left.

A FEW NIGHTS LATER, Lawrence showed up at the house, which was a bit of a surprise since I was the only one home.

"Hey, Lawrence. Jake's actually at work right now."

"Oh, that's okay, I was just in the neighborhood and thought I would stop by," he said.

"Oh, did you leave something here the other night?"

"No, I just thought I'd come by and see what was going on." Lawrence made me very uncomfortable.

"Not much. I was just heading over to the Casanova," I said looking for an escape. The Casanova Lounge was a bar on Valencia Street where Eli bartended. I don't know how the place stayed in business. The owner seemed to want to draw a very specific crowd of fucked-up artists and musicians, but none of us ever had any money. So we would drink for free until two in the morning and mope about how shitty everything was.

"Hey, do you mind if I come in for a minute, and I'll head over there with you."

"Sure," I said, letting him in. I figured he needed to use the bathroom, but as soon as he got in the door, he pulled out a couple of balloons from his pocket and asked me if I wanted any before heading over to the bar. I figured, why not? I didn't feel anything the other night, and I was still kind of curious.

"Sure," I said. "Why don't we go to my room?"

Sitting down at my desk, he opened a balloon, unwrapped the cellophane from around the heroin, and broke off a lump of the brown sticky stuff, which he placed on a little piece of foil that came from his back pocket. He then reached behind his ear, producing a three-inch straw that was kind of melted and brown at one end. Being a gentleman, Lawrence handed me the foil and the straw, which I put in my mouth so I could get my own lighter out of my pocket. I ignited the lighter under the foil, and a big cloud of smoke came up before I could even inhale.

"No, no, no . . . You're doing it wrong. Here, let me show you."

I gave him the straw and foil, he put some more dope on it, and tilting it at an angle, he slowly brought the lighter up to it. As the black spot of heroin slid down the foil, a thin stream of smoke came up, which he followed with the straw.

"There" he said after exhaling. "That's called 'chasing the dragon.'"

He handed it back to me, and this time I managed to get some of it in my lungs. It tasted kind of sweet, like brown sugar or molasses. After another hit, I realized that I felt pretty good. It was nothing incredible. I was just kind of relaxed, and whatever discomfort I had felt about being with Lawrence disappeared.

"So, what did you think of the piece the other night?" Lawrence asked me.

This was perhaps my least favorite question in the world. At least 90 percent of the time it meant coming up with some sort of believable lie on the spot. Unless I truly liked the person's work, which was rare, that question always paralyzed me. Do I say what I really think and sound like an asshole? Or do I lie, and both avoid confrontation and come across as a supportive nice guy? The I-don't-give a-fuck-what-you-think vibe I tried so hard to present may have fooled some people, but I was extremely self-conscious and cared very much what people thought. Despite my frequent tirades about almost everyone and everything, I was actually a pretty nice guy.

This attitude, along with my terrible slouch, nicotine-stained fingers, perpetual five o'clock shadow, and all-around grumpy disposition, had earned me the nickname Cranberry. According to my friend David, who had come up with it, it was on account of my being "*so* sweet, but *so* sour." When Jake had asked me earlier that day, "Hey, Oran, what did you think of Lawrence's piece?" I responded without a moment's hesitation.

"I thought it was fucking terrible . . . a total piece of shit."

"Oh come on, Cranberry. I know you loved it."

"No. Really. It was fucking horrible," I said.

"Yeah, you're right," he had replied with a laugh. "It *was* pretty bad."

For being such an opinionated bastard, my vocabulary was somewhat limited when it came to expressing my distaste for most things, especially when it came to talking about art.

"Well . . ." I said hesitantly to Lawrence, "I'm not totally sure I understood the purpose of it, or what you were trying to achieve. How did you feel about it?" This was a classic avoidance technique I had seen many people use in art school, but only one person per critique could get away with it. This was my first attempt at using that trick and I was surprised at how well it worked.

"Do you know this painting, *The Ascension of Christ* by Rembrandt?"

"No, not that I remember anyway," I said.

"Well, it depicts an ascension into heaven, or a spiritual ascension, and I was attempting to replicate that idea of ascending to another plane of existence through the use of drugs instead of religion."

His explanation seemed somewhat hollow to me.

"I didn't really get that from it. I mean, thinking about it now . . ." because I was actually thinking instead of judging, "even if I did know that painting, I doubt I would have gotten the connection from what I saw. The only references I noticed were from the title of the piece, and the conductor's baton. Like I said, I don't remember seeing that painting so I can't comment on that, but I did get the musical reference. I just thought it was kind of obvious, and it didn't really speak to me."

He thought for a moment. "You know, you could have a point. If you haven't seen the Rembrandt painting, it *would* have a totally different meaning. I spend so much time in academic circles that I guess I wasn't even aware that someone wouldn't get the reference. On the other hand, is it the artist's responsibility to censor or limit his work because the audience may or may not have the same experiences or reference points? Or do I ignore that and be true to my own knowledge? I have to think about that," he said, putting the straw in his mouth and going for another hit.

"Hey, Lawrence. Where's your accent from? I can't place it." I finally wanted to get to the bottom of this.

"Oh, it's Hebrew," he answered.

"You're from Israel? You know there's a tree somewhere in Israel with my name on it."

"Yeah," he said. "Your name means 'tree' in Hebrew."

"No . . . I mean, yeah, I know that, but back in the '70s or something, my grandma gave money to some organization that would plant a tree in Israel and put your name on it. She got one for me and one for my brother."

"Yeah. I remember when they were doing that." He started laughing. "That's pretty funny, though. Your tree just says 'tree' on it."

"Yeah." I started laughing too. "I've never thought about how ridiculous that is." I motioned for Lawrence to pass me the tinfoil and I took another hit. "Man, this stuff is good," I said. "Isn't this shit pretty addictive, though?"

"Not if you smoke it. I've been smoking it now for thirteen years," he said.

I was skeptical about that.

"Really, so nothing happens when you leave town?" I asked.

"My nose seems to run a little when I'm flying somewhere, but I'm not sure if it's the chiva," he said, referring to the street name for heroin, "or the crappy air on those planes."

"Huh. That's interesting because I would have thought . . ."

He seemed pretty convinced, so I decided to let it go. At this point it was late. The Casanova was long closed and an incredible, warm, tired feeling had come over me.

"Hey, man, thanks for coming over. I think I'm about to pass out, though." I was suddenly very out of it, like everything was happening in slow motion.

"No problem, I had a good time hanging out. I'll stop by again some time," he said, getting up to leave.

I walked him to the door, and without taking off my clothes, went straight to bed. Lying there, teetering on the border of sleep, I became aware that something was definitely different now. There were still the muffled sounds from the residency hotel, the distant car alarms, and the rumbling of buses driving by, but there was also a strange sort of silence I had never noticed before.

three

*The adventures and misdeeds of the boy and
his brother on a dirt lot in New Mexico*

HEY, ORY . . . KYLE. Wake up, guys," my mom was saying. I struggled to open my eyes. The transition to the real world was always jarring, but I could tell something was weird. The first thing I noticed was that the light was different from when Mom usually got us out of bed: it was coming from a lightbulb rather than outside. It was pitch-dark out, and a glance at the digital clock said it was 5:00 A.M. Kyle was already sitting up, and I managed to do the same.

"Okay, guys, how would you like to take a trip to Santa Fe, New Mexico?" She said it as if we had won some sort of game-show prize, and we always fell for it. We were immediately wide-awake, jumping up and down on our beds with excitement. This was what we lived for. By the time other seven-year-olds were getting up to go to school, we would be in an airplane flying to Santa Fe.

"All right then. The plane is leaving in two hours, so let's pack up quick." Kyle and I threw some clothes in a couple of duffel bags, and a few minutes later, we were ready to go.

We flew into Albuquerque, rented a car, and drove up to Santa Fe. I still didn't have a clue what we were doing there. I'm not sure if it even occurred to me to ask. As far as I knew, my mom had some sort of psychology workshop out here and we were just along for the ride. Our drive ended when we pulled into a dirt lot with one cinder-block building and five trailers scattered over the three-acre property. A sign at the entrance said Santa Fe Community School. A bald guy came out of a trailer and showed us around. Since we were closest to the cinder-block building, he took us there first. The hallway was no more than twenty feet long and separated a classroom that he said we didn't need to worry about and a cafeteria that would be a good thing to remember since that's where we would be getting our food. I was confused because he was clearly talking to Kyle and me, and neither of us knew much about psychology, or whatever it was my mom came out here for. We continued our tour around the property, but there really wasn't a whole lot to see—mostly just dirt. The only other structure not on wheels (unless you counted the outhouses) was some kind of clubhouse that the students built out of scrap wood and old doors. Even though it was barely standing, Ed, the bald guy, was very proud of it.

"You see, the way it works here is that if we just kind of stay out of it, the kids come up with these kinds of incredible projects on their own, and they have a much more meaningful experience that way than if they do something just because an adult tells them to," Ed was saying, this time to my mom, which was a relief.

"Likewise," he continued, "we have the same attitude about the kids getting into trouble. For example, if all we do is lay down rules and regulations—well, you're a parent, you know how smart kids can be—the kids don't get to experience the consequences of right and wrong actions for themselves. They either see the rules as arbitrary and rebel against them, or even worse, they might just do what they're told without questioning what's behind it. Either way, they don't get to experience that a wrong action can lead to negative consequences, and vice versa. The best way for a kid to learn is through experience."

My mom was beaming. "You really can't believe how wonderful this is. I mean, you just said it. Kids learn through experience, not memorizing state capitals. I've always raised my kids like that. You know, when Oran was around three he would just start climbing around on everything, and, instead of telling him to get down or shame him for it, I would just lay down a few pillows and let him figure it out for himself. I mean, he's either going to fall and not want to go up there again or he's going to learn to be more careful next time. If I yell at him, all he learns to be afraid of is me."

"And that's exactly how we approach the educational process here," Ed said.

They kept talking while he showed us the water pump and the

outhouses. I had rarely seen my mom interact with someone so enthusiastically. Eventually, he led us to the only tree on the whole property and a trampoline just lying flat on the ground next to it. Trampolines were one of the few things that brought out something resembling visible excitement in me, and I was extremely disappointed that it wasn't set up.

"You want to jump on it?" Ed said to me. "Go ahead."

After all that talk of learning through experience and falling off things, I thought this was one of those lessons. As if I would go jump on a trampoline that was on the ground. There's nothing like that sound your teeth make when you misjudge a jump, or think you have reached the bottom of a stairway only to find out there's one more step.

"Seriously, you can go jump on it if you want to. You can do whatever you want here."

"Yeah, Ory. You love trampolines. Go jump on it . . . if you want to," she was quick to add. I'd never heard her say that last part before, so it must have been for Ed's benefit.

"But it's not set up," I said.

"Yeah, where are the legs?" Kyle added.

"Ah, you've never seen one like this before? There's a big pit underneath. That way you don't have as far to go if you fall off. Another example of what kids can come up with if you let them fall off a regular trampoline enough times."

That's all we needed to hear. Both Kyle and I were racing to get there first. We were jumping around like maniacs, and as if to prove Ed's theories on experiential education, after a number of midair collisions, we started taking turns. I was so consumed with trying to do a backflip, I didn't realize that Ed and my mom had disappeared. By the time they returned, it was getting dark and I had come very close to landing the backflip a few times.

"Hey, guys, come here. Let's talk for a minute," she said. "So what do you think of this place? It's great, isn't it? Do you want to spend the night here?"

She was using her you-just-won-a-prize voice again. My mind was still consumed with the trampoline, or more specifically the proximity of the tree to the trampoline. It seemed that, if you gauged the jump just right, you could probably make it, but it was hard to tell where you would land afterward. If we spent the night, though, I could work out that problem the next day.

"Okay, where are we staying?" I asked.

"Well, you guys are going to stay in that trailer over there with a very nice woman named Carol. She's getting a room ready for you now. I'm going to go get a hotel room, and I'll see you guys in the morning."

"Why don't we stay with you, and we can all come back in the morning?" I asked, confused about why we had to stay with a woman we had never met before.

"Or you can stay here with us, Mom," Kyle offered.

"No, I can't stay here, but I just thought you guys would rather stay here, where it's fun, than come to the hotel where it's boring."

She had this way of telling you what it was you were supposed to do without actually telling you to do it. The choice was apparently between fun and boredom, and as much as I just wanted to go to the hotel with my mom, I knew that the *right* answer was "fun." As subtle as it may have seemed to an outside observer, I knew she wasn't asking us; she was telling us.

"Okay, guys? Let's go meet Carol."

When we got to the trailer, our bags had already been taken in, confirming my suspicion that we never had a choice to begin with. After introducing us to this woman, Mom hugged us and went to the hotel. Carol must have been in her late thirties and had short sandy hair. She seemed nice, but also kind of uninterested in us.

"Okay, so this is going to be your room back here," she said, leading us to the very end of the trailer, past a tiny bathroom with what looked like an operational toilet. By now I was certain there was more going on than Kyle and I had been told. It was all too weird, starting with Ed telling us where we would be eating, to my mom telling us in her matter-of-fact way how much we loved this place, to Carol referring to this little six-by-six-foot cubicle as "your room."

"So go ahead and get settled in, and when you're done, you can come out and watch TV. I know your mom said it's not allowed, but we just won't tell her. Okay?"

"Okay," we agreed, dropping our bags and following her back out to the living room–office.

"Aren't you going to put your things away?" she asked, noticing that we were right behind her.

"Our mom is coming to pick us up in the morning, so we would just have to pack everything back up," I said, but at this point I wasn't so convinced.

"Oh?" She was obviously surprised.

"Yeah, she's coming back. Where's the TV?" Kyle said, cutting to the chase.

"Okay, here's the TV, but you have to keep it on low because I have some work to do, and remember, don't tell your mom. She was very clear about not letting you watch TV."

MOM CAME BACK the next morning as promised and found us back on the trampoline.

"Hey, guys. How was your night? This place is really great, right? It just has a really, really good vibe, doesn't it? I mean, Ed and Carol are really amazing people."

My brain was consumed with thoughts of backflips and jumping off trees, so I wasn't really listening to her, just nodding when it seemed appropriate. But what was there to complain about when you had TVs and trampolines? I had to agree: it seemed like a great place.

"Okay. So my plane is leaving Albuquerque in a few hours, so I've really got to get going. I'll call you tonight when I get back to Philly."

The whole thing was too big for our little brains to comprehend. She might as well have been saying, "Have a good day at school, I'll be back to pick you up at three." She hugged us, walked back to the car, and drove away.

We continued taking turns on the trampoline, and when we got hungry, we went back to the trailer and ate sandwiches. Then we jumped on the trampoline some more, ate dinner with Carol, watched TV, and went to bed. We went through the exact same routine the next day, neither of us commenting on the fact that our mom had just disappeared and left us on a deserted lot in New Mexico.

I COULD HAVE LIVED with this routine of eating, sleeping, playing with Kyle, and not talking to anyone forever, but on Monday morning we were woken up at eight thirty and told to eat something now, or we would have to wait until lunch. I did my best to keep human interaction to a minimum, so without saying a word, we got up, made bowls of Cheerios, and were halfway through eating them, when Carol told us we had to go.

"Can I finish my Cheerios?" Kyle asked her.

"No. Sorry. It's nine o'clock, you have to leave. You can come back at three."

"Can I just use the bathroom real quick?" I asked.

"No. You can use one of the outhouses, though. At three you can come back and use this one."

I was no stranger to getting rushed out of the house, as my mom was always running late for everything, but I had never been rushed like this, for absolutely nothing. She ushered us out, closed the door, and just left us standing there on the little wood landing of the trailer. Still waking up, we watched as a few older kids ran toward the cinder-block building. And then dead silence, just as it had been over the weekend. What were we late for? Did we miss something? Was there somewhere we were supposed to be? What the hell just happened? Should we go to the building? I had a million questions. Kyle seemed equally confused, so I decided to knock on the door and ask Carol what was going on. There was no answer. I tried knocking again, and again we were answered by silence. I tried the doorknob out of curiosity and wasn't at all surprised to find it locked. We just sat down on the stairs and waited. I had just traded my stairway in Philly for a new one in Santa Fe.

We sat there for hours, not knowing what to do. Every so often some kids would come out of the cinder-block building, smoke cigarettes, and go back in. But aside from occasional glimpses from a few other kids off in the distance, nothing happened. At some point, maybe fifteen or twenty kids came out of the classroom and were standing around talking, but they were big scary kids. There was no way I was going to approach them for information. Eventually Ed walked by and said, "Hey, you guys want lunch?" We nodded our heads. "Well, you better get over to the cafeteria. You've got about five minutes. We stop serving food at one."

Kyle and I very tentatively walked over to the cafeteria. There were only a few people in there, as lunch was almost over. We grabbed a couple of paper bags off the counter and got the hell out of there. These kids seemed weird. They had long hair and wore sneakers with no laces and baseball hats with two long flaps coming off the back of them. I had never seen kids like these before. We got back to our steps at the trailer and found a peanut butter and jelly sandwich on white bread, a bag of chips, and a Capri Sun in our lunch bag. We ate in silence. Then we watched in silence.

Two hours later the door to the trailer opened and we were allowed back in. Afraid of the outhouses, or anything past the stairs for that matter, we had been holding our bladders all day. After we used the bathroom, Carol informed us that dinner would be at six, and we could do whatever we wanted till then. We went to what was now undeniably our room and peeked through the blinds waiting for the last of the big kids to be picked up. Then we went to the trampoline and jumped up and down for a few hours until dinner.

A ND SO IT WENT. Every day we were kicked out at nine and allowed back in at three. Every day we ventured a little farther from the safety of Carol's trailer, until eventually the three-acre dirt lot started feeling like home.

It turned out that Kyle and I were the only kids who actually lived at the school. The place wasn't set up for boarders, but some of the kids, having nowhere else to go, would hang out well beyond three. The only rule, it seemed, was that there were no rules. Anyone could do whatever they wanted whenever they wanted. Aside from five other kids whose ages ranged from eleven to fourteen, all the other students were older and apparently there because they were too smart for public school. I couldn't understand why anyone would go to class if they didn't have to, but every day, twenty or so kids would show up and go straight to the classroom, and, except to smoke the occasional cigarette, wouldn't come out until class was over at three. As I got more comfortable, I started to ask more questions.

"So what's up with all those kids who go to class?" I asked Ed one night.

"This is a school. We have classes. What's different is that we let the kids decide whether or not they want to go. We don't make anyone do anything."

"Do you think I should go to class?" I asked.

"I don't think anything," he said. "If you want to go to class, go to class. If you don't want to go, don't."

Unlike my mom, I couldn't get a read on what he was really thinking. She had this way of saying the same kind of nonjudgmental things, but through tone of voice or some sort of psychic mind trick, she was telling you exactly what she thought. I thought I had become pretty good at figuring out what people were really thinking, no matter what was coming out of their mouths, but Ed really stumped me. I had to try a different tack.

"Do you think it would be good if I went to class?" I tried.

"I wouldn't use the words *good* or *bad*. No matter what you do you're always learning something."

This guy was really tough. It wasn't as if he were uninterested or trying to blow me off—Ed could talk for hours—but I just felt like he wasn't giving me a straight answer. I wanted to hear him say, "Yes, Oran, those are the good kids, the smart ones who are going to go on to college and be productive citizens," but he wouldn't say it.

"Listen," he said, after giving it some thought. "On Monday, if you want to go to class, just go in and check it out. If you don't like it, leave."

I checked it out. I couldn't tell what the hell was going on in there. The blackboard was full of numbers, strange squiggles, and symbols I had never seen before, and they were talking about something called wormholes. I lasted all of ten minutes.

MOM MAY HAVE left us on a dirt lot in New Mexico, but she was far from an absentee parent. We spoke on the phone almost every day, and somehow she managed to be just as controlling as she had been when we lived with her. It's true we got to watch TV and eat whatever we wanted to, but we could never sound too happy on the phone because she would know in an instant that something was up.

Kyle was a little more susceptible to her mind tricks than I was, so I was always nervous that he might let something slip. In a display of my own controlling behavior, I would listen in on their conversations and cue Kyle by means of facial expressions if he was heading into dangerous territory, or start frantically jumping up and down and waving my hands if he had gone too far. Of course he knew not to bring up anything about television or candy, but my mom was a smart one and had all sorts of ways to get Kyle to slip up.

I was always the first to talk on the phone.

"So, how is everything, Oran?"

"Okay," I would say without much enthusiasm.

"Did you guys get your bikes in the mail?"

"Yeah. Thanks." I always kept my voice monotone, but in fact the dirt bikes were a godsend.

"So are you having more fun then? Making any friends?" she asked.

"Uh-huh," I grunted.

"Okay, good. Is Kyle around?"

"Yeah, hold on a second. Hey, Kyle, she wants to talk to you."

"Hi, Mom."

Shit, he sounded excited already. I tried frowning at him.

"Yeah, we're great. Yesterday I bought a rocket, and we blasted it off today, and it went like a hundred feet in the air."

I was jumping around like a maniac trying to get him to shut up, but I knew it was too late.

I couldn't hear her, but I knew what the next question would be. "Wow, honey, that sounds fun—where did you buy it?" I was just shaking my head and holding my finger up to my lips, but Kyle still couldn't see where she was taking this.

"I got it at the toy store."

"Where did you get the money?" And then he got it, and his excitement turned into a frown.

"Uh. I . . . Uh . . . She wants to talk to you again."

I didn't know how to get out of this one. I didn't have enough time to think something up.

"So, Oran. Where are you guys getting money from?"

"Uh . . . well . . . the neighbors gave us some money to pull out the weeds from their yard," I stammered.

"Oh? Wow, those sound like cool neighbors. That's really nice of them, but where are you really getting the money from?" she asked sarcastically.

"Carol," I said, folding. I didn't even put up a real fight.

"And how much money is Carol giving you guys?"

"Um . . ."

"It doesn't matter whether you tell me or not because after I'm done talking to you, I'm going to talk to Carol, and it would be better if you told me than if I have to ask her."

"Fifteen bucks."

"See, that wasn't so hard, was it? So, that would be fifteen bucks a week?"

"Uh-huh," I said. Kyle was giving me that "I'm sorry. Please don't beat me up" look.

"So, you must have a lot of money now, right?"

"No."

"Is that because you have been spending it on candy?"

"Yes."

"Okay, Oran, can you put Carol on the line now?"

I ran back to the other room and used my finger to hang up the phone and make that clicking sound. Then I released the button and very carefully put my hand over the receiver and listened in.

"Carol, I thought I made it very clear that the fifteen dollars a week was for expenses only, and not to be given to the kids. That money was to go to soap, toothpaste, laundry, and maybe a movie if they were good."

She was using her stern voice, which was somewhere between talking and yelling.

"Oh. I must have gotten confused. Yes. Now I remember that conversation. Okay, I won't give them any more money," she said in the most gracious voice she could muster.

"Carol, I just want you to be aware that even though I'm going through some heavy stuff right now and am unable to be with Oran and Kyle, they're still my kids and I decide what's best for them." Mom was getting icy now.

"Of course," Carol said. I could picture her rolling her eyes. "I would never question that you know how best to raise your kids."

"Okay, so we understand each other then?" Mom asked.

"I understand absolutely."

I didn't beat Kyle up. I just shook my head and didn't talk to him for a while. Without our allowance, it was back to stealing candy from the ampm or I should say stealing *more* from the ampm. I had found that stuffing my pants full of candy looked way less suspicious if I at least bought one thing. On Monday morning, as Carol ushered us out of the trailer, she handed us fifteen dollars each. Nothing in her expression hinted that she was doing anything wrong. We were astonished.

O THER THAN JUMPING on the trampoline, there just wasn't a whole lot going on at the school, which eventually led to trouble. The older kids who had begrudgingly let us hang around them, for the small cost of letting them play practical jokes on us, were not a good influence. They taught us how to throw rocks at cars and steal golf carts from the course down the road and showed us where they hid their stash of porno magazines underneath a floorboard in the clubhouse they had built. Worst of all was our introduction to white music. There was an eight-track cassette player in the clubhouse and a tape collection consisting of the J. Geils Band, Journey, Foreigner, Loverboy, and Toto. It made me long for Wednesday nights, which was when we got to go to the roller-skating rink. I could not wait for my once-a-week chance to hear Michael Jackson, the Gap Band, and Miami Sound Machine.

On the rare occasion when I found myself alone, I would sneak into the clubhouse, sit on the floor where no one could see me through the windows, and study those porn magazines with a passion and interest I had never experienced before. In the presence of anyone else, though, I would feign complete disinterest.

"Hey, Oran, did you check these ones out? Holy shit, those are nice tits," John or Matt or Mike would say.

I knew that picture better than anyone, but I would just say, "No, haven't seen those," and go back to reading my Conan comic book, or whatever else was lying around.

"Jesus Christ, are you fucking gay or something? Hey, Mike, I think Oran might be a homosexual."

"Lay off, Matt. He's seven years old. He doesn't even know what a boner is."

"I don't know. I think he might be a fag."

I tried to defend myself. "Okay, okay . . . those are nice tits, now shut the fuck up. I'm trying to read."

The older guys also taught us to swear. I didn't understand why this always made them laugh so hard, but I guess it was funny hearing an eight-year-old whose voice hadn't changed telling a group of teenagers to shut the fuck up. I put up with these guys mainly because I had no choice. I was ill-prepared for just how cruel kids could be, and as a result I was the perfect target for their practical jokes.

At lunch one day Matt said, "Hey, Oran, you like pickles, right? My mom keeps packing these pickles in my lunch even though she knows I don't like them. Here, you want it?"

"Sure, I love pickles. Thanks, Matt." I didn't hesitate for a second before putting the small green thing resembling a pickle in my mouth. Within seconds I was running around in circles cursing up a storm and everyone was laughing at me. "Fuck, shit, fuck . . . what the fuck? Goddamn motherfuckers." My mouth was burning up, my face was red, I had snot pouring out of my nose, and a waterfall of tears was running down my face. I ran to the sink and started guzzling water, but it wasn't helping.

"Fucking goddamned assholes!" I yelled, which made everyone laugh even harder. "Piece of shit cocksuckers!" I added. There was nothing I could do to stop the burning, or keep them from laughing at me. They had given me a jalapeño. Finally after three hours or so the burning disappeared, but I was determined to never talk to them again. It only lasted a few days. By the time it had gone through my system, and my ass had stopped burning every time I took a shit, I had forgotten all about it.

I also found out how cruel I could be.

Kyle had missed the whole jalapeño fiasco, so I decided to try the joke on him, but it didn't quite work out the same. He just cried for three hours while the teachers fed him milk and bread. No one laughed this time. Instead I got those looks that say more than words could ever convey. "How could you do this to your six-year-old brother? What kind of monster are you?" It was true. Watching Kyle cry like that really did make me feel like a monster.

That night's conversation with Mom was the worst. I watched and listened in horror as Kyle stared at me with hate-filled eyes, recounting the jalapeño incident to Mom until he broke down sobbing again. Without saying a word he held out the phone to me.

"Oran?" She only used my real name when she was pissed.

"Uh-huh," I grunted.

"How could you do such a thing? Kyle is six years old. What were you thinking?"

"I dunno," I said.

"That is not a good enough answer. I want you to think about it right now, and tell me what you were thinking."

"I dunno," I repeated.

"Did he do anything to you?"

"I dunno." I couldn't think of anything else to say.

"Let me talk to Carol."

I found Carol behind her stack of papers and gave her the phone. As usual I ran to the other room, hung up the phone as loud as I could, then picked it up in silence.

". . . I understand, but I can't keep him from the trampoline. I can't watch him all day, and the other kids use it as well so I can't make it off-limits."

"Well, he needs to learn a lesson. Did you just hear Kyle crying on the phone?"

"I heard him cry for three hours today."

"Okay, so can you ground him?"

"No. That goes against the whole idea of this school."

"Is there something we can take away from him that he likes?"

"I don't know."

"How about his bike, can you lock it up somewhere?"

"Okay, I'll lock up his bike," Carol said, but I knew she had no intention of actually doing it.

Kyle's silent treatment lasted longer than mine, probably because it worked. The more I apologized, the more he would ignore me. I had never realized how much I needed him. I did feel terrible about making him cry, but it was also a lot harder to steal from the ampm without someone to distract the clerk. Throwing rocks at cars proved to be absolutely unsatisfying by myself; plus I had finally gathered enough old mattresses, blankets, and pillows to try jumping out of the tree onto the trampoline, and I needed him to try it first in case I misjudged the placement of the mattresses. We still ate dinner together, watched TV together, and slept in the same bed, but he wouldn't say a word to me. I tried everything, from giving him Now and Laters to letting him watch *The Smurfs* on Saturday morning when I wanted to be watching *He-Man*. He may have been a retarded midget—it was still too early to tell—but he was smart enough to figure out that as soon as he started talking to me, it was just a matter of time before I would be stealing his Now and Laters and strong-arming him for the remote control.

"Hey, Kyle, I finally got enough mattresses to try jumping from the tree to the trampoline, and I know I fucked up with the jalapeño, so I'd like to try to make up for that by letting you jump first."

No response.

"Are you sure? I mean, think how cool it would be if you were the first one to do it."

Nothing.

"Okay, if you don't want it, I have no choice but to be the first one."

Silence.

I knew going into it that my last statement was a gamble, but it was my only hope. All I wanted to do was see someone else do it before me just to make sure it was possible, but I had talked my way into a corner.

I headed toward the trampoline. I was still hoping he would change his mind, but my mind tricks were not on par with Mom's. Kyle had learned that my you-just-won-a-prize voice meant something bad was going to happen. I looked back to see if he was coming, but he just stood there. I could put it off for now. But as I did every day, I climbed the tree so that I could visualize the jump. I wasn't totally positive I could make it.

When I got as far out on the branch as seemed safe, I saw Kyle standing by the pile of mattresses just waiting. Oh well, I had to do it. Better now than in front of all the older kids. I ran it through my head a few times and jumped. The branch was a good fifteen feet from the ground, and maybe twelve feet from the trampoline. I just barely made it to the outside edge, and as a result didn't get the bounce I had hoped for, and ended up landing on the other side with one leg going through the springs. Luckily I didn't get hurt, but I had barely extricated myself when I noticed Kyle up in the tree ready to jump.

"Wait! Don't do it!" I yelled. "You're not going to make it!"

"You just made it." That was the end of the silent treatment, but I was too concerned with him crashing to the ground from fifteen feet to even notice it.

"Just hold on a second," I said, lugging a mattress around to the tree side just in case he didn't make it. Then I took another mattress, and positioned it to cover the springs on the far side.

"Okay," I yelled, and he jumped.

He actually made it farther than I had, flying right over the mattresses and landing with a thud on the ground. I was horrified. I stood there stunned, imagining all the "how could you do this to your six-year-old brother" looks I was going to get on the way to the hospital, and in the waiting room, and for the rest of my life. I snapped out of it as I saw Kyle running as fast as he could back to the tree for another jump.

"Jesus Christ. Just wait one minute." I needed to reposition the cushions again, but Kyle was high on adrenaline and couldn't wait. This time he had a perfect jump and managed to land on the mattress.

"Your turn," he said.

"Oh, no more silent treatment?" I taunted him.

"Just don't ever fucking do that to me again," he answered.

"I won't."

We only got a few more jumps in before the older kids saw what we were doing and took over the trampoline. I had put so much work into setting this up, and they just bullied us out of there. I called them a bunch of assholes, and as always, it only made them laugh. We watched them from a distance for a while before Kyle said, "You want to go throw rocks at cars?"

Man, it was good to have Kyle back.

A decrepit barbed-wire fence sort of defined the perimeter of the school's three-acre lot, with long stretches of nothing between our property and the next one over. There was a tacit agreement that the Mexican family next door could use anything on our property if we could use their go-carts, so the fence didn't mean anything anyway. The entrance to the school, however, had a four-foot cinder-block wall with an opening for the driveway. It was the perfect setup for throwing rocks at cars. For one thing no one could see us, and for another, we could never see them, making our chances of hitting anything very slim.

Kyle and I walked around collecting rocks and then went and stood behind the wall. We just waited till we could hear a car come by, and when the car sounded close enough we would throw our rocks in the general direction of the sound, and I, being maybe an inch or so over four feet, would hunch back down behind the wall and listen for an impact. In six months, this technique had not resulted in one hit, and often there could be up to five of us throwing rocks at the same time. The other kids were busy jumping out of the tree though, so today it was just Kyle and me.

There was hardly any traffic. We must have waited a good ten minutes before we heard our first car coming down the road. We threw our rocks, and I peeked over the cinder blocks to see a Pacer drive by, completely oblivious that it was a target. About ten minutes later, we heard another car coming and when it sounded about right, we let loose on it. Again I peeked over the wall and saw a lowered '60s Chevy pickup driving by with a rear window sandblasted with an image of the Virgin of Guadalupe. Then I heard the sound of glass shattering, and the truck screeched to a stop.

"Shit, shit, shit. Let's get the fuck out of here," I stammered at Kyle, and we both just started running. We hid for a moment behind the schoolhouse to figure out our next move, but we could hear the truck backing up quick, and it was turning into the driveway.

"Shit, where should we go?" I asked.

"Let's hide under our trailer," Kyle suggested.

"No. That's the first place they'll look."

"Okay. Ed's trailer, then. There's an open panel we can get in through," Kyle suggested. Ed had one of those big ones that are actually two trailers put together.

We had no time. The guy had already pulled into the driveway and was getting out of the truck. Luckily, the schoolhouse was between him and Ed's trailer, so we ran as fast as we could. Kyle lifted up the access panel and we scrambled underneath. We just lay there, catching our breath, and eventually crawled over to the other side where there was a crack of light we could peek out of. All I could see was a pair of cowboy boots walking around, and then a pair of sneakers approaching them. Then the cowboy boots walked away, and the sneakers went to Carol's trailer. Ed stooped down to look underneath it. Then he went and looked in the clubhouse. Losing sight of him, I crawled back over to the other side and saw him talking to the kids who were jumping off the tree. He started heading in our direction, and I was sure he would find us, but he just walked up the stairs and went inside.

An hour or so went by before a cop car pulled into the driveway. Ed went to meet him and, together, they walked around checking every hiding place they could find. When we saw them coming toward us, we crawled all the way down to the end of the trailer as quietly as we could. A square of blinding light appeared as the cop lifted up the access panel and shined his flashlight around.

"You guys down here?"

We held our breath and waited.

"Okay, but you can't hide forever. You're going to have to come out sometime," he said, letting the door drop closed.

He and Ed went upstairs. We could hear them talking but couldn't really make anything out. We watched and waited. Neither of us had really eaten anything for breakfast, and Kyle kept whispering about how hungry he was. I told him we had to wait until it was safe, and then I'd go look for something. Long after everyone went home and the staff had all turned off their lights, I decided to see if I could break into the cafeteria or sneak into Carol's trailer to get some food. I crawled over to the door and there were two brown paper bags waiting outside.

"Here, Kyle, I found some food," I said, crawling back in. We ate our baloney sandwiches and drank our apple juice, but decided that opening the potato chips might be too loud. It was creepy down there at night, and I kept feeling things crawl over me. Eventually, we fell asleep.

H EY. WAKE UP," Kyle was whispering. "That cop is back."
       I was wide awake immediately and peeked out of the crack.

"Shit. He's coming straight over here." As I was saying this, the panel opened, and a dark silhouette crouched down and yelled.

"Okay, boys. It's time to come out now. I know you're down there and I really don't want to have to crawl in there after you. My wife just cleaned my uniform and she won't be happy if I come home all covered in dirt."

Kyle and I held our breath and hoped he would go away.

"Or I can just wait here. I don't have a whole lot else to do, so you guys think about it for a minute, and I'll be right here when you've made your decision," he said, closing the panel.

We stayed quiet for a while, but it was pretty clear he wasn't going anywhere, so after a few minutes we decided to give up.

"Welcome back, boys. You sleep well down there? Wow, you fellas look terrible."

I glanced at Kyle. He was covered in dirt from head to toe, and his eyes were completely bloodshot. I could only assume that I didn't look any better.

"Well, how 'bout we go upstairs and have a chat with Ed." Without a word we followed him into the trailer. Ed was smiling when we came in, which kind of bothered me. No matter what was going on he was always smiling.

"Okay, why don't you guys have a seat?" the cop said, pointing to a couple of chairs. "So the bad news is that what you guys did was absolutely stupid, reckless, and against the law. Not only did you break a window, but you endangered a life, and aside from the guilt you would feel from injuring or even killing someone, a crime like that could get you locked up for a long time. Can you boys read?" he asked.

Kyle shook his head, but I nodded.

"Okay, I want you to read this to your brother," he said, handing me a yellow piece of paper.

"J&B auto body, 3965 Rodeo Road, Santa . . ."

He interrupted me. "Just read that number down at the bottom."

"Six hundred dollars."

"That number is how much the window that you broke cost. Do you understand that six hundred dollars is a lot of money?"

We both nodded vigorously. It seemed like a hell of a lot of money for a piece of glass, but the Virgin of Guadalupe had looked pretty good before our rocks smashed it.

"It's enough money to bring felony charges against you if that's what he wanted to do. The good news is that he has decided not to press charges. He felt that if you were still under the trailer in the morning that it was probably because you guys are well aware that what you did was wrong, and he seemed to think that was punishment enough. I just want you to know that this was his decision, not mine, so if I have to come out here again for something like this, I will not be so lenient. Do you understand?"

Again we nodded enthusiastically.

"Good. This isn't a get-out-of-jail-free card so much as a lesson, and I hope you boys have learned something from all this."

Again we nodded, and I even said, "Thank you, sir. We promise it won't happen again."

"Very good," he said, turning to leave.

Getting off the couch, Ed said, "Officer, here is a check for the window."

"I can't take it. I don't know what's wrong with that guy, but he doesn't want money either. Do you know how lucky you guys are?" he said to us, and walked out.

Ed went and shut the door. "You guys think you're slick, but everyone saw you crawl in there. Even the guy whose window you broke saw you running in this direction. He could have come after you right then, but he wanted to see what you would do. That cop is right. You guys are lucky. Now go over to Carol's and clean yourselves up."

NOT LONG AFTER THAT we were informed that we would be taking a trip to California by way of Taos, and there would be a going-away party on Wednesday night followed by roller-skating. We were both sad to go, but it had come to a point where the cops were stopping by about once a week. We had stopped throwing rocks—that's for sure—but even though we were usually not responsible for these visits, they were almost always blamed on us. The party was in Ed's trailer, and Kyle and I sat at either end of the table. Next to me was Denis, the physics teacher. Ed was down at the other end by Kyle, and there were about ten other staff and students. There weren't a whole lot of parties at the school, but when they did happen, the adults usually shared a few bottles of wine with their meal. I don't know what possessed me, but when I had finished my milk, I just reached out and poured myself a glass of Denis's wine. Denis gave Ed a look, and Ed just smiled and shrugged his shoulders. I drank it quickly and poured another glass, and still no one stopped me, though everyone seemed to be waiting to see what would happen. The next thing I knew, the bottle was back in my hand and I just went ahead and finished it off without even bothering to pour it into the milk glass. Conversation had stopped at this point, and everyone seemed to be staring at me.

"Wow, I feel pretty good. Hey, Matt, you should try this. It's good," I said. Matt looked at Ed, who shook his head and turned his attention back to me. I had never spoken to a group this big, but I really felt good, and the words just started coming out.

"I just want to tell everyone I've really had a great time here, and I will definitely miss this place," I said, turning toward Carol. "Thank you for putting up with us, and especially our mom," which made everyone laugh. I continued down the table. "And Ed, thanks for starting this place and being such a good guy."

"Why, you're welcome, Oran. We'll miss you, too."

"And Matt . . . shit, I'll be back in a second," I said, climbing off the chair. I suddenly felt very sick, and somehow made it to the bathroom before puking all over Ed's shag carpet. The bathroom was only fifteen feet from the living room, but getting back wasn't so easy, as I kept walking into the walls. I climbed back up in the chair, and Denis asked me whether I was okay.

"I'm great," I answered.

"So, Oran," Ed said from across the table. "You know that what we're doing here is a new educational process, so I'm curious to hear—since you seem to be so talkative and honest tonight—what you might have learned while you've been here?"

My answer came fast. "I learned how to say, 'fucking cocksucker bitch asshole motherfucking shithead dick face.'"

Everyone started laughing. I was the center of attention, and since it felt like they were laughing with, rather than at, me, I kept going with it.

"I also learned that Matt looks at those magazines so people don't find out he's a fag, and that it's a lot harder to steal candy and throw rocks at cars without my favorite brother, Kyle, over there." This was also met with laughter and even a little applause.

"Then I would say that this experience has been an absolute success," Ed said, beaming. "Those are some very adult lessons you have learned, and I suspect you will have learned another one by tomorrow morning."

I was feeling sick again, so I fell off the chair and stumbled back to the bathroom. I was really fucking drunk and really fucking sick, but everyone in the other room was now laughing and carrying on, so I couldn't help feeling happy despite the fact that I was bent over the toilet puking my guts out. Eventually I stopped puking and went back to the table.

Everyone was getting up at this point, clearing the table and doing dishes. It was almost time to go roller-skating. I was on my way out the door when I overheard Ed telling Denis, "So you don't mind watching Oran tonight? This is usually Carol's only night off."

"No. Really, it's no problem," he said.

"What are you guys talking about? I'm going skating with everyone." I had waited all week for this.

"Sorry, Oran, not tonight you're not," Ed said, turning around to me. I started sobbing immediately.

"What do you mean I can't go?" Tears were running down my face. "What'd I do? No one told me I was doing anything wrong."

Ed got down on his knees and grabbed my hands. "Listen, Oran, you didn't do anything wrong. I saw what you were doing, and I made a decision to let you do it. This isn't a punishment. You're just in no state to go anywhere right now. If anyone made a mistake, it was me."

"But this is my last night to go, and you know it's the only thing I look forward to," I sobbed.

"I'm sorry, Oran. If it helps, you can blame me," he said.

"No! It doesn't fucking help! You guys are just a bunch of fucking assholes! Fuck all of you!" No one laughed this time. For once it seemed like they heard me. I ripped my hands from Ed's and ran out the door, pissed.

I went to the trampoline and lay on my back and watched the stars spin around. I'd never been that pissed in my life. Scared, lonely, insecure, nervous, anxious, and depressed, yes; but I'd never been angry like this.

"Hey, Oran." I looked over to where the voice came from and saw Ed standing by the side of the trampoline.

"What do you want?" I said.

"I just don't want this to be your last memory of being here. That would make me and everyone else very sad."

"Then let me come."

"I can't do that," he said.

"Then leave me alone."

"I can't do that either. . . . Hey, come here for a minute."

"What for?"

"Okay, I'll come over there," he said, stepping out onto the trampoline and lying down next to me.

"You know, adults can make mistakes, too."

"No shit," I said. He got a chuckle out of that, but went on.

"It's even easier to make mistakes when we're trying to do something that's never been done before, and I may have made a big mistake tonight by letting you drink that bottle of wine. I was thinking you might learn a lesson about alcohol. Well . . . that lesson will come tomorrow morning, for sure. But listen though, if all you learned while you were here was some swear words and that you love your brother, I would be satisfied and proud of my part in it. But I suspect you have learned a lot more than that, and that you might see that as well in time. Hey, you see all those stars up there?"

"Uh-huh." I didn't know what he was talking about, but I could see the stars.

"Well, I don't know all the answers to everything, actually I don't know much at all. I'm just a goofy fat bald guy who thinks the education system knows absolutely nothing, but I believe that everything happens for a reason, and that those stars up there, or the Universe, or whatever, knows all the answers and if we are open to it, everything works out the way it's supposed to.

"I don't know if you learned a lesson about alcohol, or that adults are just 'a bunch of fucking assholes,' as you so eloquently put it. I don't even know which of those lessons is the right one. I just don't want you to define your whole experience here by what happened tonight. Okay?"

I couldn't follow him, so I didn't respond. I did know that a bunch of anxious kids were waiting to go roller-skating, and that Ed was talking to me at the risk of pissing everyone else off, so it was kind of hard to stay angry even though I was trying. He grabbed my hand again, and we just stared at the stars for a while in silence.

"Hey, you ready to go?" he said.

"Where are we going?"

"We're gonna get you cleaned up, give you a cup of black coffee, and go to the rink," he said, helping me up.

"Really?" I forgot all about trying to stay angry at him.

"I'm taking a huge risk, so you have to promise me that you won't act all crazy and start yelling at everyone. People don't like seeing drunken seven-year-olds. It freaks them out. We'll see if you're okay to skate when we get there, but if not, at least you get to be with your friends and listen to your music. Okay?"

"I promise, I'll be good. Thanks, Ed."

"I don't care if you're good. Just no yelling, and try to walk a little straighter."

Even leading me by the hand, I kept bumping into him and tripping. But with a little concentration I was able to keep something of a straight line.

The rest of the night was a blur of falling over repeatedly and bothering the DJ.

"Hey, can you play 'Beat It'?"

"Sorry, kid, I just played it ten minutes ago."

"How 'bout Miami Sound Machine?" I asked.

"Nope."

"Freak-A-Zoid?"

"No, kid. I just played all of your songs."

"How 'bout 'Super Freak'?"

"I don't know what the hell happened to you tonight, but you're really starting to bother me. I was nice enough to play all of your goddamn songs, and now I want you to be nice enough to leave me alone so I can do my job and play other people's songs," he said, starting up "Fly Like an Eagle." "Now get the hell out of here, and don't come back!"

"How about 'Beat It,' then?"

"Jesus fucking Christ," he muttered. He put his headphones on, and I finally walked away.

The next day was brutal. Carol was nice enough to let me sleep in, and I just stayed in bed drinking water. She also brought me a bucket so I didn't have to go to the bathroom every time the water came back up.

It was sad leaving that place. Everyone came to see us off. Even the high school kids took a break from doing their weird math problems to come out and wave good-bye. I don't think I'd ever said a word to any one of them.

four

Tells of how the young man came to be
enslaved by the mighty god Chiva

I WOKE UP AS USUAL in my almost pitch-black room to hundreds of kids screaming and yelling from the schoolyard ten feet from the back of the storefront. Our rooms didn't have any windows, and the kids were pretty much the only way I knew whether it was day or night. Surprisingly, I didn't feel that bad. It was usually a struggle to get out of bed, but I was wide-awake, and still dressed from the night before, so I got up and went straight to the kitchen to make some coffee.

Jake was standing on the counter holding a staple gun and a flattened red playground ball—one of those all-purpose rubber ones used for everything from kickball to basketball. Every day at least one, and sometimes as many as five, would end up in our backyard, if you could call it that. We actually referred to it as "the swamp" or "the bog," because that's really what it was. Immediately outside our back door was a small fire escape that looked down into a horrifying mud pit filled with rotting trash. Four feet across from the fire escape was the fifteen-foot-high chain-link fence separating the swamp from the schoolyard, and a few hundred screaming kids. We had made a serious attempt in the beginning to clean it up, but as soon as the residency hotel upstairs had opened, we started finding all manner of weird shit out there, mostly bottles and cans, but also a startling quantity of syringes, broken crack pipes, and used condoms, as well as empty purses, leftover food, and of course, the red and yellow balls that came over the fence.

Reaching around Jake's legs to grab my French press, Jake said, "I only got one today." He was referring to the balls.

"You really are an asshole," I responded.

"Hey, you got to admit it's a good idea," he said, laughing.

Jake's new "art" piece was a bit of a sore spot for me, and he knew it. When school had started up, not only did the balls start landing in the swamp, but they were always accompanied by a group of little kids, screaming "Mister! Hey, mister!" through the door at us. Depending on my mood, I would either ignore them or go down into the pit to get their balls. It's true the kids would get annoyingly desperate sometimes, but they would be so goddamned excited and thankful when you threw the balls over that I almost always gave in. Jake, however, hated it.

"When are they going to shut the fuck up?" he would ask.

"Jesus, man, they're just kids. Chill out."

"Yeah, but when are they going to learn not to kick them over the fence?"

"Jake! They're fucking kids! Who cares?" It was a rare occurrence that I was the one preaching acceptance, but even though the kids' desperation made me kind of uncomfortable, I really had nothing against them. Jake, however, was continuously devising ways to get the kids to shut up. One day on my way to the bathroom he called out to me.

"Hey, Oran. Check it out." He was holding a ball in his left hand and a utility knife in his right. "Eh . . . what do you think?"

"About what?" I asked.

"My new piece," he responded.

"What are you talking about, 'your new piece'? You're actually going to make something?" I said.

"Hell yes, I'm making something, and trust me, *you* are going to love it."

"Oh no," I sighed. "Do you think after listening to all your bullshit art conversations that I would trust you? You know me better than that."

"Exactly. I do know you, and little Cranberry is finally going to be psyched about art again. Are you ready?" This was followed by a long pause. "I'm doing an installation with the balls."

I waited for more, but there was nothing.

"Yeah . . . and?"

"So I came up with an art piece that will finally shut those kids up.

I'm going to start collecting the balls and staple them to the wall up there. When the kids figure out they're not going to get their balls back, they'll finally stop screaming at us."

"Jake, that is super fucked up. Do you realize how fucked up that is?"

"What do you mean? You like 'fucked up.' That's your whole thing. I thought you would love it. I mean, at least you have to admit it's a good idea."

I could tell Jake was actually a little bummed out.

"It might be a funny *idea*, but it's fucking mean. Have you seen the look on those kids' faces when they lose their balls? It's the look of pure panic, like they're going to die if they don't get them back," I said.

"Good. Maybe when they find out that they *won't* die from losing a stupid ball, they'll realize it's not such a big deal, and stop screaming at us all day."

"Just ignore them!"

"No way, man, this is going to be great! So listen, if you're out there and see any balls, I need them for the piece."

"What? Are you nuts?" I yelled. "Go ahead and make your little art piece, but I'm throwing every ball I find back to them!"

"Oh, so that's how it's going to be?"

"That's right," I said.

"Okay, Cranberry, but just remember, I wake up before you."

As much as I may have believed I cared about the kids, Jake was right. If I was unable to wake up for a job, I certainly wasn't going to get out of bed to climb down into the pit and retrieve balls.

I watched Jake try to attach the new ball to what, in a very short time, had become bigger than any of us had expected. The thing was already about twelve feet wide. Not a bad-looking piece if you ignored what was behind it.

"Hey, so Lawrence came over last night," I said while I was waiting for my coffee to steep.

"Oh yeah, what did he want?" Jake asked.

"He didn't seem to want anything. I guess he just came by to hang out or something," I said.

"Huh." He wasn't really listening. Jake was starting to have trouble getting the balls to stay on the wall, because there were too many of them at this point.

"Yeah, it was kind of fun actually." That got a little more attention. "Fun" wasn't a huge part of my vocabulary at the time.

"What . . . you guys hung out? I thought you hated that guy," he said.

"I thought so, too. He's not bad, though. Anyway," I continued "you know the other night when he did his thing, I smoked a little of the heroin, and I didn't really feel anything. But last night he brought some over, and man, that shit is pretty good."

"Yeah, it smells like honey-baked ham."

"Hmm . . . I thought it smelled more like molasses," I said.

"I had some the other night, too. I kind of felt something, but I'm not sure what exactly. It was good, though?" he asked.

"Yeah, I'm kind of surprised . . . I mean, I smoked a lot of that shit last night, but I feel totally fine today, no hangover. Actually I feel good, and I haven't even had my coffee yet. Don't you think it's kind of strange that these 'hard drugs,' like heroin or coke, don't seem to fuck you up as much as alcohol or pot? I mean, last night I just felt kind of relaxed, but if I smoke even one hit of weed, I can't do anything. It seems to me they got it backward."

"That is weird," Jake said, not paying attention anymore. He was going nuts with the staple gun, trying to get the balls to stay up, but it wasn't happening.

"You think I should use longer staples, or start using nails?" he asked me.

"I'm not helping you with that thing," I answered, finishing my coffee. "All right, I'm going to go sand some pianos," I said.

As I was walking out, Jake said, "Don't forget to tell people about the Cisco party on Friday night."

"Are you serious?" I asked. We had an unplanned Cisco party back when we had first moved in, and the results had been disastrous. Cisco was a fortified wine, but it wasn't like any alcohol I had ever had before. That shit may have been the strangest drug I had ever done, and you could buy it right next door in grape, cherry, strawberry, or tropical punch flavors. Before the night was through, I had somehow gotten into three fights with my friends, and I don't fight.

"Don't you remember what happened last time?" I reminded him.

"Yeah. It was fun, remember?"

"I don't know," I said, trying not to think about my oldest friend, Jibz, whom I had hooked up with at the end of the night. I had been in love with her for as long as I could remember, and as usual, I had found out a few days later that she was with a new "serious" boyfriend. She could be single for months, but whenever we got together, she would always find someone the next day. *Why not me?* I asked myself over and over. As many times as it had happened, it never got any easier to deal with.

Depressed, I walked the ten blocks to my internship, the first two of which were spent fending off junkies trying to sell me "one and ones." I was so used to this from living in the neighborhood for the past seven years that most of the time it didn't really bother me. I just got really used to saying no twenty or thirty times until I cleared the two-block radius of Sixteenth and Mission. The thing I couldn't understand was that I had been saying no to the same people for six years. After that many nos, over that many years, it would seem fairly clear that I wasn't in the market. But these guys never let up.

"Looking?"

"One and ones?"

"Chiva?"

"Coca?"

"Outfits?"

They were like zombies who had learned a few words to trick you into thinking they were human. Sometimes they would form complete sentences like, "Come on, man. Look at me. I'm fucking sick. I need the credit." They always looked fucking sick to me with their abscesses and open facial wounds. Zombies.

"No . . . Nope . . . I'm cool . . . No . . . Not looking . . . No, really. I'm not fucking looking!" This was my mantra whenever I left the house.

THIS INTERNSHIP WAS LIKE any other internship I'd ever had—a thinly veiled scam to get suckers like me to do free labor. The thing was, all the other interns would figure it out in about a week and stop coming back. I had been sanding pianos now for three months and continued to show up. This guy, Dietrich, would scout the classifieds for free pianos, sand them down, put a coat of varnish on them, and then sell them a week later for around fifteen hundred dollars. Actually, I sanded and varnished all the pianos, and then he would come downstairs and tune them.

"Hey, Dietrich. When do you think I'll be able to start tuning pianos? I think I've got this sanding thing down."

"Did you finish the Chickering?" he asked in his weird German accent. He sounded slightly effeminate, which I had thought was pretty hard for Germans.

"Yeah, I finished it last night," I responded.

"Very good. You know that Knabe in the back. You can start sanding that one today."

"Yeah, well, I think I'm pretty good at this sanding thing by now, so why don't you give me a lesson on how to tune the Chickering?" I tried to sound pissed off, but it was pretty ineffective.

"Oh, don't worry, we'll get to that, but I'm actually working on something upstairs right now. Soon, okay?"

It's not that I wasn't aware that he was scamming me, but I had something of my own scam going. I had called Jack and told him about my idea of going into piano tuning, and if he could just help me out for a little while, I would soon be making a hundred dollars an hour tuning pianos.

"Okay, just tell Patti I said it was all right," Jack had said. Patti was his secretary, and I talked to her far more than I talked to him.

"Hi, Patti. It's Oran." I had to call her every month.

"Oh shit. How much is it, eight hundred?"

"Eight fifty."

"Okay. I'm going to the bank this afternoon."

"No problem. Thanks," I said, hanging up the phone, feeling like a piece of shit. It wasn't taking money from my dad that bothered me. He had just bought a three-million-dollar house in Santa Barbara. He could afford it. It was that I was surviving off this guy's guilt. Whenever I saw him, about once every two or three years, I always felt as if I were his dark side in physical form: a hunched-over, chain-smoking, cynical bastard who presented solid proof that he was capable of leaving his pregnant wife with a one-year-old child, and that maybe he wasn't the self-help guru he was praised as. To be fair, I never gave him much reason to think anything else of me. I experienced such an awful combination of anxiety and anger whenever I saw him that I had a hard time even talking.

I had always thought that his whole self-help shtick was a racket, but his new book exceeded the limits of what I thought was possible in terms of sheer vapidity.

"Ask me about the book," he'd said the last time I had dinner with him.

"Uh, why do I need to ask? Can't you just tell me?"

"This is how people get to write off their expenses," he answered.

"Okay. How's the book?"

"It's going great, we're still on the *New York Times* bestseller list, and we're working on the *Second Helping*."

"*Second Helping*? What's that?" I asked before realizing I probably didn't want to hear the answer.

"We're calling it a *Second Helping* of *Chicken Soup for the Soul*. Get it?"

"Yeah," I said, unable to muster any enthusiasm. *Who buys that shit?* I thought to myself. *A Second Helping?* I hadn't even been able to make it through ten pages, let alone the whole book.

There were still about five boxes of *Chicken Soup for the Soul* books in my mom's garage from when Jack had tried to get Kyle and me to walk around and sell them to neighbors. Kyle gave it a shot one day and came back with twelve bucks, half of which he was supposed to send back to Jack.

I never believed the saying "you can't judge a book by its cover." I judged things based on appearance all the time, and although I wasn't always right, I wasn't always wrong. This book's cover provided me with more than enough information to judge it by. Underneath its already cheesy title, it said, *101 Stories to Open the Heart and Rekindle the Spirit.* It looked like the Hallmark section of the drugstore repackaged in book form.

As the book started getting attention, and more and more people asked me, "Well, what's so terrible about it?" I found that my answer, "Well . . . um . . . I haven't actually read it, but come on . . . It's called *Chicken Soup for the Soul*, for Christ's sake!" was sadly not always enough proof of how bad it had to be. The next time I was at my mom's house, I went to the garage and cracked open a copy of it to get more ammunition.

The story I opened to was about a seven-year-old kid who wanted to make a bumper sticker that read "Peace, Please! Do It for Us Kids." He didn't have any money, so he asked for a loan from Jack's cowriter, Mark, in order to print up a thousand stickers. As manipulative as the writing was, I tried to keep an open mind and get behind the kid's effort—however ineffectual—to bring about world peace. A few pages in, though, the kid starts listening to Mark's *Sell Yourself Rich* series of cassette tapes, and before you know it, he starts scamming free shit from Joan Rivers, negotiating with Hallmark (no surprise), and, by the end of the story, has made almost five thousand bucks. The message was that even a seven-year-old can make money by listening to Mark's tapes. In just three pages I already felt as if I had enough ammunition, but I kept going anyway. Maybe the next story would prove me wrong. . . . A couple from Miami doesn't have enough money to go to a self-help seminar in California, and they figure out that if they tell people they are trying to get kids to say no to drugs and sexual promiscuity, they can get free airplane tickets, hotels, and car rentals. I then skimmed the first page of the next story, about a guy who comes up with an idea to help students achieve high self-esteem, and then I flipped to the last page, where the same guy has now made over a million dollars.

It's not that I questioned the integrity of the kid who wants peace, or the abstinence-promoting couple, or the self-esteem guy, but the stories had nothing to do with their altruistic goals, and everything to do with money. *The* money I was in fact living off of.

I also felt a little guilty because I had never told Jack about the trust my grandmother had left Kyle and me. The income from that was bringing in anywhere from thirty-five to a thousand dollars a month. The problem was I never knew how much was coming until the check came, and I was just too fucking lazy and maladjusted to get a real job. Dietrich was unlikely to fire me since I worked for free.

I SANDED THE KNABE for a while, and wondered what the fuck I was doing with my life. Five hours by myself in the back of a garage sanding a fucking piano by hand (the electric sander was too loud and bothered Dietrich) was incredibly conducive to those kinds of thoughts. *What the fuck am I doing with my life?* I asked myself again, and again, and again.

I locked up the shop and went home for rehearsal after work, and Sean, our bass player, was already there.

"Hey, Sean. You're early. Is Eli here?"

"No. Betsy let me in. But yeah, I did come early for a reason. I need to ask a favor," he said.

"Sure. What's up?" I asked.

"Well, check it out," he said, holding up his hand. I looked at his hand, but was clearly missing something. "I asked Christine to marry me yesterday," he said, smiling.

"Holy shit, are you serious?" And then I noticed the ring.

"Yeah, I'm serious, and she said yes."

"Wow. Congratulations, man. That's great." I did my best to sound excited for him, and I was—it was just hard for me to show it most of the time.

"I was wondering if you would be my best man," he said.

"Wow, Sean. Sure, it would be an honor," I said.

"Also, I was wondering if we could have it here."

I looked around the space. The fucked-up walls, the drywall falling off the ceiling, the paint coming up off the plywood floors, the water damage, all the buckets strategically placed to catch leaks from the residency hotel. I wondered what the hell he was seeing that I wasn't.

"I'll have to ask my roommates, but if they don't have a problem with it, then of course."

When Eli showed up, Sean showed him his engagement ring, Eli congratulated him, and we went down to the basement to rehearse for our upcoming tour of vegan cafés in L.A. and San Pedro. Afterward, I told Eli that Sean had asked me to be his best man and he started laughing.

"What's so funny about that?" I asked.

"You don't know?"

"I've never been to a wedding. I don't know shit about them," I said, vaguely recalling that I had been to a wedding once before with my mom.

"Well, two things. One, you have to give the first toast, and—"

"Are you fucking serious?" I cut him off. "What am I supposed to say?" I hated speaking in front of people.

"But wait, here's the funny part. The best man's job is to make sure the groom gets to the wedding on time."

"You have got to be fucking kidding me." Sean was notoriously late for everything, often by as much as three hours. "Oh man, I wish I had known. But I had to say yes, right? Fuck. What am I going to say about him?"

"I don't know. You better come up with something. Hey, you coming by the bar tonight?" Eli asked.

"Ah. I don't know, I'm kind of tired." I was always kind of tired. "Maybe I should just stay in for the night."

Of course I ended up at the bar. As Eli was giving me my drink, I saw Lawrence coming out of the bathroom with a straw hanging out of his mouth. It was kind of incredible. The guy had no shame. As far as I knew, heroin had not become a fashionable drug to be doing in public. He noticed me and came over to tell me about a new art piece he was working on, but I was too distracted by the straw he was chewing on to listen to him.

"Hey, you want some chiva?" He read my mind.

"Sure, but is it safe to do in the bathroom?" I asked.

"Sure. Or we could go to your place. I need to get more anyway."

I finished my beer and we left.

L AWRENCE SHOWED UP again two days later, and again the night after that. I found myself looking forward to his increasingly frequent visits, but sometimes it was hard to shake him.

The night of our Cisco party, I had magically gotten laid for the first time in six months. A girl I had never seen before showed up at our place and started staring at me from the moment she walked in. After a couple of bottles of Cisco, she led me into the hall and started making out with me. I would have invited her to my room, but the walls were still not completely built, so instead we ended up at her place with Lawrence, who had somehow tagged along with us. I kept trying to hint at him to leave, but it didn't work. By the time we managed to get rid of him at nine in the morning, I was so high from smoking dope I couldn't come. I didn't even care that much. After six months of celibacy, it should have been a big deal.

"Hey, don't worry about it," she said when I had finally given up. "It felt great anyway. You know what? I think I really like you." That was the worst thing she could have said to me.

"Uh . . . that's nice," I said. *Is she fucking crazy?* I thought. *I mean, we met last night at that Cisco party, and then I bring this creepy old guy over to her house and smoke heroin all night. She's so goddamn cute. I mean, she's beautiful. She could do a hell of a lot better than me. There is obviously something wrong with her. Shit, what was her name? Man, what an asshole, I can't even remember her name.* I was panicking, running through a list of names in my head. My first thought was Betty because she looked like Betty Page, but that just led me back to wondering what the hell she saw in me. *Something's not right with her.*

"So what do you think of me?" she asked.

"Well . . . um . . . yeah." *What the hell kind of question was that?* I had no idea how to talk to girls. "You seem very nice. I mean, we just met last night, I don't really know you that well." I think I was probably supposed to tell her she was pretty or something, but that kind of shit had a way of getting stuck in my throat.

"We should get to know each other then. I'm a rad chick."

Did she just say what I thought she said?

"What?" I wanted to make sure.

"I'm a rad chick," she repeated.

Damn, I knew something was wrong with her. *Who says "I'm a rad chick"?* I needed to get the hell out of there, but I had to figure out her name. This had never happened to me before. Finally she got up to go to the bathroom, and I jumped out of the bed and looked around for a piece of mail. I found an envelope addressed to Rosemary under a magazine on her desk, and I jumped back in the bed just as she was flushing the toilet. Damn. It could have been Rose, Rosemary, Rosy, Mary . . . Shit, which one was it?

"Hey, your friend left his tinfoil on the chair. I think there's some heroin still on it," she said as she came back. "Do you have a straw?"

"No. We could use a ballpoint pen if you have one." She went to the desk, got the pen, and put the envelope back under the magazine. There wasn't much heroin left, so I let her finish it.

"Hey, let's go get some more," she said.

"I should really get home. We've got a show at our place tonight, and it's a fucking mess from that party." It seemed like a valid excuse.

"What kind of show?"

"Eli and I have an experimental music series there on Saturday nights."

"What do you mean by experimental?" she asked. I never liked that question, because to me it meant indescribable, and, I hoped, unlike anything anyone had heard before.

"Well, last weekend we had a Japanese turntable guy named Otomo Yoshihide . . ." I started.

"Oh, you mean a DJ." She cut me off. As if I had never heard of a DJ.

"Not quite. Well, sometimes he plays real records, but this guy also makes his own needles out of shit like safety pins and electric wire, and plays sheets of sandpaper, or cardboard he cuts his own grooves into, and he had a drummer who, instead of using sticks, used microphones to play the drums. It was an amazing show. We got so many noise complaints from it that tonight we've got a shakuhachi and a koto player coming in to keep it a little more mellow." She was so utterly uninterested that she didn't even ask what a shakuhachi was. I wouldn't have been able to tell her if she had.

"Is that what you do for money?" she asked.

"Ha . . . no way. We're lucky if we get to keep twenty bucks, and that goes back into the space. I do piano restoration," I said, leaving out the fact that it was an unpaid internship and that I was living off my fucking dad. "What about you?" I asked.

"I work at a café, but I'm thinking about selling my eggs."

"What?" This time I could not have heard her right.

"Yeah. Japanese couples pay big money for Caucasian eggs."

"Jesus. How much is big money?" I was suddenly interested. The more I heard about the Japanese, the more confused I got. It seemed like it should be the other way around.

"For me, since I'm tall, brunette, and have big tits, they offered me seven thousand bucks. The couple has to see a picture of you first. Then they fly over here, fertilize the egg with the father's sperm, implant it in the wife, and go home. Then they have the baby in a Japanese hospital, and they tell everyone it's theirs."

"Holy shit."

"Yeah. So what do you think?" she asked.

"Is it safe? I mean, you only get one set of eggs, right?"

"No, I mean about getting more heroin."

"I don't know. I've done it like four days in a row. It seems like a bad idea." I was quickly losing track of how much I was doing.

"Okay, but can we do it again?" She seemed let down.

"Yeah, sure. I'll give you a call. Let me get your number," I said, putting the pen back together. I got dressed and leaned over to give her a good-bye kiss.

"Thanks, Rose." I took a chance. "I had fun. I'll give you a call tonight."

"It's Mary," she said.

WHEN I GOT OFF the bus at Sixteenth and Mission, I was immediately swarmed by drug dealers. I got about halfway down the block and without even thinking I asked this guy, "Hey, you got anything?"

"How many?" He wanted to know.

"Just one," I said, reaching into my pocket and pulling out a ten-dollar bill.

He reached up to his mouth, spit out a balloon, handed it to me, and grabbed my ten. I had always been so nervous about buying drugs, but it was the easiest thing in the world.

"Thanks," I said, starting to walk away.

"Hey, can I ask you something?" he said, catching up with me.

"Yeah?" I was about thirty feet from home, and I didn't want my roommates to see me talking to this junkie.

"Why are you such an asshole?" That threw me completely off guard.

"What? What the hell are you talking about?" I asked.

"Man, I've seen you come down here every day for years, and you just walk right by me. What? My shit's not good enough for you? Can't find your regular guy? Why have you always been such a dick to me?" I wasn't even sure I had ever seen this guy before.

"Jesus Christ, man. This is the first time I've ever bought this shit. I live right here," I said, pointing at my door. "That's why you see me every day. Hey, listen though, I'm worried about my roommates seeing me buy drugs, so . . ."

"Oh, now you don't want to be seen with me? I shouldn't have even sold to you, man." He looked genuinely hurt.

"Come on, that's not what I meant." But he was right. That's exactly what I meant. I was just so used to thinking of these guys as zombies. I had no idea they were so sensitive.

Inside I found Jake in the kitchen getting ready to go to work.

"Well, look who it is. How'd it go last night? Did little Cranberry hook it up with what's her name?" he asked me.

"Mary," I said, getting uncomfortable. I could bitch and moan forever about not getting laid, but when I actually did get lucky I always tried to avoid talking about it. My friends seemed to think I was just shy, but I thought of myself more as a celibate misanthrope. I just didn't like most people, but with women I sometimes didn't figure that out till after I slept with them.

"Yeah, her. Did you hook it up or what?"

"She was kind of weird," I said, avoiding the question. "She kept referring to herself as a rad chick." I was stretching the truth a little. She had actually only said it twice, and the second time was because I asked her to repeat it, but in my head she kept saying it over and over again like a film loop: "I'm a rad chick. I'm a rad chick. I'm a rad . . ." It bummed me out.

"Who says that about themselves?" asked Jake.

"She does."

As soon as he left, I grabbed a piece of tinfoil and went to my room. Holy shit, I was tired. I smoked the dope, put the little bag of coke in an empty Altoids tin, and somehow had enough energy to go and straighten the place up for the shakuhachi player.

I HAD HEARD LAWRENCE was having some problems with his wife and kid. He had never mentioned it to me, but it didn't seem like a good sign that he was now coming over almost every night to get high. On the nights that I went out or was downstairs rehearsing, my roommate Betsy would tell me he came by.

"Hey, Oran, your creepy older friend came by again tonight. What's that guy's deal? I told him you weren't here and he insisted on coming in anyway. What the fuck? Finally I let him use the bathroom and he was in there for like twenty minutes. Who is that guy, and why is he so creepy?" she said, visibly getting a case of the shivers.

"Listen, I'll tell him he can't come in if I'm not around." I was hoping to end the conversation.

"Okay, but who is he? Why is he here all the time? I don't like it." She wasn't letting it go.

"He's an artist . . . or philosopher, or something. I know he's kind of creepy, but I like hanging out with him."

"God. I just don't get it."

I'm not sure I got it either. All I knew is that when he was around I felt relaxed and comfortable for free. I didn't have to go out and deal with those crazy people and give them my money.

I never called Mary, but I knew it wasn't going to be that simple. When she had told me she really liked me, she sounded like she meant it. Luckily, I had an excuse ready for when she asked why I hadn't called her last week.

"Hey. It's Mary," I heard on the other end of the phone. "I got your number from Eli. I'm at the Casanova having a drink. You should come by."

"Actually I'm totally exhausted. I really need to stay in tonight," I said.

"That's fine. I'm just right around the corner. I can come over there instead." I just wanted to be left alone, but I was all tongue-tied. I was expecting her to ask why I hadn't called, so I could use my prepared excuse. I hadn't planned anything for this scenario. While I was trying to come up with a way out, she said, "I'll be over in a few minutes."

Immediately she tried to convince me to go buy some dope. It seemed easier than coming up with conversation, so I gave in. As tired as I was, I went out to see if the same guy I had bought from before was hanging around outside. He wasn't there, but some other kid approached me.

"Looking?"

I nodded to him.

"I think Javier is right around the corner. How many you want?"

"Just one," I answered.

"Give me the money. I'll be back in a second." I wasn't about to let this guy walk away with my money.

"Sorry, man, I got to go with you."

"Have you ever scored off Javier before?"

"No."

"All right. You can come with me, but I'm telling you right now, he's not going to sell to you unless he knows you."

"What, do I look like a cop?" I laughed.

"No. You live right there," he said, pointing to my door. "I'll vouch for you, but I'm telling you it's not going to work."

This guy wasn't as annoying as the other one, but it seemed even more complicated. We found Javier, who looked me up and down and said something unintelligible to the guy.

"He wants to see your tracks," he said.

"What?"

"Your track marks," he said, rolling up his shirtsleeve. His arm was dotted with red marks and bruises. It was fucking gross.

I'm never using a needle, I thought.

"Tell him I smoke the shit."

He said something in Spanish, and they started arguing while Javier kept shaking his head.

Finally he said to me, "Listen, just give me the money and meet me at the corner. Then next time you can buy straight from him." It didn't make any sense, but I reluctantly gave him the money and went to wait on the corner.

"Here, you owe me one for that," he said, dropping the balloon in my hand. "I'm Frank, by the way. What's your name?"

"I don't really want to give out my name," I said.

"What am I supposed to call you then?"

"That's the thing. You're not supposed to call me anything. I don't really do this shit. Just once in a while. I mean I live right here, man, I can't really have people calling out my name on the street. My room-mates . . ."

"Okay, okay," he said, shutting me up. "Jesus Christ, man. I just asked you your name."

"Well, thanks again," I said, walking away. I thought I heard him mutter "asshole" under his breath, but I wasn't sure. When I looked back, he was just staring at the ground. Christ, wasn't there a way to do this without hurting people's feelings every time?

"What took you so long?" Mary asked when I got back.

"Those people are fucking crazy," I said, not really answering her.

"You got it though, right?" She sounded a little desperate.

"Are you sure this is a good idea? How often do you do this shit?" I was concerned about how determined she was.

"That night with you was the first time, I swear. It was so fucking good, though."

"That's what I'm worried about." I was hesitant to do it myself after who knew how many days in a row, but I just stopped thinking about it.

"Hey, how come you never called me?" she asked after we got high.

"I've been really busy," I said without any hesitation. It was the line I had been waiting to use.

We didn't even bother trying to have sex this time.

ORAN, NICE OF YOU to show up. You know I called you a few times yesterday. Where have you been? I've got a client who wants to buy that Knabe," Dietrich said.

"Sorry. Something came up. I couldn't make it in." Mary and I had sat around smoking more dope the next day.

"Well, at least you could call me if you're not coming in."

"Or I could just not come back at all, and you could find someone more responsible to sand your pianos for free." I was cranky.

"Okay, okay . . . don't worry about it, but I need to get that piano done. This guy needs it for his daughter's birthday."

"All right! I'll do it!"

Dietrich just looked me over and went back upstairs. *Where did that come from?* I never yell at people, unless their names are Sean or Eli and I play music with them. I started working on the piano, but I didn't feel too good. *I must be getting sick. It's been a rough week, and I'm not used to this kind of life. How does Lawrence keep it up? Thirteen years? I can't even last two days. And when is that motherfucker going to teach me to tune these things? Asshole. I can't believe I'm still doing this shit. And what's up with Mary? She seems like bad fucking news. I better stay away from her. I mean, I don't even have anything to say to her.*

Nothing brings out the internal dialogue like sanding pianos.

I BOUGHT SOME MORE on the way home. Someone asked me if I was looking and I just blurted out yes and handed him a ten. I smoked a little before my rehearsal with this new klezmer band I had started playing with. The drum parts were the most boring thing I had ever done in my life. It was basically polka with more interesting melodies.

Um-pa, um-pa, um-pa. If I ever tried to do a fill or hit anything other than the kick, snare, or high hat, they would stop and tell me in the nicest way possible, "Hey, Oran, that was cool, man, but this song doesn't really need that." The only reason I had agreed to join was because they had said they were going to call themselves the Klezbians. They had just gotten their first gig at a café, and that night they told me that they had decided to change their name to the Goys instead.

"What happened to the Klezbians?" I asked. "That's the best name ever."

"Well, we decided that we didn't want to offend anyone," Adrian the clarinet player said. The band was made up of middle-aged parents except for the trumpet player and me. "You don't think the Goys is a good name? You know, a klezmer band with no Jews in it? It's funny, right?" Adrian tried to tell me.

"I'm Jewish," I said.

"You are? How come you didn't tell us?"

"Because you didn't tell me it was called the Goys. Not only is it not that funny anyway, but there's a Jew in the band. It simply doesn't work." I didn't care so much about the obvious contradiction. I just wanted them to change the name back.

"Shit. The thing is the show has already been advertised. Just don't tell anyone you're Jewish, okay? We'll change the name for the next one."

"To the Klezbians?" I asked, but I already knew I was going to quit after this show.

THE KIDS WOKE me up screaming out in the schoolyard the next morning. It caused a moment of panic before my brain turned on and told me it was just kids running around having fun, or dealing with whatever intense playground issues kids deal with. The panic subsided and was replaced by a cold, clammy feeling. I wrapped myself tighter under the blanket, waiting for recess to end, but it didn't help. Even when they got called back in for class, I couldn't fall back to sleep. I just kept tossing and turning, thinking that the last month of hard living had finally caught up with me, and I was coming down with the flu.

Then the panic came back. *Fuck, fuck, fuck,* I said to myself as I flashed through the last few weeks. *Lawrence, Mary, then on my way home from Mary's, the next night, the next morning, then Mary again. Has it been that long? When did Lawrence start coming by? A month ago? I can't even remember, and it's been a blur since then. What the fuck were you thinking? It's so obvious. How could you be such an idiot?* I had read enough William Burroughs books to figure out I didn't have the flu. Even though I had never really understood at the time what he went through when he described withdrawal, his descriptions matched the way I felt now. *How could I let this happen? I knew Lawrence is full of shit. I didn't believe him for a second about not getting addicted in thirteen years. Motherfucker's at the house every night. But it's not as if I've been nodding out or anything. Actually, I've been getting a lot done. I'm not as tired as usual, not as anxious or depressed. Shit, it's only been one or two bags a day, and I don't even feel that bad. I can totally deal with this. If I don't smoke any of that shit today, I'm sure tomorrow will be fine.*

I got out of bed, climbed down the ladder, took out my piece of tinfoil, and rooted around for the three little pieces of plastic I had thrown in the trash. There was a little bit of brown residue on each piece, which I scraped off with a pocketknife. I got enough out of it for a small hit, and within seconds I felt better. *You fucking idiot. You just said you weren't going to do this thirty seconds ago. Oh well. You already fucked up today.*

There was a sinking feeling in my chest as I walked out of the house to get more. The feeling of impending doom. It went away when I got back to my room and smoked a little of it. *Fuck it. It'll be fine. I'll deal with this tomorrow.*

five

*Wherein the boy encounters a holographer,
a born-again Christian, and his Jewish
grandmother, and lives to tell about it*

E D DROVE US FROM Santa Fe to Taos, New Mexico, in his falling-apart Toyota Celica and dropped us off at a deserted Buddhist retreat up in the hills. There were a few people around, but no one paid any attention to us. We slept in a geodesic dome and spent our days jumping on yet another trampoline, a big round one that proved to be a disappointing, less bouncy substitute for the one back in Santa Fe.

Four days later, Wavy Gravy and his partner showed up with their group of jugglers, acrobats, hippies, and clowns to set up for a month of Camp Winnarainbow. It was a traveling camp at the time, and they had just come from Woodstock. I hadn't juggled much while I was in Santa Fe, but I quickly got back into it and even started branching out a little with gymnastics and tightrope walking, neither of which I was very good at.

The camp's next stop was in Mendocino, California. Kyle and I tagged along with the hippie clowns, who were our counselors, and we slept in tepees with a new batch of kids for the next month. I was always nervous as hell around other kids, and I could never figure out how to make friends with them. But one kid in particular made me more nervous than I had ever been in my life. Her name was Jibz, and unlike me, she had no problem making friends. The first few days of camp were nerve-racking for almost everyone, but Jibz was running around on day one as if she had already been there for a month. She seemed to be free of the ever-present, all-encompassing self-consciousness that made me do shit like practice juggling six hours a day in an effort to avoid exchanging words with other kids.

I didn't know what I wanted from her, but whenever I saw Jibz making crazy faces, or coming up with the most awkward dance moves I had ever seen in my life, onstage, for everyone to see, I would get a feeling I had never experienced before. The feeling was similar to my normal fear and anxiety, except that I wanted to run toward it, rather than away. I practiced juggling even harder. Since there was no way I could ever get the nerve up to approach her, I hoped that maybe, if I became the best juggler ever, she would approach me. After the first four weeks neither had happened, but I had learned to juggle five balls.

M OM MET US in California to explore the idea of relocating to the Bay Area. We lived with her temporarily at a hotel in Corte Madera, across the street from a strip mall and directly behind Highway 101.

We took day trips to Stinson Beach, Muir Woods, the Exploratorium, and Haight Street. Mostly we had fun, but I never understood why we kept going back to the Haight; it was crowded, the stores seemed to sell nothing but colorful junk, and everyone was always asking for money. "Spare change for some acid, man?"

Haight Street's only redeeming quality was its proximity to Golden Gate Park, the Double Rainbow ice cream store, and a place called the Holography Museum, which we had become fond of. The Holography Museum was actually a store, a dark, quiet room displaying three-dimensional portraits, a few space ships, and models of Saturn. As much as they intrigued me, I could only spend so much time looking at them.

Bob, a guy who volunteered a few days a week and made holographs himself, could spend hours explaining the science behind it, but it still made no fucking sense. Mom would pretend to understand him, and they would talk forever while Kyle and I stood out on the sidewalk, fending off hippies who seemed to think it was cute or funny or something to ask us for spare change.

"Spare some change for a bomb, little guys?"

"Sorry. I don't have any money," I answered honestly.

"Come on man, even a nickel . . ."

"I don't even have any pockets," I said, drawing attention to the black satin pants Mom had commissioned a woman at the dry cleaners to make for me. I had to hide the occasional quarter I would steal in my blue-and-white-checkered Vans. Whenever I managed to get a dollar's worth of change together, I would go to the gas station by the hotel and trade it in for a bill. Walking around with more than a dollar in change in my shoes would start to hurt like a motherfucker, especially when a coin got stuck behind my heel. The bills were much more comfortable.

I suspected that Mom had a thing for Bob, especially when she asked us what we thought of him. She had a way of auditioning prospective boyfriends to us, even though I had never seen them lead to anything. Not that she waited for an answer.

"He's a cool guy, right?" she said. "I mean, anyone who devotes their life to holography has got to be pretty cool."

Having no response to that line of reasoning, we nodded in agreement. We were focusing more on eating our It's-It ice cream sandwiches before they melted than on Mom's thing with Bob.

"Great, because he's agreed to let you guys stay with him and his wife while I wrap things up in Philly."

BOB, HIS WIFE, Sarah, and their two kids, Vanessa and Andre, lived in what had once been a public elementary school in San Rafael. They had converted one of the classrooms into a living space and another one into Bob's holography studio. Kyle and I slept in another classroom that served double duty as a bedroom and storage space.

Mom had shipped my juggling equipment and unicycle from Philadelphia, and I was content to hang out in the former schoolyard practicing by myself, until one day when I heard Kyle get spanked by Sarah. It must have connected to something primal in me, because after I found the door locked, I started slamming my body against it as hard as I could to break it down. When that didn't work, I screamed about the merciless retribution that Mom was going to bring upon them when I told her they hit Kyle. The threats didn't work either, so I ran down the hall and reluctantly took off my shoes to put what little change I had into a pay phone.

Mom was furious. She had a million conditions when it came to leaving us with other people, but the only absolute rule, the one that she could 100 percent never excuse, was the condition that Kyle and I never be physically hit. She told me to pack our stuff and she would be there as soon as possible. After calling Bob at the Holography Museum and threatening him with cops, lawsuits, and prison, she drove straight to the airport and got on the first flight to San Francisco. I was still on the phone when Kyle ran past me straight to the bathroom and locked himself in.

I didn't know what Kyle had done, or how bad he had been hit. He refused to speak to me through the bathroom door, but I was relieved to see the plate of food that Bob left out for him was gone. Kyle didn't come out of the bathroom until the next morning, when he heard Mom's voice in the hall raising hell. I got him and our bags to the car, while Mom and Sarah went nuts on each other. It looked as though it was going to get physical a few times, but Bob did a good job of keeping them apart.

We spent that night back in the same shitty hotel in Corte Madera. The next day we got in the car to "run some errands" and ended up at the San Francisco airport to drop off Mom and pick up Grandma Ada.

"Why, hello, boys. How was New Mexico?" she asked while pinching both of my cheeks and shaking my face around. Thirty seconds later, she finally let go and moved on to Kyle. "Now come on and give your grandma Ada a big kiss. Look how much you've grown. Such big boys."

Grandma Ada rarely said anything that warranted a response, or even made one possible. When she did ask a question, it always led directly into some other train of thought.

"Would you just take a look at that," she said as we were crossing the Golden Gate Bridge. Overtaken by the majesty of it all, she wasn't paying any attention to the road. "The light is magnificent. Have you ever seen anything like the light reflecting off those hills? You never answered me about New Mexico, boys. You know that's where Georgia O'Keeffe did some of her best work. The sky is so much bigger in the desert, and the light is so different that it creates an alternate perspective for the artist. Isn't it amazing how the differences in regional climate and light can affect the art in that area? Oh, the colors Gauguin started using when he went to Tahit—"

"When's Mom coming back?" I cut her off, or she would have gone on forever.

"You should be excited to see your grandmother. Mom didn't tell you I was coming, did she?" This time she paused after her question. Mom hadn't told us anything about it. She probably thought we would have temper tantrums and refuse to get in the car.

"No. Why did she leave again?" I asked.

"Boys, your mother is going through some stuff right now, and I offered to come and take care of you until she gets it worked out. Isn't that exciting? Just us three getting to . . ."

"When is she coming back?" This time it was Kyle who cut her off.

"Well, right now we're going to the hotel, and . . . oh dear, you children must be starving. I'm going to make some ratatouille for dinner. Your favorite . . . I bet you didn't get ratatouille in New Mexico, did you? I started putting just a little bit of basil in it since the last time you guys came to Flori . . ."

"When is she coming back!" I yelled.

"Now, Oran. There is no need to yell. I can hear you perfectly fine. She'll call us when she gets home."

Goddamn, that took long enough.

"What's wrong with her?" asked Kyle. I, too, had no idea what was going on.

"Oh dear. I've been asking myself that same question since she was seven years old," she said to herself. "Your mother's a bit meshugenah is all. I don't know what happened to that girl. She used to be so cute in her little dresses; everyone loved her. You should have seen her back then . . . the way she'd play that piano. Ah," she sighed, "I can still hear her doing Beethoven's Fifth from the living room as if it was yesterday. The proudest day of my life was seeing your mother play at Carnegie Hall when she was thirteen. Then . . . I don't know what happened. She changed. Arthur and I did everything for her. I don't know why she hates me so much."

We had heard this too many times and we weren't interested in what Mom had done when she was thirteen. We wanted to know what was going on now. It was no secret that they had a tense relationship, but while Mom could go on hour-long rants about what was wrong with Grandma, Grandma usually just called Mom meshugenah and went into some cute childhood story or another.

According to Ada, all three of us were nuts, but considering that Kyle and I were living everywhere from Guatemala to New Mexico, going to hippie camps, and living with a holographer, of course we were bound to be crazy. What other outcome could there be? None of this would have happened if Mom had just married a nice Jewish boy.

How could she turn out so meshugenah when both Grandma and our grandfather, Arthur, *rest his soul*, had done nothing wrong? They bought Mom the right dresses and gave her the right education, played her the right music, and took her to the right museums. All the things Ada never got growing up. Her seven brothers and sisters had raised her after their parents died in a car crash, and as far as she knew, she was the last one standing. Arthur had died of cancer when I was a year old, and he was one of the few people on the planet who Mom didn't have anything bad to say about.

Mom just didn't like cute little dresses, she didn't like the right music, and she absolutely hated art as a result of being dragged to countless museums as a kid, all so that she be cultured enough to meet a nice Jewish man, settle down, and raise a nice Jewish family. Instead she became a renegade-feminist-antiestablishment-intellectual-new age hippie psychologist who was against everything Ada stood for.

Mom was having trouble lining up new living situations for Kyle and me. After living with Grandma at the hotel for a few months, we moved to an apartment in Tiburon. We tried to make the best of it, but none of us wanted to be there. Kyle and I weren't settled enough to even think about going to school, and hanging out with Grandma twenty-four hours a day was tough, to say the least.

Fed up and stir-crazy, we somehow got ahold of a blow-up raft and paddled into the San Francisco Bay. Hours later, we washed up somewhere near San Quentin. It was already dark when, wet and shivering, we hauled our little boat over the huge black boulders onto the side of the road. We waited near the DO NOT PICK UP HITCHHIKERS sign, hoping that someone would pick us up and take us home. A woman stopped and was nice enough to drive us back.

After giving us endless big wet grandma kisses and then pinching our cheeks harder than ever, Ada promptly took out a knife and started stabbing the boat. Kyle and I grabbed a couple of steak knives and joined in.

Taking care of us, however, proved to be too much for the poor woman, and other arrangements were soon made. Mom couldn't find anyone to take the both of us, so Kyle went to a foster home with a nice Catholic woman named Pam, and I ended up going to live with Fred, a Sufi clown from Camp Winnarainbow. He was one of my favorite guys, but he had since renounced his Sufi past and converted to born-again Christianity. Mom didn't seem so excited about my staying with them, but I had always liked Fred. The next decision was whether I should go to the born-again-Christian school with his kids or attend the public school near their house. I elected to go to the Christian school so as not to make any waves, but there was only one way Mom would allow it: she refused to sign the corporal punishment release required for admittance.

"Okay, honey. I want you to listen to me very carefully," she told me after signing all the school's paperwork. "You can't tell them this, but I didn't sign the release card. Most likely they'll just assume I did and won't even look. I absolutely cannot sign that thing, so if they find out, you have to go to public school."

"Uh-huh," I agreed.

"This is the important part. If they let you in and you do get in trouble, you need to promise me that you will scream and yell as loud as you can that your mother never signed the release, and she will sue them and shut them down for good if they ever lay a hand on you. Can you make that promise?"

"Okay."

"Good. Let's just hope it doesn't come to that."

A S SOON AS MOM dropped me off, Fred opened my bags and went through each article of clothing I brought with me. He was unfolding my E.T. shirt when, without any warning, he began dry-heaving, dropped a shirt on the floor, and started babbling in some unknown language that sounded a lot like baby talk. I thought he was having a seizure. Whatever was happening resembled an after-school special I had seen where this otherwise normal kid would fall down and start shaking for no particular reason. The kid on TV didn't make the sign of the cross and start hissing at T-shirts, though. Fred backed away from the shirt, still holding his fingers in the sign of the cross until he made it out of the room. He returned moments later, still babbling in that weird language, with a pair of salad tongs he used to pick up the shirt and carry it to the trash.

"E.T. is in place of God!" he yelled at me. He offered no further explanation as he continued going through my stuff, and I tried to figure out what I had done wrong. *E.T.* was my favorite movie, and I too was starting to feel like I was stranded on the wrong fucking planet.

At grace that night, he made reference to the incident and thanked Jesus for getting him through it and giving him the courage to throw Satan in the trash and banish him from this God-fearing house. He threw out the salad tongs as well, since it was likely that Satan had time to enter them from my shirt. His wife, who had been completely silent since I had arrived, served us salad with forks and spoons.

Other than the impressions I got from my mom about Reagan, Nixon, Kissinger, and my dad, Jack, I knew next to nothing about Satan. Fred was the closest thing I had ever seen to my conception of the devil. Even more frightening to me was that someone could change so much in so short a time. I didn't know my dad at all, really, but I couldn't picture him freaking out over a T-shirt. I decided right then and there that I would keep my mouth shut unless opening it was absolutely necessary. I secretly thanked Ada for being Jewish. I had no idea what being Jewish meant, other than that I could not possibly be one of these people.

So that's what I told everyone at school when we were out in the yard and everybody was arguing about who God loved more: Billy or Michael.

"God loves me more because my dad owns a Christian bookstore!" yelled Billy.

"Oh yeah, well, where was your dad on Sunday? I didn't see him at church," countered Michael.

It was insane. All over the school, everyone seemed to be saying the same kind of shit, except for in the hall next to the pastor's office where all you could hear were the screams from the kids whom he was paddling. I wanted to talk to those kids, the ones who hadn't gotten wrapped up in this nonsense, but after he had paddled them, it was too late. They sounded just like everyone else.

Whenever they tried to rope me into their God arguments, I responded by telling them I was Jewish. Again, I wasn't sure how it was all related, but I said it anyway because it always got the response I was looking for.

"God hates Jews," they told me matter-of-factly in the yard. In class, during Sunday school, Bible study, and even from the pulpit, they had a slightly subtler way of saying it, but the implication was clear: Jews were bad. *Thank the fucking Lord for that*, I thought to myself as I watched a few hundred upstanding citizens babbling like a bunch of babies.

It didn't take much to get the paddle, otherwise known as Big Bertha. They always did it with the windows open. You couldn't see the kid getting hit because of the curtains, but you could sure as hell hear them. The thing reportedly had big holes cut out of it to reduce wind resistance, and it left marks in the shape of perfect circles. You could tell which kids had been paddled, because they would do a kind of jump-and-wince thing whenever they heard it.

One day before class, I pushed a girl who was drinking at the water fountain. The push was unjustified and admittedly intentional. I desperately needed some water before class, and she was taking far too long.

"I'm telling on you" was all she said when she turned around, and I could see in her eyes that she knew exactly what that meant: Big Bertha.

I was fed up with the whole thing, so I pushed her again to make sure it wouldn't be an empty threat.

Ten minutes later, the pastor showed up in my history class, where we were reading the Book of Genesis. I stood up the moment I saw him; he didn't even need to call me.

"My mom didn't sign the consent," I told him as we walked down the hall.

"Nonsense. Everyone signs it."

"Not her."

"Everyone signs it," he repeated as we entered the secretary's office. I refused to go any farther, thinking that this was the perfect time and place for the secretary to look at her records. The file cabinets were right behind her.

"Let's go," he told me.

"Not until you look at the card. She would never sign that thing."

"We're not going to look at the card, and you're going to come with me right now. I already told you, everyone signs it, otherwise we don't let you in. That way we don't have to look at the card every time some bratty kid thinks his mom would never sign it. So let's go. Now!"

"If you lay a hand on me, my mom will sue you and she will shut this school down. She did not sign that card!" I screamed in absolute panic.

Mom's plan was not working. *Why wouldn't he pull out the card?* The next thing I knew he had me in a bear hug and was carrying me into the office. I was struggling, but the fucking pastor still managed to bend me over his chair and get my pants down. As far as I could tell, I was screaming louder than any kid I had ever heard, and he hadn't even hit me yet. Just as he was about to come down on me with the wrath of Big Bertha, the secretary ran in holding the card.

"Stop," she said to the pastor. "You need to look at this."

He was still holding me with one arm and had to lay Big Bertha on the desk to take the card. It took a moment for him to figure out what he was looking at. On the line that Mom was supposed to have signed her name were written the words *Do not hit my son* in the same flowing cursive she used for her signature. He stared at the card, dumbfounded. He was literally an arm's length from losing his fucked-up school. I squirmed out of his grip, ran outside, and pulled up my pants.

IN THE MEANTIME, Mom had moved to a houseboat in Sausalito. But whatever she was going through in Philadelphia had obviously come with her, and she was still unable to take care of us. Fred, who seemed to be under the impression that he had been some kind of positive influence on me, refused to drive me into the hands of the devil. Mom couldn't be fucked with, though, and her threats of filing kidnapping charges finally turned him around.

On the way to Mom's houseboat, I had to listen to him for an hour about how I was definitely going to hell, and that now he probably was, too, for delivering a defenseless child into the hands of Satan. He wasn't even sure if he could get the taint of my sin out at the car wash, which meant there was a very good chance that his wife and kids were going to be dragged down as well, and it was all my fault for not rejecting Satan when he guided my hands toward that little girl's shoulders and told me to push. I remained silent the entire drive. I was trying to remember whether I had packed my sticker collection during the rush to get out of there. Thinking about other shit was the only way I knew of to keep the taint of Fred away from my brain. I thought I heard him sniffling as he pulled to a stop in front of the docks, but I refused to look at him. I got out of the car without saying good-bye and walked onto Berth C looking for the blue houseboat.

I had been to the houseboat a few times on weekend visits, but the little floating community was so different from a regular neighborhood that I could never remember where her house was in relation to the seventeenth-century Victorian houseboat, the early Dutch-settler houseboat, or the one made out of bicycle rims and colored Plexiglas. If you ignored the fact that her house was floating in the San Francisco Bay, the place looked relatively conservative. It was a modern design, painted pastel blue, and it basically looked like the top story of a duplex, sticking out of the water. In my excitement over having escaped the Christians and of seeing Mom again, I was a little loud and clumsy when I entered the boat.

"Ow! Oran! Close the door!" I heard her voice in a kind of whispered yell.

"Mom!" I shrieked, excited to be hearing her voice again.

"The door. Please. Please close the door," she implored.

Whatever it was my mom had been going through had now taken physical form. She was totally paralyzed on the left side of her body, and any light gave her excruciating headaches. I closed the door and felt my way through the dark to find her. When I did, I gave her a big hug and cried.

I cried because I had been holding it in for three months, and I cried because I was with my mom again, and I cried, and cried, and cried. And when I got it all out, I could see that she was crying, too.

"It's okay, I'm back now. You can stop crying, Mom."

But Mom was crying from the physical pain of hugging me, and crying because of the physical pain of crying, and crying because she couldn't take care of me.

The next day I went to stay at Kyle's foster home for a few days while arrangements were made for me to go back to Santa Fe, this time by myself.

six

E VERY NIGHT BEFORE going to bed I told myself, *This is the last time I'm going to smoke this shit. I'm going to quit tomorrow.* And every morning I would climb down from my loft and root around in the trash for any remnants of dope that might be in there.

I was now a full-fledged self-hating heroin addict, but life seemed to be getting better. I had finally told the piano guy to fuck off, and at the suggestion of my mom, I wrote up a business proposal to build a recording studio down in my basement. Money was now turning into an issue. I was spending thirty to forty dollars a day on my habit, and the money from my dad wasn't cutting it. As much as the dope was helping me imitate real human beings, I wasn't so good at it that I could hold down a nine to five.

"Jack wants to know where you guys want to eat," Mom asked while we were discussing Jack's upcoming visit. I hadn't seen him in at least a year, but he was coming to town for a few days to do one of his human-potential training sessions.

"Chez Panisse," I answered without any hesitation.

"Whoa, Oran. That's a bit fancy, don't you think?"

"You know what? He can fucking afford it. We've lived three blocks away from it for twelve years and have never eaten there. He's probably been there ten times without inviting us." I was even more agitated on the phone than usual, probably because I was talking to my mom about my dad. Either of those situations alone was enough to send me in to a yelling fit.

"Okay. Calm down, I'll ask him," she said.

I got over to Mom's house in Berkeley an hour before we were supposed to meet Jack, so she could go over my proposal with me. When Kyle and Jack were both there, we walked over to the restaurant. As a kid, I had stopped to look at their menu almost every day and would wonder what Rabbit Loin, Green Bean, and Rocket Salad with Roasted Figs and Basil tasted like. Or what a Grilled Wolf Ranch Quail with Stone-ground Polenta, Sweet Corn, and Torpedo Onion Rings even looked like. Since we were going for lunch, there was nothing so exotic on the menu. But for dinner that night they were serving a King Salmon Carpaccio with Farm Egg and Chervil; a Saffron Risotto with Shellfish, Lemon, and Prosecco; a Grilled Yellow-fin Tuna with Fennel Pollen, Braised Fennel, and Green-Olive Relish; and for dessert, Caramel–Ice Cream Crêpes with Summer Lady Peaches. What the fuck?

We all ordered the salmon. They brought it out in a brown paper bag. I was skeptical, but it was the best salmon I had ever had.

"So how is the piano tuning going?" Jack asked, while we were getting our dessert.

I couldn't believe they were charging twenty dollars for a peach, literally a sliced peach with nothing else—until I tasted it.

"Actually, I wanted to talk to you about that. Holy shit, where did they find this peach? You've got to try this." I couldn't believe it came off a tree. "Oh yeah. So the whole piano thing was a scam. The guy wasn't teaching me anything. I quit."

"What the hell am I giving you eight hundred bucks a month for if you quit?"

Normally I would have shriveled up and agreed with him at this point, but I had smoked just enough dope in my mom's bathroom before lunch to keep my confidence up.

"Well, here's the deal. I don't like taking that money either, so I came up with an idea to start a business and stop relying on you. I would need to borrow some money to get started, but it would be a loan, and I would be able to pay it back in two years."

I pulled my handwritten proposal out of my pocket and went over the itemized list of equipment, rent, building supplies, and construction deadlines. On a different sheet of paper I had drawn up a payment plan including a hand-drawn line at the bottom for my signature.

"So, what do you think?" I asked, as he was looking it over.

"Sure, it sounds great, but I have two concerns. One, what happens if you invest this much time and money into it, and for some reason you lose your warehouse space? And two, I hate to say this, but you just don't have a good track record with money."

"Listen, I'll pay you back no matter what. The worst-case scenario is that I have to sell the equipment and get a job. Either way, you still get your two fifty a month."

"Okay, I'll do it," he said hesitantly, pulling out his checkbook. "But if you don't pay me back, I will never lend you money again. If you do, maybe this could lead to something bigger." He then handed me a check for ten thousand bucks.

"Don't you want me to sign that agreement?" I asked. My voice was shaky from holding that much money.

"No. The ten thousand dollars is nothing to me. I don't care whether you pay it back or not. This is about you being responsible and keeping your word. If you don't, that's fine, but no more money from Jack."

N OT WANTING TO fuck up my one chance at owning my own business, I got to work the next day. It took a week just to get all the materials from the hardware store to the storefront on Mission Street. I would leave them my driver's license in exchange for the use of their pushcart and spend the day hauling lumber and drywall back to my place. Next, I covered the floor and the walls of the basement with sheets of plastic, and then I started framing out the two new rooms. My dope habit was slowly getting bigger, but I needed it to get through the ten-hour days I was spending on the studio. On top of that, I kept ending up in more bands, including a garage band with Eli and Jibz called the Roofies and a Slayer cover band called Sleigher. We wore Santa Claus hats and wrote Christmas lyrics to all the songs. We played "Reindeer in Blood," "Mandatory Yuletide," "South Pole of Heaven," "Seasons Greetings in the Abyss," and "Angel of Mirth," to name a few. It was the hardest music I had ever played, but it was worth it just to see people excited and singing along at our very first show. I was playing in four other bands as well, and I was still the token Jew in the Goys, which I hadn't managed to quit.

I was getting increasingly nervous about being the best man at Sean's wedding. Not that I had to do anything other than get him to the ceremony on time and make a toast, but I didn't have much faith that I was capable of either of those things. Waking up before twelve was almost impossible, but I ended being so anxious about the toast, getting Sean there on time, and not dropping the ring that I ended up not getting any sleep anyway. It didn't help knowing that this girl Heather was going to be there. It's true I would get crushes on almost every girl I saw, but these were mostly phantoms I would pass on the street and never see again, or girls I would sneak glances at on the BART. Before we'd even make it through the tunnel we would have been married, had kids, and gone through an ugly divorce, and I'd walk to my mom's house with a resentment against them. I would also get crushes on girls I saw regularly in the neighborhood, in bars or at shows, but I would avoid talking to them at all costs. If an exchange of words was unavoidable, I would either get paralyzed and fuck everything up or they would say something idiotic, and I would lose my crush. If they didn't say something stupid, I would usually find some way to judge them, even if it was as minor as their platform shoes, which, for some godforsaken reason, had come back in style. And finally, if they had passed all these tests, it was pretty clear that they shouldn't be going after me. Something must be wrong with them, even if I couldn't figure out exactly what.

Heather was an exception to the myriad intentional and unintentional defense mechanisms I had developed over the years to keep myself lonely and miserable. She was smart, cute, cynical, funny, talented, didn't wear those fucking shoes, and most important, in the three years I had known her, had never once exhibited any interest in me whatsoever. She was perfect.

"Hey, Oran. You know Heather's going to be at the wedding. Alex, her ex, just moved to Spain. You can finally get your chance," Sean had told me after rehearsal a few nights earlier.

"You mean my chance to fuck it all up?" I asked.

"Dude, you've been asking about her forever, and she's finally single. That's all I'm saying." Sean loved talking to just about anyone, so he couldn't understand the paralysis I would experience in the presence of girls.

"Thanks for the thought, but you know how I get."

"Goddamn, man. Just say hi to her, okay? She's awesome."

"All right. We'll see what happens. I don't want to think about it anymore." But all I could do was think about it.

I kept thinking about it till we got to the Japanese tea garden up at Golden Gate Park. I thought about it through the ceremony, and I thought about it some more through dinner. Actually, I was fucking obsessed, but I couldn't for the life of me bring myself to say hi to her.

The only reprieve I got from the anxiety of being around Heather was the anxiety of having to do the toast. I had come up with the first half of the first sentence and had drawn a blank. When it seemed as though it was getting close to that time, I ran to my room, smoked some dope, and managed to calm down enough to make my voice shake less. When I got back, I resisted every instinct I had to turn around and run away. Instead, I grabbed a glass of wine, tapped my spoon against it, and waited for the room to quiet down.

"When Eli first told me that the best man's job was to get the groom to the wedding on time, I almost asked Sean to find someone else. As we all know, getting Sean anywhere on time can be an impossible task." I knew that line would be a success, considering at this point in the evening it was still an intimate gathering of bandmates and relatives, all of whom dealt with Sean's habitual lateness regularly. I wasn't so sure Sean would laugh, but he did. I went into some awkward ad-lib about how we met, and when it seemed like I had been up there long enough I ended with, ". . . but as you all know, Sean is such a talented musician, and good friend, that he has always been worth waiting for." *Totally lame*, I thought to myself as I sat down and tried to forget about it. *And I didn't say anything about Christine. What an asshole.*

After dinner the party livened up pretty quickly. The band started playing, and everyone started getting smashed. The ceremony and dinner had been a small gathering, but not because Sean and Christine lacked friends. Sean had been playing music in the city for years now and knew just about everyone, and slowly but surely, the place filled up. I found Jake and just kind of stuck with him. I was pretty intimidated by this crowd of Mission hipsters who had taken over our house, even though I had a pretty good idea that I was one of them.

"So what's going on? You talk to Heather yet?" Jake asked.

"No, man. I can't do it. She freaks me out," I answered.

"Jesus, do it for me then. You've been talking about her for how long now? It's driving me crazy. 'I saw Heather walking down the street today . . . I ran into Heather at the store . . . Heather this . . . Heather that.' Just go talk to her. She's right there."

I couldn't help glancing over to where he was looking, and I made eye contact with her by accident. I quickly looked down at the floor and turned back toward Jake.

"Damn," I said under my breath.

While Jake was imploring me to just go over and talk to her, I heard a voice from behind me say, "Hi, Oran."

I turned around and it was Heather.

"Hey, Heather, how's it going?" My heart was racing and sweat was starting to bead up on my forehead and upper lip, which made me more self-conscious and made my heart beat faster, and made me sweat even more. All I could do was stand there and try to look calm. I moved over a step, hoping to let Jake into the conversation, but he had vanished.

"I just wanted to come over and say hi, since I didn't get a chance all day." She looked like a grown-up version of a Margaret Keane painting: big eyes, small face, little-boy haircut. So fucking cute.

"Your toast was hilarious. Someone needed to say that."

"Yeah, well, I was just trying to be funny, but I was a little worried about bumming Sean out. That guy can be a little sensitive, you know?" I was surprised that my mouth was moving and words were coming out. I was calming down a little bit.

"Jeez, you're telling me? I'm in a band with him, too, you know," she said.

"By the way, I wanted to tell you, that last show I saw at the Chameleon was great. You're an amazing drummer."

"Yeah, right. What a disaster. Jeff Ray and his fucking guitars. It's like the Three Stooges up there."

"But there are five of you," I pointed out.

"Yeah, but the only way I can deal with it is to pretend that Tracy and I just happen to be onstage watching *The Three Stooges*. That way it's actually pretty funny seeing those three guys run around changing instruments and tripping all over their cords. Otherwise, I'd lose my mind. How's Optimist International doing?"

"Sean didn't tell you about San Pedro?" I asked her, kind of surprised.

"No. I knew you guys went down to L.A., but he didn't say anything about it."

I told her a few stories from our recent tour of Southern California and noticed that my anxiety had all but disappeared. I was more or less able to be myself around her. We continued talking for a while, and I kept waiting for her to say something stupid, or me to say something stupid, or anything that might give me the slightest reason to judge her, but it never happened.

"Well, I think I've had too much to drink, but I need to say bye to a few people before I leave. It was good talking to you."

"Yeah . . . okay." There seemed to be a moment of awkwardness where we couldn't tell if we should hug, shake hands, or . . . then she walked away, and my paralysis came back full force. *Shit. Did it go okay? Did I say anything dumb? Should I have asked her if she wanted to get a drink sometime? Fuck. I think I just screwed the whole thing up.* I needed to talk to someone.

I looked around the crowd to find Jake, but he had already reappeared in his old spot right next to me.

"Finally. So what happened? You guys were talking forever."

"I don't know," I muttered.

"What do you mean you don't know? Did you get her number, or ask her to go out?"

"No. I don't know how to do that."

"What the hell were you guys talking about for so long?"

"Stuff," I said. While Jake was trying to get information out of me, someone grabbed me around the waist from behind. When I turned around to figure out what happened, all I saw was a blur of people dancing.

"What was that?" I asked Jake.

"I don't know, it happened so fast, but I think that was Heather."

"Heather? What was she wearing? Was it like a white lacy thing?"

"Yeah. That was her. Oran, she just gave you a hug from behind." He said it as if a "hug from behind" were a thing I should somehow know about.

"What should I do?" A flood of longing, excitement, anxiety, loneliness, and, finally, depression hit me.

"Cranberry! She just came up to you and gave you a hug from behind! Are you crazy? Go outside and find her! Now, man!" He said the whole thing loudly and slowly to make sure I could understand him.

"Uh . . . I'm sure she's gone by now," I said, contrary to everything I was feeling. I did want to run after Heather and tell her that she was the cutest girl ever, and that I had a crush on her from the moment I saw her, and I couldn't stop thinking about her, and if she just gave me a chance . . . but I couldn't fucking move.

"Did you hear what I said?" His voice was getting louder. "Go! Go now, Cranberry! I don't see you going!" I had never seen him so frustrated before. "Ahh! Jesus Christ, you're killing me, man."

"Maybe I'll call her tomorrow," I said, depressed and confused. I wanted her to hug me again. It felt nice. Damn.

Jake lowered his head in total defeat and said, "Un-fucking-believable, man. Un-fucking-believable."

———

I DECIDED I WAS going to call Heather, I just wasn't sure when. First of all, I had to get my shit together and stop smoking dope. It was a good incentive. I hardly ever ran into her, so I knew it was just a matter of time before some other guy wouldn't stand there like an idiot the next time she felt like hugging someone and running away. What the hell was wrong with me? Before I got the chance, though, I ran into her and Sean at the Casanova.

"Hey, Heather, it's good to see you. Twice in one week even."

"Yeah. Well, I don't usually come here, but we just got out of rehearsal and . . . hey, you want to get something to eat? I'm starving."

I wasn't hungry, but I wasn't going to let her run away again.

"Yeah, where do you want to go?"

I didn't even say hi to Sean. We just started heading back out the way I came in.

"I don't know. I just want to get out of here. I don't really like this place." She seemed agitated about something. We started walking up Valencia, and I asked her if she had made it home okay after the wedding. She looked at me kind of suspicious. "Uh, what do mean?" she asked. It would have been a perfect opportunity to ask her about running out of the wedding the way she did, but I dropped the ball.

"Oh, just 'cause you said you were pretty drunk. That's all." She seemed relieved that I didn't bring it up.

We were coming across Seventeenth Street, and Heather said, "Hey, do want to go in that alley and make out?"

Holy shit. I was stunned. Even I couldn't fuck this one up.

"I can't think of a single thing in the whole world I would rather do," I said.

We didn't talk for a while after that. We just hid in the dark, making out, oblivious to the legendary reek of Clarion Alley. There were also some incredible murals in there, but at night it just smelled like rotting trash and urine. I lost my sense of time, but at some point I said, "Wow, you have no idea how long I have been wanting that to happen."

"Really? Even at the wedding I couldn't tell at all. Me, too, though."

"Ever since the first time I saw you. It was your first show with Sean, like three years ago," I said, remembering how mesmerized I was by that train wreck of a first show.

"I got you beat. You were one of the first people I noticed when I moved to San Francisco. You used to serve me coffee at the Art Institute Café."

"No way. I would have noticed you."

"Nah, I was just this shy little punk-rock girl. I had a shaved head and I just lurked around. I didn't talk to anyone."

"Shit. I feel bad that I don't remember," I said, trying to visualize her with a shaved head.

"Hey, I've got another confession to make. At the wedding, that was me who hugged you and ran out of there all crazy. I was just so frustrated. I didn't know what else to do, so . . ."

"I kind of figured that out, but I wasn't sure," I lied.

"Wait. That's not the confession. I was so frustrated from talking to you that on my way home I walked into the Casanova and grabbed some random guy, and . . ." I waited for her to finish. "I can't believe I'm telling you this, but I took him home. I just didn't know what else to do. That's why I needed to get out of the Casanova and looked at you strange when you asked me if I got home okay. I thought maybe you knew."

"I didn't have any idea. Well, I'll take it as a compliment, I guess, but I wish you would have taken me home instead."

"Me too. Believe me. But tonight I have to go home alone," she said.

"What? You mean I basically got some random guy laid the other night and now you have to go home alone?" I said, pretending to joke. I mean, who else could this happen to but me?

"Yup, but don't worry. I'm not going anywhere."

"You just said you were going home." I was joking this time, and she laughed. I didn't try too hard to get her to change her mind for two reasons. One, I never tried too hard, and two, I hadn't brought any dope with me. I would have gladly traded spending the night with Heather for a morning of being dope sick if that's how it was going, but she was determined to leave by herself.

"Okay, but promise me you won't go in any bars on your way home," I said, giving her a final kiss goodnight.

"I promise."

I watched her walk down the street till she disappeared. Then I started home down Seventeenth Street. I needed to avoid the Casanova because I couldn't stop smiling. I didn't want to freak anyone out.

I was still smiling the next day, and for the next week, and the next month. For the first time I could remember, I was pretty psyched. I had an amazing girlfriend, and I started my first recording job the day after I finished soldering the last of the three hundred cables. The first band was two black guys of questionable sexual orientation, and even more questionable musical skill, called Rocket Science and the Nigger-Loving Faggots. With a name like that, you didn't need to be good. Their lack of skill ended up working to my advantage anyway. Since the drummer seemed to think the microphones were actually tiny little drums, I got an extra two days of work just trying to mute all the mic hits out of the mix. I ended up making twice my rent in the first four days of business. With my new smile, and a rate of fifteen dollars an hour, getting clients wasn't a problem at all.

What I couldn't understand was how the better things kept getting, the more I seemed to hate myself. It didn't make sense, because I'd always believed that if I just got this, that, or the other thing, I would be fine. I had the girlfriend, the recording studio, my music, my friends, and . . . I was a junkie, and a lying piece of shit.

As long as I was working, or playing music, or hanging out with Heather, I was fine. I had somehow managed to believe my own lies enough to convince myself I was doing great, until I started getting goose bumps, my nose started running, and I had to excuse myself to go get high. I dreaded it. Every six hours I would face the most hateful, venomous, self-critical motherfucker on the planet, as I hid in the bathroom, smoking enough dope to get well. Coming out, I would completely forget all about it and jump right back into whatever I was doing, oblivious that I had just been doing heroin. It was the only way I could keep the act going. I was actually the worst actor in the world, but I had figured out that if I believed my own lies, I could fool anyone.

My version of reality was questionable before I ever started using dope, and now it had split off into two distorted versions of itself: the one where for the first time in my life I felt comfortable enough in my own skin to talk to people and be witty, and charming, and tell them how great everything was going, and the one where I was in my room, chain-smoking Pall Malls, looking at pornography on my computer, doing dope, and telling myself what a fucking piece of shit I was until the inner dialogue got so brutal that the only way to shut it up was to smoke enough heroin to pass out.

I didn't have a plan for when these two realities collided. The first time it happened, I had broken one of my rules. I had a whole bunch of rules. One of them was not bringing dope to Heather's house. As a result, I would wake up sick, in a puddle of sweat every morning, as if I had literally taken a shower in my sleep. I don't know how she put up with it. Twice, though, I ended up at Heather's house with dope on me because I hadn't planned on going there, and as long as I had it with me, there was no way I could keep myself from doing it. I knew women faked orgasms all the time and got away with it, but I had never faked one before, and aside from my bad acting skills, there's another far more obvious problem with men faking orgasms than women.

The first time I did it, she didn't say anything, but it made me feel fucking awful. I told myself I was a terrible person, which was nothing new, but I was used to only allowing myself to feel that way in the privacy of my own room, not in my girlfriend's bed. The second time I tried faking an orgasm, she brought it up and I was caught totally unprepared. For all the rules and systems I had set up not to get caught, I hadn't come up with a plan if I did. My two realities had collided, and it was as if I was as surprised as anyone else that I was a junkie.

"Hey, I wanted to ask you this last time, but what happened?" Heather asked after I had recovered from my lame act of being out of breath and relaxed.

"What?" I asked. I had heard her, but I needed time to come up with an answer.

"What just happened?" she asked again.

"What do you mean?" I was starting to panic.

"You did that once before as well."

"Did what once before?" I was racking my brain, but I couldn't come up with anything even remotely like an excuse.

"You know . . . didn't finish?"

"Uh . . . well . . . shit . . . Oh man, you're going to hate me." I was looking for the right words. How do you tell your girlfriend you're addicted to heroin?

"I'm addicted to heroin," I said, and immediately started crying uncontrollably. As much as I was afraid she would kick me out then and there (I wouldn't have blamed her if she had), it was a relief to finally tell someone. Although my orgasm had been an act, the crying was real and fucking pathetic, and I couldn't stop. I hadn't expected to break down like I did, but keeping it a secret was killing me. Heather was staring off into space with a totally blank expression.

"I should probably leave," I blubbered. "Really, it has nothing to do with you. You shouldn't be involved."

"How long has it been?" she finally asked. She was scrunched up in the far corner of the bed, against the wall.

"I don't know. Maybe five months now, something like that. I fucking hate it. I just got physically addicted is all, and I've been too stressed out and busy to quit. And I'm just smoking it," I said, as if that somehow made it better. It sounded better to me at least. I believed every word I was saying.

"Okay, listen. You don't have to leave, and I don't hate you. I'm actually relieved that you told me. I thought it was something much worse. But you have to stop. I don't know what I can do, but I'll help in whatever way I can. You have to take this seriously, even if it means getting out of town for a while. It's way more important than your bands or your studio. I'm serious. You have got to quit soon."

I was amazed she didn't throw me out. Jesus, I would have broken up with me years ago if I knew how. And she even said she would help. I started to regain my composure a little.

"Hey, what could be worse than what I just told you?" Because I really couldn't imagine what that could be.

"Nothing. It doesn't matter."

"What is it?" I said, and with that she burst out in tears.

"I thought it was because I was too old," she cried. I didn't know what to say. It would have never occurred to me that she had been thinking that. I always forgot that she was a few years older than me because she definitely didn't look it. Why didn't I see it? What else would she have thought? What a selfish asshole I was.

"Whoa. Heather, I'm so sorry. I had no idea. That couldn't be further from the truth, I swear." But I knew it wasn't going to help. It wasn't the issue.

She kept crying, and I decided I was going to get clean for real. It was dawning on me for the first time that no matter how much of a secret I kept it, my drug use was affecting other people. I didn't really care about myself, but Heather didn't deserve any of this. If I couldn't do it for myself, at least I could do it for her.

WALKING HOME THE next morning, I noticed a small sign on the door of this fancy-looking acupuncture place on Valencia Street that said ACUPUNCTURE FOR HEROIN ADDICTS, $5, 7–9 A.M. It was unnerving. I wasn't a big fan of signs from God, but I couldn't ignore it after what had happened last night. *Why had I never seen it before?* It was about eight o'clock, and, despite a ton of apprehension, I walked in.

The waiting room was dead silent and there wasn't anyone at the desk. I was about to leave when a woman appeared, and simply said, "The sign?" pointing at the door. I nodded and she led me back to another room with six tables and motioned for me to lie down on one. I had no idea what to expect, but for five bucks it seemed like it was worth a shot. I lay down on the table and the woman tapped three needles into each of my ears and left. It felt like a lot more than an hour went by before she came back and took the needles out. As I walked back out to the waiting room, she was leading someone in, and without a word I handed her five bucks and left. It was about ten thirty, and I realized she had just left me there till her first real client showed up.

I went home, starting to feel pretty shitty. I looked through the phone book under "addiction" and called a few advice hotlines. One place was right around the corner, and I made an appointment to go talk to them.

"So how long did you say it's been?" this older black guy asked me from across his desk. I had made the appointment for three o'clock, and I managed to hold out on buying dope till about two thirty. I always ended up getting too high when I held out so long.

I zoned out for a second and had to ask, "I'm sorry, what was that?"

"How long you been using dope, man?"

"Four or five months . . . something like that."

"Uh-huh, and you think you could kick by getting acupuncture, and coming here for counseling?" he asked me with a hint of *boy you must be crazy* in his voice.

"I don't know. I mean, I'm only smoking it. It shouldn't be that bad. Right?"

"Honestly, I have no idea. Our clients usually detox at the Salvation Army or somewhere and do the counseling to stay clean, not get clean."

"But it could work? Maybe?" I really wanted him to agree with me.

"Maybe it could. We start at eleven in the morning. Come by if you feel like it."

I never went back. I tried the Haight Ashbury Free Clinic next, and they gave me a bag of Extra Strength Tylenol and some shit for stomach cramps. The stuff was worse than a placebo; it actually made me feel shittier. Heather didn't bring it up too much, but about once a week she would ask me what was going on and I'd give her a doctored-up progress report. I was managing to cut down a little, but shit came up all the time that seemed like a valid excuse to use. I couldn't do a full day in the studio if I was sick. I couldn't play those Sleigher songs if I was sick. I couldn't go out if I was sick, and I definitely couldn't tell people how great I was doing if I was going through heroin withdrawal. About all I could do was lie down on a table with needles sticking out of my ears. Since that first morning I walked into the acupuncture place I hadn't exchanged words with the woman who worked there. I would go in and she'd stick the needles in my ears until the first customer arrived. I was the only person who showed up for the 7–9 A.M. junkie special. I felt guilty toward the acupuncturist too. She must have been waking up at six in the morning for five extra bucks, and I really wasn't showing much progress.

A FTER ABOUT A MONTH of this really trying routine, I got a phone call from a bass player, Jeremy, who asked me if I could go on tour in three days with his band, Caroliner. Their drummer, Mike, had just quit over some girlfriend drama.

"I've never heard them. What kind of music is it?"

"You've never heard of Caroliner? How is that possible? They've been around for sixteen years. I thought everyone knew about them."

"I've heard *of* them, but I thought it was just some generic noise band. I didn't know you and Mike were in it." Mike was an amazing drummer.

"Yeah, we've been in it for a few years now. I can't believe you've never seen us. It's perfect for you."

"I don't know. I can't keep up with Mike, that's for sure."

"You don't have to. Just do whatever you want. It'll be perfect. I promise."

"Shit. Three days? Let me call you back in a minute."

I hung up and called Heather at the photo gallery she worked at to tell her about the phone call from Jeremy, and without any hesitation she said, "Call him back and say yes. Don't think about it. Just tell him you're going."

"Yeah, but I mean I've never even heard them before. What if it's the worst thing ever?"

"That's not what it's about. You have to go," she said. "Listen, I got to get back to work. Call that guy back and tell him you'll do it!"

"Okay," I said, getting ready to hang up.

"And find out when you'll be in New York. I'm going there for work in two weeks."

Typically, I would have liked at least to hear the music, and maybe meet the folks in the band, but Heather was right. It had nothing to do with whether I liked the music or the people, for that matter. I had to get the fuck out of San Francisco. I spent the next few days with Jeremy, a banjo player named Thomas, and Cheryl, the violin player, going over the songs. It was the best band I had heard in San Francisco, and I was surprised I had never seen them before.

The singer was apparently too busy dealing with last-minute tour stuff to come to rehearsal. When I told Sean I was leaving, he asked me what I thought of Grux.

"What?" I couldn't understand him. It sounded like he was eating a piece of celery and talking at the same time.

"You mean you don't know Grux? Oh, man . . ."

"Wait. Say it one more time. I might have met him." It was a weird name. I couldn't be hearing him right. Grux?

"*Grux!* The main guy! The singer!"

"No. I haven't met him yet, he's been busy trying to reschedule a bunch of shows since we're leaving three days late."

"Well, seriously, man. You should try to meet him before you get in a van with him for a month."

"Why? Is he weird?"

Sean laughed at that one. "Is he weird? Dude, his name is Grux, and he's been doing obscure noise music for sixteen years. He is the textbook example of weird."

"Well, I'm pretty used to weirdos by now, and I already said yes."

"Yeah, but . . . Oh well. I guess you'll find out."

He wasn't the only one to ask about Grux. It seemed that everyone I called to say good-bye to, or reschedule recording sessions with, said the same thing.

"What do you think of Grux?"

"I haven't met him yet."

"What! And you're . . ."

"Yeah, yeah, yeah . . . I heard he's weird."

"Weird? That's a bit of an understate—"

"Listen, I have to make some other calls," I said, cutting them off.

How bad could this guy be? I was only going to kick dope anyway. I didn't see how this guy could make matters worse than they already were.

I devised a system to taper off by filling a nasal spray bottle with heroin and water, and the idea was to sniff just enough of the stuff to get well when I was really hurting. Then every night I would top off the bottle with water, slowly weakening the solution. I would supplement as little dope as possible with large quantities of alcohol to take the edge off. I could only hope that the two hundred bucks I had spent on heroin was going to be enough.

The plan may have made sense logically, but I had a feeling it wasn't going to be so easy.

seven

*In which the boy finds himself living among
misfits, radicals, anarchists, and robots
while performing daring feats with a band
of clowns*

I ARRIVED AT THE SANTA FE Community School only to leave
the next morning for their annual field trip to the International Free
School Convention. The previous year we had spent a fun month driving
to Boston and back, and this year the convention was in Miami. There
were about fifteen of us in an old International school bus, and as nice as
it was to see Ed, Denis, and the rest of the group—especially after being
around the born-again Christians—it just wasn't the same without Kyle.

When we got to Houston, we were closer to the ocean than many of
the kids had ever been, so we took a detour down to Galveston. It was
the ugliest beach I had ever seen, covered in spots of crude oil and surrounded by offshore wells and tankers. Ed told us that anyone who wasn't
back in forty-five minutes wouldn't get to go to Disneyworld.

Never having seen waves before, most of the others were scared to
get in. It wasn't even the ocean, it was a gulf for Christ's sake. Ignoring
the SEVERE UNDERTOW signs, I put on my shorts and went for a swim.
When I turned around a few minutes later, I could barely see the bus
parked on the side of the road. I started swimming back, but I wasn't
making any progress. So I tried harder, even though it didn't seem to
make a difference. Panicking, I put even more effort into it, but I could
only keep it up for so long. The moment I started treading water to catch
my breath, I could feel myself getting sucked back out. I panicked again

and put everything I had into it, but I was starting to have trouble staying up. Then I really started freaking out. I began to scream for help, but that wasn't helping me catch my breath either, and I could barely keep my head up. I never stopped struggling, but at some point, my efforts just weren't helping anymore and I started going under.

I don't know how he found me, but out of nowhere an arm reached down into the water, got me in a headlock, and pulled me up. It was Denis, the physics teacher. The timing was eerie. Another few seconds and it might have been over.

When we got to Orlando, Ed made good on his threat of not letting me go to Disney World and made me wait in the parking lot. I tried every combination of crying, swearing, yelling, and blaming, all to no avail. For five hours I sat in the bus, seething. I thought it went against Ed's whole philosophy of learning from our mistakes, but he said that when our mistakes affect other people, those who are affected get to decide the consequences. I had held up the group for over an hour while I was out there drowning.

The trip was terrible, but during the month I was away, Mom had moved out of the houseboat and into a huge mansion rented in San Rafael. When I got back, I was happy to finally be reunited with Mom and Kyle. Even Laurel, our old housekeeper, had come out to join us. Mom wasted no time in finding me a new juggling teacher, and Kyle and I started taking gymnastics and breakdancing classes as well.

On Sundays Laurel took Kyle and me to her church, which couldn't have been more different from the one I had gone to with Fred. Laurel's crowd sang, danced, started shaking, and fell down. Even though the preacher read from the same book, it came out sounding totally different. I still wasn't buying into it, but at least they were having fun. Even I couldn't help dancing once the gospel band got going.

It was just like old times with all of us back together again, and Kyle and I even got to experience public school for a few months, until Mom asked me what I thought about the idea of joining a circus.

THE AUDITION WAS at a big compound called The Farm in San Francisco's Mission District. I juggled in front of a few people, who then asked me why I wanted to join the circus. I told them, "I just want to make people happy," which was the stock line I had been using whenever I was asked why I juggled. This explanation always made me feel like a liar and a fraud, but no one ever questioned it. After seeing my mom hand a check to the woman who appeared to be in charge, I was informed that I had been accepted. The exchange of money was never mentioned to me, but it was hard not to wonder how much passing the audition had to do with that check. It worked the other way around with the rest of the performers. At the end of the week, Leticia, the director, would walk around and hand *them* checks. It bothered me that I had been accepted because of a payoff rather than my skill as a juggler. Granted, I had just turned nine years old, but I was by far the best juggler there. I tried to put it out of my mind, thinking this was just a trial period. Once they realized how talented I was, they would start paying me instead of the other way around.

Shortly after my audition, Mom worked out a deal with my school where I was able to get credit for "life experience" in the circus, so I stopped going to class and started taking the bus to San Francisco every day for intense rehearsals.

The circus was small. There were only five performers, which meant that just being a juggler (me), or a tightrope walker (Francesca), or trapeze artist (Pierre), or an acrobat (Robert) wasn't enough. Even though each of us had our specialty, we all had to do a bit of everything. Leticia, who didn't really have any circus skills, was the director and main clown. For ten hours a day I practiced acrobatics, tightrope walking, stilts, trapeze, and slapstick. When I wasn't working on that stuff, I was teaching the others how to juggle. It was hard work, I was always sore, and my armpits were in constant pain from jumping off a three-high twenty times a day.

The three-high was the most dangerous part of the show, so we had to practice it incessantly, as there was no room for error. It was a difficult trick. Francesca would jump up on Robert's shoulders using his calf as a kind of springboard to launch off of. I would do the same thing to get up on Pierre's shoulders so he could transfer me to Robert and Francesca. The complicated part was getting from Pierre's shoulders to Francesca's. We had tried various ways of getting me up there, but almost all of them ended up with me swinging through the air in the harness I was attached to. Francesca wasn't tied in, and if I didn't send her off balance while trying to get on her shoulders, I would usually knock her down when I came swinging back in her direction. Robert, who was trying to hold all of us up, didn't seem to be enjoying it much either, but Leticia was adamant that this was going to be the grand finale with me juggling three clubs up on top. Eventually I figured out how to get up there, but the next problem was how to get down. The idea was for all three of us to jump at the same time, cued by a count-off from the band. The band hadn't started rehearsing with us yet, so Leticia would count off for us. Francesca would jump backward to get out of my way while I fell straight down to be caught by Robert. When he did manage to catch me, he would grab my underarms so tightly that after five attempts what started as a yelp of pain became a scream. By the twentieth jump I was forcing back tears. This went on every day, with Leticia reminding us there wouldn't be a harness in the show, which caused Robert to grip my armpits even harder. It didn't take me long to start hating that guy.

THE FARM WAS part circus rehearsal space, part punk-rock club, part apartment complex, part animal farm, part community garden, part preschool, and part anything else that could bring in a few extra bucks. When the circus finally started the new season, I began staying at The Farm since there was no way I could make it from Marin County to wherever we were performing by 6:00 A.M. The guy who ran The Farm, a lawyer named Andy, assured my mom that I would be fine there, and I started sharing an apartment that was built into one of the two airplane hangars attached to the back of the main building, with a night nurse from San Francisco General Hospital. The other hangar was home to a group called Survival Research Laboratories, which built huge, evil-looking robots whose only purpose was to destroy each other. Although I hated waking up at 5:00 A.M. and not getting home till 10:00 P.M., I enjoyed living in that madhouse. The residents were mostly self-obsessed creative types who held menial jobs in order to support their art.

My roommate, whom I rarely saw because our schedules were so different, seemed to be the exception. The only thing I could find out about her that might be considered unique was that she chewed tobacco. At least she had left a can of Skoal lying around in the apartment, and having nothing better to do, I decided to try it one night. I immediately started sweating and puked all over the floor before I could make it to the communal bathroom down the hall. I couldn't understand why anyone would chew that stuff. I remembered getting sick when I drank that bottle of wine, but mostly I remembered being funny and entertaining. This stuff only made me sick. I still felt nauseated the next day while performing in Tracy, a town between San Francisco and Fresno. I couldn't be certain whether I was still feeling ill from the chewing tobacco or from the ninety-degree heat and Tracy's overwhelming smell of manure. In either case, it was all I could do not to vomit standing on top of the three-high for our grand finale.

O UR SHOW WAS split into three parts. The first part we referred to as the Adult Show. The story line was a political commentary on the Reagan administration, as told through juggling, trapeze, tightrope walking, and a misguided elephant that would repeatedly appear onstage to ruin our acts. I was too small for the elephant costume, which required two people to operate. Everyone but me took shifts in it since it came out to ruin everyone's act at least once. The audience would go nuts every time it came out to knock me over, right as I was about to be the first person ever in the world to juggle fifteen balls. The Adult Show got that name not because of the political theme, but because before I had joined, only adults performed in it.

The big selling points of our circus, at least when it came to applying for grants, were the second two parts: the Workshop and the Kids' Show. Our audiences consisted of kids, ages five to twelve, and their parents. After we in the Adult Show did our thing, four of us would hold workshops with the kids for another hour or so, teaching them to walk on the tightrope, juggle, do somersaults, and so on. Pierre got to sit the second half out, since it would have been a terrible idea to let inexperienced kids swing from the forty-foot trapeze. It didn't even seem like a very good idea to let *him* do it. Instead of a net, we put a six-inch-thick piece of foam directly under the trapeze, and Robert would stand there, pretending to be ready to catch him should he lose his grip. The four-foot strip of foam was all for show. Once Pierre got swinging, it was far more likely that he would have landed out in the audience, or hopefully on top of the truck parked backstage, than into the armpit-destroying hands of Robert.

My workshops ranged in size from ten to twenty-five kids, depending on the turnout, and I had only an hour to get them ready for the Kids' Show. I wasn't a very good teacher, but there were always two or three kids who could actually keep three balls in the air after only an hour. I became pretty good at spotting the ones with no talent and would hand them some scarves to throw around. There was always at least one crier, but most of the kids were pretty excited to be in the circus for a few hours, showing off their new skills, juggling scarves or doing somersaults in the ring. I didn't like being around kids that much and didn't really know how to talk to them. They all seemed so immature and direction-less to me. The workshops were one of my least favorite parts of being in the circus.

I had a lot of least favorite parts.

Waking up at 5:00 A.M. every morning sucked. I hated Robert more than anyone, but he lived closer to The Farm than anyone else, so he was there every morning to pick me up. Getting rides from Robert sucked.

Upon arrival at the site, I had the unfortunate job of picking up dog shit. I wouldn't have been so opposed to it had the job not come with the official title Pooper Scooper. It may have been intended to make the job cute-sounding, but for some reason that title had the opposite effect on me. It was actually a high-pressure job, considering we couldn't really begin setting up until the area was shit-free, but instead of lending a hand, everyone else would stand around impatiently, watching me pick up feces. If we were really running late, the other members would walk around looking for dog shit, and yell, "Pooper scooper!" at the top of their lungs. I would then run over and pick the shit up with one of my clear plastic bags. Picking up dog shit sucked.

After setting up, which took about four hours, it was time to get into costume in preparation for the arrival of the kids, who would start show-ing up around 10:00 A.M. I had to put on a pair of blue tights, a red leotard, and a pair of shorts that had been painted to look like Jackson Pollock made them. Then I would walk around the audience in full clown makeup and hand out brochures. Being a clown was one thing, but *feeling* like a clown sucked.

Setting up, performing, and then teaching, often in ninety-degree heat, was a tough job. It was usually three o'clock by the time we took off our outfits, at which point it was time to tear down. Tearing down after what had already been a grueling ten-hour day really fucking sucked.

I did my best to smile and keep my feelings to myself. I even told people that being in the circus was fun. Every kid's dream. That kind of shit. A local news station shot a segment on me and when they asked why I wanted to be in the circus, I gave them my stock answer. What else was I going to say? I had no idea why anyone would want to be in the circus, but when I saw myself on TV, it did look pretty convincing. No one seemed to question my enthusiasm, which is why I was stunned when Leticia told me I wasn't going to be performing in the next season.

"You're kicking me out? What did I do?" I asked her. I was devas-tated, not because I would no longer be in the circus, but because I was being rejected. It was my first clear sign of failure. What had I done wrong? I worked my ass off for these people. I didn't know what to say. I was paralyzed, which was the only thing that kept me from crying.

"Listen, you didn't do anything wrong. It's just a lot of work taking a kid on the road, and . . . well, actually, it's even harder dealing with your mom. We've all got too much going on to be able to talk to your mom every day, and frankly, it's not so easy to tell whether you're here because you want to be or because of her."

I stared at her, trying to figure out the answer to that one. Not my answer, but the right answer. In that moment it seemed as if the rest of my life depended on it.

"Of course I want to be in the circus. This is what I do. I don't have anything else."

Leticia looked at me dubiously. "Okay, but we've all been under the impression that if it wasn't for your mom, you'd be doing something else. I mean, you're a great juggler but. . . . Listen, this is what we'll do. You can't come on the road with us, but we'll keep you on for the local shows. Okay?"

I was still seething when I smiled and said thank you. It was only a few minutes before I found myself wishing that they had just kicked me out. I didn't want to spend fourteen hours a day with these motherfuckers, who didn't want me around anyway. Assholes. Come to think of it, I did hate the circus, but I really wanted to live at The Farm again during the next season.

TO MAKE MATTERS worse, my mom, Kyle, and I moved to Berkeley, shortening the commute to San Francisco considerably. When spring came around, and we started rehearsing again, I didn't get to live at The Farm anyway. Mom decided that instead of waking up at 5:30 in the morning, I could just as easily wake up at 4:00 and take BART in to the city. Every kid's dream.

It was another six months of unrelenting physical pain, and if I thought I was tired before, I was now always on the verge of exhaustion. I was lucky if I made it home by ten, but no matter how tired I seemed to be, I would get insomnia from thinking about the various problems I had with almost everyone I knew: Leticia, for being a bitch; Robert, for his unrelenting abuse of my armpits; and of course my mom for waking me up at four every morning after not sleeping because all these people were out to get me. It was getting harder to hide my discontent, except for those couple of hours when I put on my clown makeup, leotard, and tights and did my best to pretend I was enjoying myself.

I was becoming more and more drawn to The Farm. The punks, hippies, anarchists, and other indefinable weirdos held a strange attraction for me. I didn't have a room there anymore, but I was able to talk Andrew into letting me sleep in any available corner of the place, rather than come back and forth from Berkeley. I usually slept on or behind the stage, but when they started having more punk-rock shows in the main space, he gave me a key to the preschool downstairs.

It wasn't the best arrangement, considering the stage was directly over my head. It was so noisy I couldn't sleep at all, but in the beginning I was too afraid to go upstairs. Judging from the characters drinking and smoking outside, it didn't seem to be much of an atmosphere for kids. After the third night of trying to sleep through one of these shows, I gave up and went upstairs to see what was going on.

There were hundreds of people up there. The most insane people I had ever seen. Mohawks, leather pants, tattoos, nose rings, and one guy who had shaved most of his head except for two very realistic devil horns that he had sculpted out of his hair. These people looked how I felt. Pissed off. I liked them even though I was completely invisible. No one bothered me up there except Andrew, who spotted me and asked, "Aren't you supposed to be sleeping?"

"How the fuck am I supposed to sleep through this?" I yelled at him.

"Listen, I don't care what you do. I'm only bringing it up so if your mom asks me why you fell asleep in the middle of your show tomorrow, I can tell her I told you to go sleep."

"Don't worry about it, I won't tell my mom. What's going on in there anyway?"

"These guys are called the Circle Jerks. What do you think?" he asked, grinning.

"It sounds like shit," I said, leaning close to him so as not to offend anyone. As much as I was drawn to the crowd's look and demeanor, the music was terrible.

Like most white music, the stuff lacked any soul whatsoever. So much so that it almost seemed intentional, as if a whole lot of effort went into taking every ounce of soul out of it. How did people dance to this stuff?

I found out when I walked into the theater. At ten years old I was still a foot and a half shorter than most people there, and they were packed in like sardines. It took me almost five minutes to get ten feet into the place to see what was going on. Insanity. A circle of spectators was watching fifty or so people running around in circles and beating one another up. Every few seconds someone would climb onstage and jump out on top of the audience. I'd never seen anything like it.

I watched for as long as I could, but without any warning I kept getting slammed into by these huge, sweaty, leather-clad punk rockers. I made my way to the bleachers in the back of the room, hoping to find a safer place to watch from. Even though I had to wake up in a few hours, put on my leotard, and juggle for the kids, I decided to hang around. The circus seemed lame compared to this, but why did the music have to be so shitty? No wonder everyone was flailing around, hitting and kicking each other.

The next day was brutal. I had stayed up for the last band, Black Flag, and didn't get more than three hours of sleep. I was glad I saw them, though, because watching the singer of Black Flag run around in his underwear like an asshole made me feel slightly better about having to wear my fucking leotard the next day. I was over it. Sick of commuting, sick of waking up at 5:00 a.m., sick of wearing my hideous clown outfit, and most of all, sick of pretending to everyone and my mother that this was what I wanted to do with my life. I was fucking tired of the whole thing.

This time I knew I wasn't going to be asked back, which was fine with me, because I had a secret fantasy of going back to school and being a normal kid for once in my life. I didn't know more than one or two other kids my own age, and the people I called friends were ten to fifteen years older than I was. I couldn't wait for the season to end, even though it meant no more hanging out at The Farm. In the meantime, I decided I would go to as many punk-rock shows as I could, regardless of how tired I was. It turned out I really could juggle in my sleep, but the backflips and tumbling were hard. Aside from clearing the park of dog shit, I had pretty much stopped helping out with any of the setup. I told Mom I wanted to go back to school, and she agreed that it wasn't a bad idea.

eight

*In which our subject tries to escape from
the powerful clutch of Chiva and is
transformed into a bull-person*

CAROLINER PICKED ME up at seven in the morning in an old
'64 stretch Suburban airport limo. There were five of us in the
band, so, with two people up front, the other three got their own bench
seat. It was more comfortable than touring in Eli's old Datsun. I decided
to take the first stretch up front and see how nuts this Grux was for
myself. Not that there was any rush. I had a whole month to get to know
these guys.

"Grrrrrreh," he said as I climbed in.

"Hey, I'm Oran."

"Grux," he responded, but it didn't sound a whole lot different from
the grunt he had greeted me with. We drove in silence for a long time.
There was no doubt the guy was kind of strange. He had obviously made
his own clothes out of God knows what, and he was wearing a pair of
homemade cardboard sunglasses with long sharp angles that shot out all
over the place, covering everything from his cheeks to the top of his
forehead. All of it—clothes, shoes, sunglasses, and probably even his
underwear—was covered in Day-Glo paint. I couldn't help thinking that
if he had been wearing regular clothes he would have been absolutely
unnoticeable. Almost invisible.

After about an hour or two, he said, or rather grunted, without looking at me, "So what's your deal?"

After all that silence, it didn't seem like a few more awkward minutes would hurt.

"What's my deal?" I eventually said, hoping he would figure out that it was a stupid question.

"What do you do? What do you listen to? That kind of thing. Your deal."

"Well, I'm not sure what my deal is, but yeah, I play music, and I listen to it, as well."

He waited for more, but I left it at that. It was his turn to look at me as though I were crazy, which is what I was going for. Then he called back to Jeremy.

"Where'd you say you found this guy?"

Jeremy was asleep, so we drove on in silence for a while longer. I had pegged Grux as being just as uncomfortable and awkward as me, only he had developed a different system for getting by in a world that he didn't understand. It was pretty clever, really. Where I acted cool and indifferent in order to keep people at arm's length, Grux's method was to wear Day-Glo-covered homemade clothes and communicate through a series of grunts and yells.

"Seriously, though. What do you listen to?"

Again I decided it was a stupid question, so I decided to give him a stupid answer.

"Nirvana . . ." I said, coming up with the most unhip band I could think of in the obscure noise world. "Pearl Jam, shit like that."

"Fuckin' cool, dude. Wow, you're really cool, man. Hey, Jeremy!" he yelled back again. "I thought you said this guy was perfect. Where the hell'd you find him again?"

Jeremy wasn't waking up for anything, but Thomas, the guitar/banjo player–leader in absentia, yelled back. "Leave him alone, Grux. He's fucking with you. Don't worry about it."

"Ergh," he grunted, giving me a weird look, then focusing back on the road.

At the first gas stop, I switched seats with Thomas to try to get some sleep.

Before we got back in the Suburban, Thomas told me, "Hey, don't worry about Grux. He's just not used to talking to people who don't worship him. You're throwing him off."

"Don't worry about it. I'm having fun up there. I just need to get some sleep. I was up all night trying to get my shit together to leave."

We had an eleven-hour drive to Salt Lake City. I mostly slept. When we got there, I was definitely feeling dope sick. I wanted to ride it out as long as possible before I started tapering off. I just needed to drink as much as I could before the show, then do just enough dope to feel well before playing. I went up to the bar and ordered a drink. When the bartender came back with it, I asked him if the band got any drink tickets.

"Oh, you're in the band? No, sorry, I can't give this to you."

"Fine. How much is it?" I always got pissed when they wouldn't even give you a drink.

"No. I can't sell it to you either. I can't serve you at all," he said, taking the drink off the bar.

"What are you talking about, you can't serve me?" I stared in horror as he poured the beer in the sink.

"Utah state law. Bar and restaurant employees can't drink on the job. According to the state, you're officially an employee of the bar tonight, so I can't serve you, period."

"Are you fucking kidding me?" I asked.

"Not at all," he said without the slightest tone of sympathy.

"Well, is there somewhere else I could go?" I asked, but I knew from the drive that there was nothing remotely in walking distance.

"You could, but then I wouldn't be allowed to let you back in because you would be intoxicated while on the job. Believe me, there's no way around it." He had clearly been through this conversation a million times before.

"Holy shit. I have never heard of anything so insane in my life."

"Welcome to Utah."

"Well, Utah fucking sucks."

"Yup." There was no argument there.

"How about after I play? After I've done my job." Some fucking job. Drive twelve hours for this, and so far it didn't seem like anyone was even going to show up. I was looking for any loophole at all.

"I could serve you after you get paid, but that usually happens after we shut down the bar."

I walked to the bathroom pissed off, dejected, and nervous about playing my first show with these guys after only two rehearsals. By accident, I snorted more of the dope than I should have and ended up getting pretty high. I had to be careful. The whole point was to make it last as long as possible.

When I came out, the other guys had started bringing the equipment in, so I went to help out. They had told me the shows were something of a production, but I had no idea to what extent. After we brought our instruments inside, Grux climbed up to the roof of the Suburban where he had built a wooden box that was about six feet wide, by three feet high, and fifteen feet long. Once he got it open, he started handing down all manner of . . . I didn't even know what. There were laminated posters, backdrops, strips of cloth, Day-Glo-painted stage props, crumpled-up balls of what could be costumes, masks, long strings of black lights, boxes of duct tape, clothespins, thumbtacks, and all kinds of other shit I couldn't describe except as piles of Day-Glo-painted crap. One thing looked suspiciously like a three-foot-tall by three-foot-wide Day-Glo boot. Maybe that other thing was a hat? It took about forty-five minutes just to bring it all inside.

Since I had no idea what to do with all this stuff, I watched as the other guys transformed the stage into a neon Day-Glo alternate universe that looked like some sort of bad fever dream. The only recurring themes seemed to be cows and pioneer wagons, but the colors didn't seem to fit unless the pioneers had gotten smallpox or eaten some moldy bread or taken some peyote from the Indians. I guess a lot of shit could have, and probably did, happen to the pioneers that we would never know about. There was also apparently a lot of shit happening in San Francisco for the last sixteen years that I and—judging by the size of the crowd—no one else knew about.

After one local act, which was some kid screaming over a drum machine and rolling around on the floor for fifteen minutes, Jeremy handed me a costume sewn out of painting canvas with intricately designed patterns drawn all over it and a mask that might have resembled a deformed bull-person if you were on acid—or had snorted too much heroin in the bathroom, as I had.

The show was a disaster as far as I could tell. I had written notes all over my drumheads in order to remember the songs, but the holes in the mask didn't even come close to lining up with my eyes, so for the most part I couldn't tell what was going on. Eventually I found a way to hold the mask in position with my teeth, so I could look out through the mouth hole, but the colors onstage were now so vivid and disorienting from the black lights that it was still nearly impossible to read my notes and watch for the visual cues at the same time.

Grux didn't seem to be faring much better than me. On the occasion that he entered my field of vision, he seemed completely tangled up in wires, tripping over the three-foot boot he was wearing on one foot, knocking over amplifiers, and falling off the stage. He may have been singing, but I couldn't tell. Mostly he seemed to be trying to get off the ground, only to trip over something else and end up back on his ass. There were only five people in the audience, and they stayed as far away as possible, where it was safe. It was more like a dress rehearsal than anything.

By the end, the only two people left were the guy we were staying with and the kid who did the opening set, so we decided we might as well use it as a rehearsal for real, and we went over a few more new songs. *What a fucking mess*, I thought, although I had been thoroughly entertained by the chaos of it. Wearing the mask had the amazing effect of making me not give a shit what happened. After the show everyone agreed that, aside from me fucking up a few of the changes—which was understandable given the circumstances—it had been a total success.

"Hey, Jeremy, where'd you say you found this guy again?" Grux yelled. But this time it seemed to carry a whole different meaning. He confirmed it by asking me, "Where the hell have you been?" He was clearly incapable of making direct compliments, but I could tell he was trying in his own way to show approval. I got out of my costume as quickly as I could, hoping to get to the bar for a drink, but it was too late. The bartender had shut it down.

"Did we even make any money?" I asked him.

"Nope. I guess technically you were a volunteer. I don't know what the law is for volunteers."

"Jesus Christ. Utah fucking sucks!" I said with more gusto than the first time.

"Yup."

W E HAD A BLOWOUT the next day in the middle of Wyoming. Grux was nearly decapitated when he went out to inspect the damage. The iron lock ring that held the tire to the rim had popped off and chased us down the highway, missing Grux's head by less than a foot before smashing through the back window a few minutes after we pulled over. It was extremely unnerving to think that this inanimate object had been following us for that long without us knowing it.

I'm not normally superstitious, but Grux had been talking about the founder of the Church of Satan, Anton LaVey. The story was about how when he was cleaning out LaVey's basement after he died, a huge swarm of flies had appeared out of nowhere in order to thwart Grux's attempts at moving LaVey's stuff out.

"So what do you think they were doing there? You think it was Anton reincarnated as a swarm of flies?" I asked, humoring him.

"I don't know what they were there for, but they seemed pissed that I was fucking with his shit."

"What'd you do?"

"I was scared. The air was black with buzzing flies, man. I ran upstairs to tell his daughter, Karla, and she told me not to worry. *They're just trying to scare you, but they don't have any power anymore. If you ignore them, they'll leave you alone.* That's what she told me. Freaky. When I went back down, they were gone."

After all this talk about the supernatural goings-on around the recently deceased founder of the Church of Satan, it was hard to shake the idea that this iron ring was trying to kill Grux. For what, I had no idea. I didn't know him that well yet. We were apparently going to meet another high priest from the Church of Satan when we got to Denver.

We arrived late. At least that's what they told us when we pulled in. It was Goth night at the club we were playing, so we had to be done by eight. I still didn't know what was going on with the whole stage setup, but I pitched in as much as I could. We only had an hour and a half to set up and put on our 1800s Day-Glo pioneer show before we needed to clear out for the children of darkness. It was pretty dismal, but at least they let me drink.

Jeremy spotted me at the bar and came over to tell me, "You know, Grux doesn't like it when we drink."

"What are you talking about? Why would he care?" I asked. This was the first I had heard of this, and it didn't seem like it was any of Grux's business.

"He hates drugs and alcohol. He's never had anything, not even a cup of coffee."

"Maybe that's why he's so crazy." I wondered if Caroliner wasn't somehow the result of not having the luxury to drop a hit of acid every once in a while, like us normal folk.

"Yeah, well . . . anyway . . . I would just try not to let him see you drinking. He can get kind of nuts about it."

"Don't worry about it, Jeremy."

He was acting so nervous, but what the fuck? I come out with these guys on three days' notice, and they're going to give me shit about drinking? It doubled my resolve to drink as much as possible, which was proving to be problematic anyway since we were so busy setting up and then playing before Goth night got rolling. I slammed that one beer as fast as

I could, but we were in such a rush, we had to go right onstage after that.

There was no opening act and maybe ten people showed up, which was an improvement over the five we had in Salt Lake. We ran over schedule despite only playing a twenty-minute set. Afterward, we had to tear down immediately, while a line of angry Goth kids waited outside to come in and do whatever it is that Goth kids do. Unfortunately, we had to load out of the same door that they were lined up at, and each time we came out with a load, they let us know how displeased they were by shooting angry glares at us. Their consternation was exponentially more effective through all the eyeliner, mascara, and black lipstick they wore. *How did they turn out like that?* Maybe their parents loved them the way they were, but we wanted to get the hell out of there.

Driving away from the club, I asked Grux if the Satanic priest had ever shown up.

"Who? Boyd? Yeah, he was there. He was telling me some shit about owls and Indians."

"Damn. I wanted to meet that guy. What'd he look like?" I asked him.

"He was the guy wearing all black."

"The guy? Almost everyone there was wearing all black. I must have thought he was there for Goth night."

That made Grux laugh, which was unusual. "Ha. I wish he could have heard you say that."

That one beer hadn't done much as far as supplementing my dwindling supply of heroin, but I did my best not to overdo it. I was almost out.

FOUR DAYS ON THE ROAD and the sickness hit me like a Mack truck as we pulled into Lawrence, Kansas. I had been letting myself get pretty sick for about a month now, so I thought I would be prepared, but I found out quickly that I had never even been close to experiencing full-blown withdrawal. It was beyond horrific. Everything hurt. Bones, stomach, skin—and it was no easy task holding in the diarrhea that was threatening to explode at any minute. We made it to the club just in time for me to avoid shitting my pants. I was in so much pain and so fucking scared, yet I had to pretend that everything was fine. When Thomas commented on my pale complexion, I told him my stomach was hurting.

"Must have been something I ate," I said with as cool a demeanor as possible, but I was sweating bullets, and it was pretty cold out.

"Jesus. Tell me you didn't eat that spaghetti last night. Did you?"

Grux had cooked about fifteen pounds of spaghetti and tomato sauce. It was the first thing he made that appeared to be somewhat edible before he decided to mix a five-pound can of peanut butter in with it. None of us ate that night besides Grux, who couldn't stop telling us how good it was. But as long as Thomas was asking, I might as well lie and blame it on Grux.

"I had to. There was nothing else to eat." It was a good excuse, and maybe we would get some better food out of the deal. I didn't lift a finger for load-in or setup that night. I just sat at the bar and drank shots of whiskey. I finally had my chance to get wasted, but it didn't seem to be doing a damn thing for the dope sickness. It only added fuel to my self-pity. All I wanted to do was curl up and die, but I had to play the drums instead.

The show went surprisingly well—it was maybe even the best one yet—and I actually felt some relief as soon as I put on my mask. Once in costume, I didn't have to put on an act. I could be as sick, sweaty, and miserable as I wanted, which made a huge difference.

Playing also gave me something to focus on other than wanting to die. When I took off my mask, though, the thoughts of death returned with a vengeance. The thing was, I didn't really want to die forever. I just wanted to be dead for the next week or so. At least until the worst of it was over. I ordered another drink, but people were trying to talk to me, and I was in no shape to talk about anything other than myself, and that was not a good subject. I had to get out of there and talk to someone I knew.

Grux had a device from RadioShack that when you pressed the button made the sound of a quarter dropping into a pay phone. I convinced him to lend it to me, and I went out to explore Lawrence.

It took me a while to find a pay phone that worked, because the phone companies had been getting wise to the gadget I was using. The newer phones would connect you straight to the operator who would read off your location and tell you the cops were on their way, but eventually I found one that accepted the sound of fake quarters. I called Heather, and the moment I heard her voice I started sobbing.

"It's fucking bad. Way worse than I thought. How could I have been such an idiot? Fuck . . . fuck . . . fuck . . . and these people I'm with are fucking insane!"

"Ha! And you're not?"

"Not what?" I asked, either not understanding or not paying attention.

"Insane? I mean, this whole thing is insane," she said, trying to make a point I was unable to grasp.

"Well, I might be a little insane due to the circumstances I'm in, but these people are really crazy. They put peanut butter in their spaghetti and wear homemade sunglasses!" But even that didn't sound crazier than what I was doing. I couldn't articulate what I wanted to say, but I didn't call her to get laughed at. She could hear me getting defensive and changed the subject.

"Hey, O, you're going to get through it. You're not the first person to go through this. Just think about all the other people who've been through the same thing."

I thought about it, but it didn't help. "Yeah, but I'm not those people. I don't think I can do it. I thought I brought enough stuff to last two weeks, and it's already gone. It's so fucking bad. So fucking bad." Repeating myself was the only thing I could think of to convey how horrible I felt.

"I'm sorry, O. I wish I could help, but what can I do? It doesn't even matter whether or not you think you can do it. At this point you don't have a choice."

"Yeah, you're right. I don't have a fucking choice. Why did I do this? I'm such a fucking idiot," I said.

"Think about it this way: you still have seven days before you get to New York, so by the time you see me you'll be all better."

"Okay, where am I meeting you again?" Talking to her wasn't helping. I suddenly wanted very much to get off the phone.

"It's on the corner of Houston and Lafayette, a huge brick building. Just go in and find the Scott Nichols Gallery."

"Okay." I wrote it down. "I'll see you in a week."

"Good luck, O."

THAT NIGHT I TOSSED and turned on a hardwood floor, my skin alternating between freezing and scalding, and my head filled with thoughts of . . . I thought about all sorts of shit. My mind was racing all over the place. Mostly I just tried to repeat my mantra, "It's bad . . . this is so fucking bad," until some crappy childhood memory would come out of nowhere only to be replaced by, "I wonder what happened to so and so from high school?" . . . and on and on till I reined it in and got back to my mantra. Occasionally I would hear a truck speed by on the highway, and I thought about how nice it would be to take a casual stroll right into one of those big motherfuckers, and just like that . . . nothing.

W E BROKE DOWN in Kansas City the next day, and I decided to try taking NyQuil. I was so tired, it seemed like I just needed a little something to knock me out. It made me more tired but it didn't put me to sleep, so I figured another bottle would do it. That had the same effect, and it wasn't till I drank the fourth bottle that I realized the shit wasn't going to put me to sleep. It was just immobilizing me to a point where the slightest movement demanded an ungodly amount of effort.

It didn't slow down my brain, though. It just made my thoughts more ugly. They were no longer appearing in the form of childhood memories, or anything I could attach much meaning to. Weird blurry figures appeared, and what seemed to be animated piles of grayish meat. It was as if I were living inside a Francis Bacon painting or Peter Greenaway movie. Or a fucking Caroliner show. I tried to take off my mask, but it wasn't a mask. I was a deformed bull-person in an 1800s band. We were trying to make our way west for some reason, but the farther west we went, the more deformed we got and the brighter the colors became. We were forgetting how to talk like people, but we could understand the cows, and they kept telling us to keep going. It was a slow journey because I could see only out of my mouth, and Groat Pulp, our leader, kept putting dirt in the spaghetti and tripping over his gigantic foot. Gris Welled, the banjo player, was trying to tell me something in the old language, and I vaguely recalled that I hadn't always been a bull-person named Both Oars. I was a human person lying in the third row of an old airplane limo heading east, not west.

"Huh . . . what?" I said, opening my eyes.

"Hey, Oran, sorry about waking you up, man, but we're in St. Louis. You can stay in the van if you want, but I thought I should tell you where we're going in case you woke up later." Thomas was whispering, as if he could convey the message subconsciously without really having to wake me up.

But I was wide awake and had been for almost three days now. I was just too physically tired from the NyQuil to move. "Okay," I said.

"We're going to a club down the block with a big neon sign. Just tell them you're with us and they'll let you in."

"Okay. Thanks, Thomas."

"No problem. Hope you feel better."

We had the night off, which was a relief, as I could not imagine playing a show in my condition. Eventually I did get up and walked around looking for food. I ordered lasagna at a diner, stared at it for about twenty minutes, and headed over to the club, leaving the food untouched.

The club looked like an MTV set, or a Mafia club in a Hong Kong action movie, and there were hundreds of good-looking kids standing still, intently focused on one of the most boring bands I had ever heard. When I was in the van, at least I knew the shit in my head was just that—shit in my head. What I saw in that club was real, and in that moment, still sick, and feeling the toxic aftereffects of the NyQuil, reality was way too much for me to handle.

I went back to the Suburban, hoping to escape back to the land of Day-Glo cow-people, but it never came. It was just my saliva on the cold vinyl of the bench seat and silence for the next three days. I had ceased talking, except to update the others on the state of my "insomnia." They were all pretty nice about it, despite the fact that I had stopped taking part in any of the loading or setting up. The only relief I got was when I put on my mask and played for the increasingly larger crowds. I started looking forward to our shows with an almost religious fervor, because the other twenty-three hours of the day were unbearable.

W E WERE IN DETROIT when Jeremy came and found me in my usual spot, lying horizontal in the third row while everyone else was setting up.

"Hey, man, I found this guy who says he has some methadone. You want some?"

Even at this point I was still trying to hide what I was going through, so I tried to control my excitement and said with a hint of disapproval, "Why would I want methadone?" Did he know what was going on? Did all of them know?

"Don't tell Grux, but I just kicked dope a week before we left because I didn't want to go through it on the road, and . . . well, I just thought that you were . . . uh, never mind," he said, getting ready to shut the door.

"Hey, Jeremy, wait. You're right, it would probably help with this fucking insomnia. Where is this guy?" I was still unable to admit it.

"He's across the street, but I can go get it."

"Nah, I'll come with you." I wanted to see who he was so I could maybe get a few more pills later on without Jeremy seeing me. We crossed the street, and this regular-looking guy pulled a prescription bottle from his pocket and handed us each a pill.

"Thanks, man. How much do you want for these?" Jeremy was already taking his, but I knew that if I took mine now I would be catatonic by the time we played.

"Don't worry about it," he said.

"Cool. You sticking around for the show, man?"

"Fuck yeah, I drove up from Chicago to see you. You guys sounded amazing last night, but I couldn't see shit. Too many people."

"Yeah, it was insane."

It had seemed as though there were five hundred people packed into this little Greek bar in Chicago, which was a startling turn of events for us. It was too bad I missed most of it, but I had spent the majority of the night down the street lying on a pile of secondhand clothes in a thrift store owned by a guy in one of the bands we were playing with called the Beast People.

"What is this place?" I asked the methadone guy, looking up at what must have been a fifteen-bedroom brownstone mansion. "You been here before?"

"Yeah. It's some kind of anarchist collective. They got a 1 percent interest loan from the Catholic nuns and bought the place," he explained.

"Wow. There's so much wrong with that I don't know where to begin. First of all, isn't an anarchist collective a contradiction of terms? And second of all, since when do Catholics buy mansions for anarchists?"

"Detroit is fucking weird, man. That place there," he said, pointing to the mansion next door, "is owned by the communists. Same thing. Nuns bought it for them."

"Really? You think they'd buy me a mansion if I told them it was for satanists?" Just knowing I was finally going to get some sleep tonight had put me in a better mood.

"I'm pretty sure they already bought one for the satanists. I think it's one of those across the street." We were both looking up and down the block for any sign of satanism, but there was nothing obvious.

"Shit. What about a house for atheists?"

"Maybe, but then you'd have to live in Detroit. And believe me, you don't want to live here without believing in something."

We went inside to see the Beast People rolling around naked on the floor, covered in black and brown greasepaint and wearing unidentifiable animal masks. I think they were an a cappella act, but the sounds they were producing were totally inhuman. I was glad I hadn't seen them before I drank the NyQuil.

Next up was a more straight-ahead band, but not too far into their performance, someone in a blue whale suit ran in screaming and started attacking the audience before chasing the band offstage. I almost lost the guy with the methadone in the confusion, but I found him right before we went on and convinced him to give me a couple more pills. He still refused to take any money for them. Once again, I found myself having to sleep on a hardwood floor, but after being awake for five days I could have slept on a pile of nails.

The next night we played in a building owned by the Cleveland Communist Party since the 1930s, but since party membership had been on the decline, they had donated the first floor to a bunch of runaway teenagers, who were allowed to do whatever they wanted with it.

A couple of frat boys had apparently beaten up Grux during our set, but it was always hard to tell when the line had been crossed from good-natured violence to mean-spirited violence. The fight had gone down outside of the narrow vision of my mouth hole, but Grux looked pretty bad after the show. They had gone after him with a ladder, but he couldn't run with his three-foot boot on, and I doubt he could see any better than I could. I took only half of a methadone pill that night and slept on the stage with four cute two-week-old kittens. They were still cuddled up with me when I woke up the next morning, finally over the withdrawal.

I felt great, but Grux was bruised up beyond belief, and his mood was deteriorating. He claimed it was the result of getting closer to New York Shitty, as he called it, but now that I wasn't so sick and self-absorbed as I had been, it was clear that no one was doing that well. Cheryl had had it with Grux and was on a hunger strike due to the lack of anything remotely edible. Thomas, who was a pretty quiet guy to begin with, had receded even further into his silence, and Jeremy was limping around in severe pain as a result of not taking off his shoes.

"Jesus Christ, Jeremy," Thomas said as we all stood around looking at Jeremy's green foot in the parking lot of a truck stop. "You've been wearing them since we left?"

"I took 'em off to take a shower, but . . . yeah. They smell so bad I got to keep 'em on."

"Come on, man. If you don't give them some air, you're going to lose your foot. It'll be fine if we just leave the windows open," I said.

It didn't work, though. Even when he tried sticking his foot out the back window, it caused all of us to gag, and we had to air out the Suburban at the next exit while he put his shoes back on. It was an unfortunate example of the good of the many outweighing the needs of a few, or in this case, one. I gave Jeremy the rest of my methadone, hoping it might help with the pain, but there was nothing else to do about it.

After Buffalo, we got a much needed day off, so Thomas could hang out with his family. I woke up early and caught a train to Manhattan to meet up with Heather. I didn't know what was happening to me, but for the whole seven-hour train ride down, all I could think about was sex. It came out of nowhere, and I kept having to shift around in my seat to hide what was going on. I hadn't experienced anything like this since high school. It occurred to me that my lack of sex drive may have been at least part of the reason I had been so productive over the last six months. I wondered if there was some sort of substitute that would curb my sex drive the way heroin did without the nasty side effect of addiction. I had heard about kings in olden times putting saltpeter in visiting princes' wine (or was it sex offenders in modern times? I couldn't remember), but I don't think it took away the urge, just the ability to perform. I needed the opposite of that.

God, I couldn't wait to see Heather.

RUNNING LATE, I found Heather waiting outside for me. I was actually a tiny bit proud of myself for having just gone through the worst experience of my life and come out the other side, and Heather was the only person on the planet who knew about it. We went straight to her friend's apartment, and on the way there I gave her a short recap on my adventures of the last two weeks, but didn't go into too much detail about kicking. Other than not sleeping, the crawling skin, the nausea, the aching, the sweating, and the diarrhea—the boring shit everyone has heard about a million times—I couldn't find the words to describe it. What does any of that mean to someone who hasn't been through it? It didn't matter. It was just good to be around someone I wasn't lying to. Heather's friend was out of town, so we had the place to ourselves. After what must have been another hour of talking about myself, it finally occurred to me to ask how she was doing.

"Fucking Scott is driving me crazy," she answered.

"What's he doing?"

"Oh you know, just being Scott." Her boss was always driving her crazy, but that was the only reason she ever gave me. He seemed like a nice enough guy to me.

"How's New York been? Have you seen any friends? Has it been fun at all?"

"No! I'm here for work! I sit in that fucking building all day talking about Ansel Adams to idiots! I wish I was on vacation, or touring across the country, playing music with crazy people, but I'm not! I'm fucking working!"

Whoa. I had never seen Heather like this, or I had been oblivious to it before. Wrapped up in my own shit for as long as I had been, I'm not sure it ever occurred to me that she might have problems of her own. Of course that made me start thinking about myself again and what an ass-hole I was for being so selfish. It felt as if the dynamic had shifted, but I couldn't put my finger on it.

"Hey. Tomorrow night we're doing an improv set under a different name. If there's another drum set, why don't you play with us?" I said, partly trying to change the subject, and hoping to give her something fun to do in New York.

"I don't know about that. I can't play that stuff."

"What stuff? There is no stuff until you play it. It'll be fun. You just said you wished you were playing music."

"We'll see."

"Good," I said, leaning in to kiss her.

She was still preoccupied about something, and the sex felt a little one-sided, as if she wasn't really there. It made me feel kind of gross about myself afterward, as if I had just experienced what it was like to fit my mom's description of all white men everywhere. Usually, just think-ing about sex made me feel guilty of that, but I had never experienced it in real life.

"I'm sorry," I said, for no reason in particular.

"About what?"

"Everything."

I MET HEATHER the next night after work, and we headed up to Harlem on the A train. The crowd was neither communist nor anar-chist, but some weird brand of negative urban hippie I hadn't encoun-tered before. Long hair and beards were not to be mistaken for peace and love. There were little groups of people hiding in dark corners whis-pering to one another, lest they be overheard and judged by another little group of whispering people. As more and more of these quiet hippie art-ist types showed up, the small whispering groups morphed into a larger silent group. It was an uncomfortable atmosphere, and Heather really didn't want to play. I wasn't sure I did either, but I kept trying to talk her into it anyway.

"Don't worry. We'll be wearing masks. If it really sucks, no one will know who was up there anyway," I said.

"I'll know," she responded. I didn't have an answer for that one. No one ever judged me as badly as I judged myself.

"Well, yeah. You're right, but look at these people. They're just here to be seen anyway. They're going to like whatever we do just because they're supposed to."

Since we were performing under the name of the Commode Minstrels, not Caroliner, we had to come up with a different idea for the masks. We all had clean laundry, courtesy of Thomas's family, so I thought of wearing underwear. It wasn't all that creative, but we didn't have time for anything more elaborate. Heather joined us in donning our various tighty whities, boxers, and long johns, and we played forty-five minutes of some of the most jarring, unlistenable music possible. As I expected, the audience loved it. It had very little to do with us and almost everything to do with alcohol.

The next morning I said good-bye to Heather, and the band began its journey back to California. After kicking dope I found that life on the road rather agreed with me. Our only responsibility was to show up at the next club on time. The shows got progressively worse as we made our way back west. We played for video game nerds in Philly, empty cages that were supposed to contain naked women in South Carolina, alcoholic ghost people in New Orleans, one confused guy in El Paso, and a pretty good sampling of almost every stereotype Los Angeles had to offer.

As Grux said, "the best thing to ever happen in L.A. was us going home."

nine

Is where he gets some new clothes

AFTER FINISHING OUT my fifth-grade year at Malcolm X Elementary School on the south side of Berkeley, we moved across town, two blocks away from the Arts Magnet School. Considering my history as a performer, it didn't seem that far-fetched that I would qualify for admission, but something to do with racial quotas prevented Kyle and me from being eligible. Instead we were to be bused a few miles away to Columbus Elementary. Mom tried every method of persuasion she could before deciding to boycott the Berkeley public school system and charge them with engaging in reverse racism, which according to my mom wasn't as bad as the regular kind but was pretty bad nonetheless. I said goodbye to my dream of a normal childhood and reluctantly went along with the boycott.

The truant officers came around every couple of days to try to get us to go to the other school, but Mom just lectured them on how she never would have joined the freedom rides if she had known it would have ended up keeping her kids out of school.

"But, lady, your kids got to go to school. It's the law."

"First of all, my name is not lady. You can call me doctor. And second, when a law doesn't make any sense, I'm just supposed to follow along? There wouldn't be any civil rights if we had just mindlessly obeyed the law. That's the problem with this whole country, and frankly it's the last thing we expected to encounter when we moved to Berkeley."

"Okay, lady. I mean doctor. But can't the kids go to Columbus until we get this figured out?"

"No way. This boycott is in response to an unjust system that victimizes kids because of the color of their skin. If the school was full, then that would be one thing, but can you honestly say that it makes any sense to keep my kids, both of whom are very involved in the creative arts, from going to the Arts Magnet School because they are white? Reverse racism is still racism."

"I'm just doing my job, ma'am."

"Yeah, that's what they said in Germany."

I turned away in embarrassment. Sending us to Columbus Elementary was a far cry from sending us to the gas chamber.

"And I'm not a ma'am, either," she added. "I'm sorry about your job. Will that be all?"

"For today. But we'll be back. You can't keep your kids out of school forever."

"Oh, really? These are my kids, and I am not raising them to mindlessly participate in a system whose only concern is filling quotas and has no respect for the individual, especially when the victims are innocent kids. So don't bother coming back if that's what you intend on asking me to do."

Not surprisingly, a different truant officer would show up every day, each one higher up in the chain of command, until the superintendent himself came by.

Kyle and I were shut out of that meeting, but afterward Mom called us downstairs and said, "Guess what? The boycott worked. You guys are starting at the Arts Magnet School tomorrow." It was confusing after all that to find only two other white kids in my class. What kind of quota were they trying to fill?

WHILE IT MAY have been my secret fantasy to start living a normal life, the other kids didn't view me as normal. It took me almost six months to realize that one reason might have been that I was still wearing these shiny black satin pants, a red muscle shirt, and either Capezio dance shoes or checkered Vans. It was too weird to even make fun of, so for a while the other kids just left me alone.

Once a year Mom would get five pairs of the pants custom made for me, and she would buy an equal number of red muscle shirts, which she liked because they were made of a 100 percent cotton, not an easy thing to find in the 1980s. Kyle's wardrobe consisted of a couple of identical kung fu uniforms, and—when those needed to be washed—the satin pants and muscle shirts I had grown out of. My only friend, it seemed by default, was one of the other white kids, Muni. The other white girl was so awkward that not even the teachers could talk to her. I never heard her say one word.

I realized I couldn't keep wearing this same uniform every day if I had any hope of fitting in at all, so at Christmas break Mom took us to the mall to get some new clothes, protesting the whole way there that we looked fine. She objected to the fact that we would now have to waste valuable time thinking about what we were going to wear just so we could look like everybody else. She was so against the idea that I figured we would go in and grab some stuff off the rack and be done with it, but eight hours later I was in tears, pleading to just go back to Berkeley and get some more satin pants made. It felt as though we had tried on everything in the mall at least three different times. Every time I tried a new shirt, it meant retrying all the pants I had already put on to see how they went together, and just when we thought we were done, Mom would see something she hadn't seen before, or she would catch me glancing at something, and we'd have to start the whole process over again.

The mall was absolute hell, but I did come out of there looking a little less vaudevillian. Walking back to the car, we could have almost been mistaken for a couple of normal kids, except for the fact that we had somehow ended up getting our ears pierced. The part about looking like everyone else did concern me. I just didn't want to look like a clown.

THE CHANGE IN STYLE worked as far as getting the other kids to talk to me.

"What are you, some sort of fag or something?" Akbar asked me when I came back from break. Akbar was the most popular kid in the class. He was charismatic and good-looking, and his dad was well known for owning the Black Muslim Bakery. Despite the insult, it was the first time anyone other than Muni had talked to me since I started going to school, so I took it as a good sign.

"Would you call Mr. T. a fag?" I asked him.

"Well . . . uh, no, but . . ."

"Anyway, you're only gay if you pierce your right ear, not your left," I clarified.

Soon after that I was allowed to join the basketball games at recess, and it kind of sort of seemed as if I had friends. I was getting a little too comfortable with them, though, because when I called Akbar "blood" one day, trying to get him to pass me the ball, he spat on the ground and said, "Uh-uh, man. You ain't my blood."

"Come on, cuz. I didn't mean anything by it," I responded.

"What's wrong wich you, honky? You ain't my cousin neither."

I had never thought about what these words meant and assumed that they were just terms of familiarity. Now I realized they were about race. My new clothes may have helped, but there was no way I was ever going to completely fit in. I had been calling Muni and Kyle *blood* and *cuz* for so long it was just part of my vocabulary, and I kept using the terms out of habit until I had almost no friends again. I didn't understand why we couldn't all be *bloods* and *cuzzes*.

After all, we had learned in class that everyone originally came from Africa. We also learned about a lot of the atrocities "my people" had done to other people that didn't look like me, and I could understand why the other kids didn't want me to call them *blood*. I didn't want to be associated with white folks either. In American history we learned about the genocide of the Indians, slavery, the lynching of black folks by the KKK, and the shooting of white folks who helped blacks in the civil rights movement. In California history class we learned about Japanese internment camps and Cesar Chavez's struggles to help the Farm Workers Union. At home I learned about Ronald Reagan's secret war against the Sandinistas in Nicaragua and the lower classes right here at home. In my ten years of life, I really hadn't seen many examples of white people, or more specifically white men, that negated any of these horror stories.

I don't know if it was because of white guilt or what, but I ended up joining a South African Dance Troupe and spent my weekends up at UC Berkeley protesting U.S. involvement and support for apartheid. When Kyle and I started taking part, there were no more than ten or fifteen people following this guy with a bullhorn who would yell at students to boycott the university. As more people joined the protests, he started organizing sit-ins and got people to handcuff themselves in front of doorways. In a very short amount of time, there were a few thousand people marching onto campus demanding that the UC system divest its money from South Africa. What had started with a guy holding a bullhorn had turned into a national movement.

For the most part the protests were peaceful, and the police only focused on those who were obstructing access to buildings or roads, but as the gatherings grew in size it became harder to know what was going to happen. Riots had broken out a few times, and Mom was worried that if Kyle or I got arrested, she would be deemed an unfit mother and they would take us away from her. Instead of not allowing us to go, however, she made some kind of arrangement with Wavy Gravy, our old camp leader, that if either of us got arrested, we should tell the authorities that we were under Wavy's care and should be returned to our mother.

Because of my new guardian, I was now free to do whatever I wanted as long as it didn't interfere with any of my ten other extracurricular activities, which included tap dancing on Monday, jazz and modern dance class on Tuesday and Wednesday, South African percussion class on Thursday afternoon (before heading to gymnastics class), and Capoeira on Friday night. Saturdays were usually my day to go and protest apartheid or nuclear weapons, and then on Sunday I would take BART into the city to the juggling meet in Golden Gate Park. It seemed like every minute of every day was accounted for. No wonder I couldn't get out of bed in the morning. I might as well have stayed in the circus. The fatigue, coupled with the thought of having to do it all over again the next week, was overwhelming. I felt like that Greek guy who pushed a rock up a hill every day, just to watch it roll back down.

Mornings were always horrific, and I pretty much hated everyone and everything until about noon. Mostly I hated my mom, whose job it was to get me out of bed. She tried all sorts of ways to get me up, but the most ruthless trick was the water treatment: threatening to pour a bucket of cold water over me. In the beginning, it worked like a charm, but one day I was too tired to care if she poured cold water on me or not and found out that she was incapable of bringing herself to follow through with it. Instead she talked Kyle into doing it, and it worked. I jumped out of bed kicking and punching Kyle. I then crawled back under the covers, threatening to beat the shit out of anyone who ever tried that on me again.

"You motherfucking cocksuckers!" I yelled at them. "I'm coming into your fucking rooms tonight, and I'm gonna pour water on your heads. See how you fucking like it." I was wide awake, seething with hatred. I stayed in bed out of protest.

"Come on, honey. You have to get up. Remember how hard we tried to get you into school? We can't let them down after all that."

This was another thing she brought up every morning.

"I don't give a shit. You don't pour water on someone when they're asleep, for fuck's sake."

"I didn't do it. Kyle did. I would never do that to you."

"You fucking told him to do it. That's even worse."

"Oran David Canfield! Get out of bed right now!" she yelled, trying out authoritarianism.

"No."

"This instant!" It was rare that she tried the same trick two sentences in a row.

"Fuck you."

"What did you say?" She was almost laughing at the absurdity of it, which pissed me off even more.

"You heard me."

"You just said that to your own mother? Well, since none of this is working you leave me no choice but to come over there and physically get you out of bed."

"How about leaving me the fuck alone?"

"I can't do that, honey, because then you won't make it to class, and I'll look like a bad mother," she said, getting closer to the bed.

"I don't care what you look like," I said, at which point she grabbed my arms and tried to pull me out. I started thrashing my arms around, trying to scare her off, but she didn't give up. She got her arms around my waist, and I flinched and let out a little laugh despite being as angry as I ever had been. I could see the lightbulb turn on above her head when she realized what just happened.

"Aha!" she said, going for my armpits this time.

"Goddamnit." I was trying to yell through the most painful involuntary laughter I had ever experienced. "Fuck you!" I screamed, leaping out of bed. "That is totally unfair. Don't you ever do that to me again."

But she did. Almost every morning I woke up to the threat and eventual execution of the "tickle treatment."

Kyle never had a problem waking up, and in retaliation for getting beat up over the water treatment, he somehow snuck into my room, and I woke up naked with my wrists handcuffed together behind my back. It was unclear how Kyle had come across a pair of handcuffs, or why he didn't have a key for them, but I showed up late to school that day with a note from the police officer who had been called to let me out of the things. I couldn't understand how Kyle didn't get in trouble for that one. I got in trouble for everything. When Mom caught me eating a hamburger, she dragged me to the McDonald's, asked to speak to the manager, and demanded that they tape one of my school photos to the wall and never serve me again. The punishment for handcuffing your brother in his sleep was laughter. Even the cop laughed at me.

ten

Tells of a series of bad decisions, which lead to a terrible fall

DRIVING INTO San Francisco was always an amazing experience, even if I was only gone for a few hours. This time I had been away for a month, and I was coming home to an awesome girlfriend, my new recording studio, and a bunch of bands, and we still had our Saturday night improv noise thing going. It was the life I had always envisioned for myself, ever since my days at The Farm. Using some kind of bizarre logic, I decided that if I felt this good clean, just imagine how good I would feel if I got high. I didn't see any danger in it because it was fairly obvious that the only reason I got addicted in the first place was because I had been so sad and depressed at the time. Feeling good was a totally different scenario, and anyway, after that fucking tour, I deserved to do it one more time.

An hour later I was hiding the straw and the foil wondering, *What the fuck is wrong with you? You stupid piece of shit. I can't fucking believe you would do this shit again. And after everything you just fucking went through?* My internal dialogue was interrupted by the phone ringing. It was Heather calling me back from work.

"Hey, O. I'm leaving now. I can't wait to see you. Where did you want to meet?"

"Well, actually it turns out I'm super wiped out from the drive. I didn't get any sleep last night, and I think I just need to take it easy."

"Uh . . . I'm pretty tired, too. But I thought since you just got back . . . that . . . you know we could just be tired together."

"Yeah . . . I don't know . . . I mean, I won't be any fun to hang out with, you know? It was a pretty rough month, and I've been around people twenty-four hours a day. I think I just need to be alone right now."

"When have you ever been fun?" she asked.

I tried to force a laugh, but there was too much truth in that joke. "Listen. How about tomorrow? I'm just too out of it right now." It was the wrong thing to say. The whole situation was wrong and I knew it. Heather had rehearsal the next night, and an opening at the gallery the night after that, and still I made up excuses not to see her on the only night she was available. I couldn't face her after I had just spent a month trying to get clean, only to relapse the moment I got home. My theory about feeling too good had turned out to be wrong. *At least I only fucked up once*, I thought. *I just won't do it again.*

The problem was that I didn't feel quite so good about myself the next day, and the urge to get high was overwhelming. Since Heather was busy anyway, why not just one more time?

There was always an excuse that, no matter how unbelievably ridiculous it may have sounded after I got high, made more sense than anything in the whole world beforehand. I tended to make the worst decisions stone-cold sober and could only see how stupid they were after it was too late. This went on until I was right back to where I was before. Lying to Heather, faking orgasms, waking up sick. The same exact bullshit all over again. I don't know how she didn't see it.

It stopped being the same when I started running out of money. The tour had wiped me out. What little money I had left from my dad's loan, I had spent on the road, and the three hundred dollars that Grux had given us when we got home didn't last too long. I figured if I switched over to using needles just until I got some money, I might be able to make it through until I got some work, without getting sick. Seeing all that smoke when I exhaled seemed like a waste. A needle seemed a lot more efficient.

I also came up with a new idea to quit. It was something I had read about on the Internet called "rapid opiate detox," where they put you under general anesthesia and give you an opiate blocker called Naltrexone, which would kick all the heroin out of your system in a matter of hours instead of days. When you woke up the next day, you would be clean. The big issue with it was that it was only being done in Canada and cost ten thousand dollars. If I had ten thousand dollars, I wouldn't have had to quit. A little more research taught me that Naltrexone was also used to deter heroin addicts from relapsing and could be found at the local pharmacy for five bucks. I could just do it myself for a savings of $9,995. What a rip-off.

Meanwhile, lying to Heather was stressing me out so much that I broke up with her. My rationale was that I cared too much about her to see her wasting her time with a pathetic piece of shit like me. Racked with guilt and self-loathing, I admitted to her that I had started using heroin the moment I got back from tour.

"I just need some time by myself to sort all this shit out," I told her, bracing myself for at least a little drama.

"Okay. Good luck with that," she said sincerely. Even though I broke up with her, I couldn't help but be disappointed at how easy it had been.

To complicate matters, Jibz had finally decided that I was the right one for her after all. I couldn't have agreed with her more, but heroin, while fucking me up in so many ways, did allow me to see through the distorted lens of emotions that I usually based all my decisions on.

With my *feelings* no longer in the way, it was obvious to me that it just wasn't going to work out between us. Not now, anyway.

She didn't give up so easily. In a complete role reversal, she tried to convince me that we were always meant to be together, she just never saw it before. It was the same line I had been using on her for years, which made the situation harder to get out of. The only excuse I could come up with was that I was a junkie, thinking that would surely scare her away. But it only made her more determined. She wanted to save me.

Jibz was the only other person besides Heather who knew I was doing drugs. I told her about this rapid opiate detox thing, and that I was going to do it at a motel my roommate worked at in the Marina. She offered to come with me and be there when things got rough, but I decided I'd better do it on my own. I didn't want anyone to see me squirming around in a pool of sweat while vomiting and shitting for six straight hours.

From the accounts I had read it was definitely going to be bad, but I had been through some rough shit before and figured I could take anything for six hours. A common theme was that the Naltrexone detox wouldn't kill you, but it would sure as hell make you wish that it had. Trying not think about it, I checked into the motel, poured myself a cup of water, and swallowed the harmless-looking pill.

It got so bad so fast that within an hour I wished I were dead. My skin was going from freezing to burning so quickly that I couldn't tell which was which. It was also the first time I had experienced what literally felt like crawling skin—not goose bumps, or a chill, or that weird shiver I would sometimes get after taking a piss. It was as if my skin had decided it wasn't in the right place and was trying to figure out where it was supposed to go.

At the same time, I was trying to navigate my way back and forth from the bathroom through a whole new space-time continuum I didn't understand. My trips from the bed to the bathroom every few minutes felt like a mile each way. I tried just hanging out on the toilet because, no matter how many times I puked, or shit, there was always more. When there was finally nothing left to puke up, I dry-heaved until I was so parched that I needed water. But I couldn't keep the water down for more than a few seconds. On the few occasions that I did, it would come out in the form of diarrhea a few minutes later.

Eventually my skin, having given up on trying to find out where it should go, just crawled off my body, leaving raw flesh and exposed nerves. Everything hurt. The sheets, the pillow, my T-shirt, my underwear, and my body hair felt like steel wool against my body. Just as I had been warned, the idea of killing myself was going around in my head like a tape loop, but I couldn't think of a single painless way to go about it.

The most fucked-up part—the thing that I had not seen mentioned once by anyone who had gone through it, was how this stuff affected one's sense of time. I stared at the red numbers on the digital clock and it would take at least an hour for a minute to go by. I could deal with the pain, the puking, and the diarrhea, but this time warp I had gone through was fucked up, especially since there was a horrific psychedelic element to the whole thing. Time had slowed down so much, I felt as if I were rolling around in a blur of raw flesh at ten times the speed the rest of the world was operating on.

Looking for any form of escape, I tried turning on the TV. Just the light from it gave me sharp pains in the back of my eyeballs, and the people on the infomercial were far scarier than what I was dealing with. Even on mute, the TV put out a high-pitch hum that I found unbearable. I turned it off and went back to watching the minutes slowly tick away on the clock.

It felt as if I had been alone in that room for at least a week when sunlight started appearing around the edge of the curtains. With the sun came a small bit of relief, as the pain and hallucinations started to recede.

I watched it get brighter, thinking this must be what spring is like in Iceland because it felt like two more days went by before I heard a knock at the door.

I had agreed to let Jibz come and check on me in the morning, but now I wished I hadn't. I still felt gross, like a shell of a human being, and my body had been put through the wringer. I put on some clothes before letting her in, and they felt like sandpaper against my skin. Everything was uncomfortable. I opened the door and tried to say something, but I got choked up and started crying. Then she was crying. When I calmed down, all I could tell her was that it had been rough, which must have been obvious enough just by looking at me. I thanked Jibz for the soup and crackers she brought and asked her to leave, which made me feel like a real asshole.

All I managed to get down was a saltine. It felt as if I were eating metal filings. Seeing Jibz had made me so antsy that all I could think about was being anywhere other than where I was, which is always a difficult predicament to be in. I got in my car and drove home, puking up the cracker out of the window at a stoplight.

Once again I couldn't see the harm in doing a little dope just once. Not even close to fully recovered from the horrors of last night, I needed desperately to feel better. The Naltrexone was supposed to block opiates for twenty-four hours, and the dope caused another violent fit of coughing and vomiting before I felt better. Five minutes later, I was cleaning up the puddle of vomit on the floor, feeling as if last night had never even happened.

I called Jibz to thank her for coming by, and to let her know that I was finally clean. This time for good. Our old band, the Roofies, had reformed when she got back, and we had rehearsal the next night.

When Jibz showed up for band practice, she couldn't get over how much better I looked, considering what she saw the day before.

"Yeah. That stuff was terrible, but it really worked."

Of course I had to use up what was left of the dope that morning, which led me to buy more.

"You want to come over to my place?" she asked when we were done rehearsing.

I wanted to go to my room and be by myself, but I couldn't think of a way out of it. It was just so depressing. I felt like a bad actor in a fucked-up soap opera as I went through the motions of making out with her. I did want to give it another chance, I was just too stressed out with all the shit that had been going on, and the last thing I wanted to do was start lying and faking orgasms with someone else. I couldn't even get that far with Jibz.

"I'm sorry. I'm just too stressed out," I said.

"Too stressed out for what?" she asked.

"Never mind. Nothing," I answered, realizing I was actually being a bit presumptuous in the first place. It gave me a new resolve to clean up my act, though. This time for Jibz. Even so, I avoided her as much as possible over the next few weeks while making preparations to do the rapid opiate detox again. But there was no fucking way in hell I was going to be conscious for it.

A couple of weeks later I rode my bike down to Pill Park in the Tenderloin and bought what I was told were Klonopin off a Vietnam vet. Not telling anyone about what I was doing, I climbed the ladder up to my loft and settled into my bed before taking the Naltrexone and Klonopin. They both kicked in just when I realized I needed to take a piss. As I approached the edge of the loft to climb down to the bathroom, there appeared to be two ladders. I must have picked the wrong one because the next thing I saw was the floor coming up fast.

eleven

In which the young boy comes upon an
evil dictator and starts a revolution

IF THERE WASN'T A PROTEST going on, Kyle and I would usually
head up to UC Berkeley anyway and try to make a couple of bucks
juggling. I had a routine that was mostly bits and pieces stolen from other
people's acts, but I never got the same response from these jokes that my
older colleagues did.

"And now, ladies and gentleman, five balls," I would say, starting to
jump up and down while only juggling three balls. I rarely got more than
a chuckle from that joke, but I still thought it was funny.

Kyle, whose job it was to hand me things while I performed and collect the money after I was done, somehow got a lot more laughs than I
ever did. It started one day after my five-ball joke. One at a time, he was
supposed to throw in two extra balls, and I would catch them while I
continued juggling, transitioning from the joke to actually juggling five
balls. By accident, he threw both at the same time, and I ended up dropping everything. The crowd got a laugh out of it, but I was mortified that
he had fucked up the trick.

Another time he threw me a lit torch while I was up on my six-foot
unicycle, but his aim was off. Not only did I catch the side of the torch
that was on fire, but I also lost my balance and fell. I had to let go of the
other two torches I was holding in order to not fall on my head, and one
of them knocked over the open container of kerosene. Before I knew it,

I was lying on the ground a few inches away from the three-foot flame of ignited gas. The audience went nuts for that one. We collected almost sixty dollars from that crowd, but I was humiliated.

After that Kyle changed his job description from assistant to saboteur, always trying to find clever ways to make me fuck up and look like an idiot. The fact that we were making more money was little consolation. Those assholes didn't care about skill anyway; they just wanted to see me fall down and light myself on fire. If I didn't hurt myself, we were lucky to make thirty bucks in a whole day. We'd spend half of it on candy, split the other half, and then tell Mom that we only made five bucks.

"Five bucks? What happened to the rest of it?" she'd ask.

"The rest of what?"

"The money?"

"I swear. That's all we got," I lied.

Eventually Mom figured out we were spending our measly earnings on candy and video games. She came by our usual spot to surprise us, and we weren't there. I don't know how she tracked us down, but I was just about to get a replay on Bride of Pinbot when she found us at the arcade with our pockets full of candy. Luckily she didn't have any of my school photos with her or I'm sure she would have tried to ban me from the arcade the same way she did at McDonald's.

Mom's obsession for always knowing exactly where we were and what we were doing was taking a toll on her. I would have been more than happy to disappear and give her some space, but she had come up with a plan to get us out of the house and know what we were doing at the same time. Saying good-bye to the political protests and street performing up at UC Berkeley, Kyle and I started taking the train out to San Jose on weekends to stay with a family who was extremely active in the juggling community.

Barry was a computer programmer who ran the International Juggling Association with his wife in his spare time. Ironically, Barry was a terrible juggler, and his wife, Sue, couldn't juggle at all. I never understood why they were so involved in the grunt work of running the IJA, but it was unbelievable how much paperwork it generated. Their house was filled with file cabinets stuffed with documentation on who could juggle how many balls or clubs or rings, and for how long; breakdowns and descriptions of the artistic versus technical skills of each of these jugglers; what juggling organizations they belonged to; whom they studied under; their relatives; and so on. He was the J. Edgar Hoover of the juggling world. Although I never asked, I assumed they had a file on me as well.

Spending time with them actually made my mom look slightly less obsessive. They had two kids, Marc and Scott, who, like me, had to juggle at least an hour a day. It didn't seem to help them that much. On Saturday nights we all went to a local church where they belonged to a juggling organization called Safety in Numbers.

At this point, I was up to seven balls, but I usually couldn't keep them in the air for more than thirty seconds. My record was around a minute, but it wasn't long enough or solid enough to include in a routine. I could keep five clubs in the air for slightly longer. I had been working on seven balls and on five clubs for almost six months and wasn't getting any better. I felt as though I had finally hit a wall, but I kept at it anyway.

While I was in the gym practicing, Kyle spent his time trying to catch a rabbit we had seen hopping around on the church grounds. When he finally did catch the thing, we smuggled it back to Berkeley in a paper bag. Mom didn't know what to do about the rabbit. We already had two peacocks living in the backyard. The peacocks didn't belong to anyone, and no one in the neighborhood seemed to have any idea when or how they had gotten there. She let us keep the rabbit in the house that night, but the next morning there was shit and piss everywhere. Monday was show-and-tell at school, so we got the cheapest chicken wire cage we could find, put a bunch of shredded-up newspaper in it, and brought the rabbit to school.

Of course, I had to go directly from school to tap dancing class, so I convinced my teacher, Carol, to let me leave it over night. After repeated requests to take the poor rabbit home, he was still hopping around in his cage in the back of the classroom a month later. I brought food for him, but I hated cleaning out the cage and only did it when the smell got really bad. It pissed me off, because in my mind it was Kyle's rabbit, yet I was the one who ended up being responsible for it.

Mondays were the worst. Aside from being a terrible day in general, after two days with the windows closed and nobody to clean up after the rabbit, the classroom always smelled awful. I didn't want to deal with Carol's threats of what she was going to do if I didn't take the rabbit home, but I was even less excited when a substitute teacher walked in holding a scarf to his nose. Carol could be vicious, but everyone liked her. Her brand of nastiness was always entertaining, as long as I wasn't the focus of it. I could tell that this substitute teacher was an asshole the moment he walked in the room, and I was not mistaken.

"What's that smell?" he asked, scanning the room. "What is that rabbit doing in here? Whose rabbit is that?"

Since I had decided it was Kyle's rabbit, I didn't say anything. Neither did anyone else, until he threatened to take away our recess if we didn't tell him. Everyone pointed at me.

"You get to stay here during recess to clean that cage," he told me. "Okay. My name is Mr. Lutkenhouse," he said, causing a chorus of moans throughout the class. "Yes, I was told you call your teachers by their first names here, but when I was a kid, 'mister' was a title of respect. So I don't care what you call your other teachers, you will call me Mr. Lutkenhouse."

I had never acted particularly rebellious before, but this guy's presence had triggered eleven years' worth of the antiauthoritarian conditioning I had grown up with. He started calling roll, and when it got to me, I once again decided to say nothing.

"Oran?" he said for the third time, looking around the room. I was nervous as hell, but I couldn't answer him.

"Does anyone know where Oran Canfield is?"

"That's Mr. Canfield," I answered.

"What did you say?"

"You can call me Mr. Canfield," I repeated.

"Okay, Mr. Canfield. You can go to the principal's office." He looked as though he was shaking, and I could swear his skin had turned a redder shade.

"Thank you," I said, getting up to leave.

"After you clean the rabbit cage during recess," he said, causing me to reluctantly sit back down.

"Yousef? Is Yousef here," he went on.

"Do you mean Mr. Daryiush?" Yousef asked him.

"Mr. Whateveryousaid, you can go to the principal now."

Ten more kids went to the principal's office, and it was looking as if class was just going to be Quincy Blue, Akbar Bey, and me. I couldn't imagine what class was going to be like with only three students, but eventually, the principal, Wendy, brought the other kids back to class and told them to take their seats.

"Oran," she said. "I will see you in my office at recess."

I was still afraid of this guy, but I was feeling pretty cocky about the fact that I had started and seemed to be winning this little sixth-grade revolution. Knowing he couldn't send anyone else to the principal, Mr. Lutkenhouse resigned himself to using our last names.

"Where do you think you're going, Mr. Canfield?" he yelled at me as I headed for the door at recess.

"I believe you heard the principal tell me to see her in her office," I said, gloating.

"Fine. I guess you and I will be having lunch together then," he said. It was only ten thirty, and I couldn't see the day getting any better.

I was hoping Wendy would send me home, or just keep me in her office.

"What happened? This is very unlike you," she said.

"I don't know. I really couldn't help it. That guy's an asshole. I don't like him."

"I can tell. Listen, though. Carol is going to be out for two days, so you're going to have to deal with him. I don't like him either, but that's who they sent. Please, try to do what he says until Carol gets back."

There were still a few minutes left of recess, so I went back to class and cleaned up after the rabbit so I wouldn't have to do it during lunch. The rest of the day went without incident, but every moment was a struggle.

The next morning, I pretended I was sick.

"Too sick to make it to that audition after school?" Mom asked.

I was supposed to try out for a Coca-Cola commercial. I had done a few local commercials for JCPenney and was hoping to get a national one. I had heard that the Mikey kid from the Life Cereal commercials had made ten thousand dollars just for the shoot and was still getting royalties every month on top of that. I was going to walk in that afternoon, and the casting people would know I was the one for the job the moment they saw me. I wouldn't have to audition or anything. That was my fantasy anyway, since I hated auditions. I took rejections very personally, and so far that's all I had ever gotten. JCPenney had cast me in two fleece-wear commercials because they wanted someone to ride around on a unicycle in a sweat suit. No audition necessary.

"That teacher is an asshole. I'm telling you, something bad is going to happen if I go to school today," I told her.

"Come on. Aren't you being a little dramatic?"

"You haven't seen this guy. Believe me, if you saw him, you would know what I was talking about."

"Sorry, Ory. I've got clients coming in all day. You have to go." She was surprisingly empathetic.

If for no other reason than to promote this softer, gentler way of getting me out of bed, I got up and put on my clothes. The look on my mom's face scared me, though. I could tell she was actually worried.

MR. LUTKENHOUSE MADE it obvious that he hated me. I could see it in his eyes when he called out "Mr. Canfield" during roll call. I was determined not to say a word the whole day, lest I say the wrong thing and get detention. I wanted that ten thousand dollars from the Coke commercial, even though I had never seen the seven hundred bucks I had supposedly made from the other ones. I succeeded in not saying anything, until I found myself having to stay after school anyway and write three hundred sentences as a punishment for reading my book.

Mr. Lutkenhouse handed me a piece of paper after I failed to put my book down within thirty seconds of our reading period being over. It was a Xerox of Carol's favorite punishment, having to write *Making noise in the learning environment is disturbing and therefore prohibited.* The "X 25" was in Mr. Lutkenhouse's handwriting at the bottom. It was obvious that he had been waiting all day for me to make the tiniest slipup.

"No," I said, looking up from the note. I felt like he had just taken ten thousand dollars from me.

"What did you say?" he asked. I could see his face instantly getting darker.

"I said no. I wasn't making any noise."

"No, what? You weren't making noise? Or you're not going to write the sentences?"

"Both. I was not making noise, and I'm not writing those . . ." Before I could finish answering, he lunged at me, and without even knowing what happened, I found myself on the other side of the table with Mr. Lutkenhouse facing me from where I had just been. His face was not only red, but at this point the veins were popping out of his neck and he was shaking with anger. He tried to grab me again, but I just kept running around the table. He stopped and stared at me for what seemed like an eternity and then jumped on top of the table and dove at me as I was trying to run away. I was lying on the ground in shock when he grabbed me by my collar and lifted me off the ground. The class was in an uproar, everyone was yelling, but no one was louder than me. When we got to the door, he threw me against it, and I fell to the ground. Again I tried to run, but before I could get away, he grabbed me and threw me against the door a second time. The third time he got me by the neck and didn't let go. He dragged me out the door and carried me out to the hall where he lost his grip. There was so much screaming and yelling going on that by the time Mr. Lutkenhouse made it to the hall, Kyle's fourth-grade class next door was already there, waiting to see what the hell was going on.

Mr. Lutkenhouse was bent over, trying to get a better handle on me, when Kyle saw that I was the one getting beat up. In an instant, Kyle was on Mr. Lutkenhouse's shoulders trying to get him to let go of me, while I was flailing around as if I were in one of those *Laurel and Hardy* skits where the little guy's arms are too short to punch the big guy. Somehow he managed to shake Kyle off him while holding me in the air by my collar. He then carried me down a flight of stairs to the principal's office, where he threw me over the counter, and I landed on top of the rather surprised secretary, Yvette. Looking back at the door, I saw Mr. Lutkenhouse leaning against the doorjamb, trying to catch his breath. His face was covered in blood.

"Oran? Is that you?" I heard Wendy's voice from the principal's office.

I tried to answer, but nothing came out. I felt fine for a minute, but panicked when I realized that I wasn't able to move or breathe. Eventually I was able to take some small breaths, which then turned into rapid, shallow hyperventilation. I was still on Yvette's desk crying and hyperventilating while a bunch of adults stared at me, waiting to hear what happened.

Nobody asked Mr. Lutkenhouse for his version, and no one went after him when he turned around and walked away. By the time I had recovered sufficiently to talk, a cop and a doctor had shown up on the scene and a lawyer was on his way. The cop took down my story and the doctor checked for injuries. I had somehow made it through the ordeal with no visible signs of abuse, which was odd considering the shape Mr. Lutkenhouse was in. I couldn't figure it out. I repeated the story for the lawyer, and he asked, "Did you hit him?"

"I don't remember hitting him. I mean, he was holding me by my neck. I was freaked out. If I did hit him, it wasn't intentional," I answered truthfully.

"I'm sending you home for the rest of the day. We'll call you in a little while and see how you're doing," the principal told me.

On my way out, the cop was in the hallway studying a trail of blood that still hadn't been cleaned up.

twelve

A reconstruction of confounding events,
as our protagonist tries to escape the noble
intentions of his friends and family

"WHERE ARE WE?" I asked, finding myself in a car speeding down the freeway. I couldn't lift my head off the rear dash to see who was in the car, but I heard my mom's voice.

"Ory, is that you? Who's the president?" she asked me.

"What are you talking about? Clinton," I said, having a vague memory of someone else asking me the same thing.

"Good, it's you. We're in Berkeley."

"Almost at my house," Kyle added from the driver's seat of his Honda Civic. I still couldn't lift my head, but I managed to turn it enough to see my mom's boyfriend, John, sitting in the backseat next to me. "Welcome back," he said. I tried to piece a narrative together, but nothing made any sense.

The last thing I remembered was being in a hospital elevator with Jake, when one of the passengers started yelling and pointing frantically behind me. I turned around as the doors were closing, and saw that my IV bag was still out in the hall. As the elevator started going down, I managed to rip the IV from my arm just in time to see it yanked up and out through the door. Jake had been taking me outside to smoke a cigarette, but I had no recollections beyond that. *How the fuck did I end up in Berkeley, who did Mom think I was, and why could I feel the car upholstery rubbing against my bare ass?* Nothing terrified me more in that moment than being naked in a car with my fully clothed family members. The fear gave me enough of a jolt to lift my head and get a more accurate picture of the situation.

I saw that I was wearing a baby-blue hospital robe, but it was only a slight relief. I still felt naked, and vulnerable.

"Jesus. What the fuck happened? Where are my clothes?"

"We were hoping you could tell us what happened. The doctors had no idea what was wrong with you."

"What do you mean? Didn't they run any tests on me?" I asked, trying to figure out how much they already knew. Then some of it started to come back to me.

I had been in a hospital room with close to twenty people standing around my bed. A doctor was leaning over me.

"Who's the president?" he asked.

"Clinton," I said.

"Okay, much better. Now can you tell me what day it is?"

"Monday."

"Actually it's Wednesday, but you seem to have come back to us. Good work. I'll check back in a little while," he said, leaving me to face the crowd of people. *How did they all fit in this tiny room?*

My vision was so blurry I couldn't tell who exactly was there with me, but I recognized Jibz's voice.

"Have you been using heroin again?" she asked.

I tried to focus on her and found that I had been experiencing a serious case of double vision. What I had thought was twenty people merged into nine. I looked around to see Jibz, Jake, Aaron, Betsy, Eli and his girlfriend Beth, Kyle, Mom, and John.

"I don't know what you're talking about," I told Jibz.

"I found some needles in your room. Did you start using heroin again?"

"Jesus Christ. What were you doing in my fucking room?" I tried to yell but didn't have the energy.

"Come on, Oran," my mom said. "We've been here for three days now. I asked her to go see if she could find out what happened to you."

"You've got to be kidding me. You guys are fucking sick. Waiting around for three days so you could give me a fucking lecture? Where are my cigarettes?" I said, trying to sit up.

"Hey, Ory. No one's here to lecture you. We've all been worried sick. Who waits around a hospital for three days to judge someone?"

I looked around at all the people judging me. "Exactly. Who does that?

And what the fuck happened to my cigarettes? I need to get out of here."

"Are you crazy? You can't leave," Mom said.

"Would someone at least get me a fucking cigarette!" I yelled.

"Easy there, Cranberry," Jake said. "Listen, let's you and I go get a cigarette, and we'll come back and figure out what to do next. Okay, buddy?" I nodded.

Jake helped me out of bed, and we headed to the elevator with the IV rack in tow. But I couldn't remember anything between then and waking up in Berkeley.

"So are you going to tell us what happened?" Mom was asking me, as my awareness returned to being in Kyle's car. "Was Jibz telling the truth? Have you been shooting heroin?"

I was so ashamed that I couldn't answer her. I just stared out the window at the other passing cars.

"All of us have been waiting around at the hospital for three days wondering if you were ever going to come back to us. Now, come on, have you been doing heroin?" she pressed.

"Goddamn! Yes, I've been doing heroin. I was trying to quit, and I fell out of my loft. Okay?"

"Hey, man. She's not trying to lay a trip on you, but come on . . . You're her son and she's just trying to figure out what's going on so she can help," John said.

"We all are," Kyle added.

"Okay. So now you know. And what the hell happened to my clothes?" I asked again as Kyle veered off the freeway.

"I don't know. Aaron was trying to find your things, when Jake came running back to tell us you left the hospital," Mom answered, giving up on the questioning.

"We ended up driving all over the Mission looking for you," John piped in.

"What? Where could I have gone like this?" I asked, leaning over to get a visual confirmation that I wasn't wearing any shoes either.

"Oh, Ory. You should have seen it. We finally found you on Sixteenth Street with your ass hanging out of your robe, talking to a couple of drug dealers," Mom said with a laugh.

I couldn't help but laugh with her. The whole idea was ludicrous. I couldn't believe I managed to walk a whole mile dressed like this without getting picked up by the cops or somebody, and what the hell was I planning on buying the drugs with? My robe?

"Are you fucking kidding me? What the hell was I doing?"

"I have no idea, but those dealer guys were glad to see us. You were acting so crazy that they were more than happy to help us get you in the car." She was still laughing.

We were all laughing. What else was there to do?

I MUST HAVE BLACKED out again, but this time only for a few minutes. When I came to, Kyle was laying out a sleeping bag for me in his basement recording studio. I looked around, trying to get my bearings, and asked, "What happened to Mom?"

"Man, are you serious? You just said good-bye to her two minutes ago."

"Listen, Kyle. I'm totally sorry about all this." I didn't know what else to say to him.

"Just go to sleep. I'll see you in the morning." He headed upstairs.

"Hey, you got any clothes?" I called after him.

"I already gave them to you. You put them on top of the records," he called back.

I looked around the room, which was filled with over ten thousand records. Kyle was a DJ and hip-hop producer. A few years earlier, when his collection had been half that size, Kyle and I drove across the country to Orlando, where he had enrolled in college. We loaded all of his records into a U-Haul trailer, which was so heavy it kept lifting the back tires of his Honda off the road. We took shifts driving eighty miles an hour the whole way, taking our only break in New Orleans on a Saturday morning. There wasn't a whole lot going on that early, and after eating a bagel and cream cheese, we were back on the road. We ended up driving into Orlando exactly forty-eight hours after leaving Berkeley. He was going to school for audio engineering and had never lived on his own or taken a cross-country road trip. All he got to see was the shitty view from I-10 for two days. After going to a Walgreens to buy some dishes, utensils, and trash bags, he drove me to the airport. A few hours later I was on my way back home, wondering how I could be such an asshole to leave my little brother stranded in Florida all by himself. The trip could have been a great opportunity to try to make up for not being a very present older brother, but I didn't manage to figure that out till I was on the plane going home.

I found the clothes Kyle had laid out for me. After I changed out of my robe into a pair of boxers and a T-shirt, I lay down on the sleeping bag, feeling like a total asshole.

I FELT LIKE EVEN more of an asshole the next morning when I walked up the stairs from Kyle's recording studio. I was wearing a pair of his baggy hip-hop pants and a shirt that hung down to my knees, and my feet were crammed into a pair of Nikes a size and a half too small for me. Surprisingly, other than my scrunched-up feet, I felt pretty good physically. I just desperately wanted to get a cup of coffee and smoke a cigarette before I got on BART to go home.

"Hey, Kyle, you up?" He was obviously still asleep, but I couldn't sit still.

"Wha? Oh, hey. How you feeling?" he asked, rubbing his eyes.

"Surprisingly good," I said. "Get up. Let's go get a cup of coffee."

"Oh man, I'm still sleeping." But there was something odd about the way he said it. In fact, he seemed pretty wide-awake and alert for some-one who had only been up for thirty seconds.

"Okay, I'll bring one back for you. I need a couple of bucks, though." Whatever few dollars I had were left at the hospital.

"I can't let you go," he said nervously, getting out of bed. "Mom told me I had to keep you here."

"What the fuck are you talking about? I'm only walking two blocks to Peet's. You can come with me, but you can't stop me from going."

"Sorry, Mom said I can't let you leave."

What the fuck did she have to do with it? I was grateful to Kyle and everyone for finding me last night, but I was fine now, and I wanted to go home.

"What are you gonna do? Tie me to a chair?" I started walking down the stairs to the front door.

He threw up his arms but made no attempt to come after me. The door was locked from both sides with a deadbolt that you needed a key to open.

I felt bad for Kyle, but there was no way I was going to let him lock me up in his apartment. Going back upstairs, I told him, "Listen. I don't want to get you in trouble with Mom, but you can either let me out through the door and tell her I climbed out the window, or I can just go ahead and climb out the window."

"Man," he said with a sigh. "I'm not letting you out of the door or the window."

"Okay," I said, opening the window and climbing out without even looking to see if I could make it down.

Kyle was instantly on the phone with Mom, and I realized after I got outside that there was nowhere for me to go, and it was about a fifteen-foot drop down to the sidewalk. But instead of going back inside, I held on to the window frame and watched Kyle defend himself on the phone.

"There's nothing I can do, Mom. He's hanging off the side of the building." He rolled his eyes at me, which was our code for Mom being on one of her rants that no one could defend themselves against.

"She's calling the police," he said, hanging up the phone.

"The police? What are they going to do?" I asked, still holding on to the windowsill.

"Man, I don't fucking know," he said, exasperated by the whole situation. Kyle sat down and took a deep breath, I repositioned myself on the windowsill, and we waited for the police to show up.

H EY! YOU okay up there? What's going on?" A cop yelled up at me from the sidewalk, as another stepped out of the car. It couldn't have taken them more than five minutes to show up.

"Yeah. I'm fine. I'm just trying to get out of the house. My brother's got me locked in," I answered.

"Okay. I want you to go back inside and tell your brother we want to talk to him." The other cop walked to the door and started pounding on it.

"This is the police! Open up!" he started yelling.

Kyle shook his head and started for the stairs, while I climbed back in through the window and followed him down.

They asked both of us to come outside, where they separated us to figure out what the hell was going on. I couldn't hear what Kyle was saying, but I told my cop everything that had happened from the hospital till they showed up.

"Okay. So you weren't trying to hurt or kill yourself?" he asked me after I told him my story.

"No. I just wanted a cup of coffee."

"Stay here for a minute," he said before walking over to Kyle. This time I could hear every word because the cop started screaming at him. "Being a drug addict is not illegal, but kidnapping is one of the most serious crimes in the state of California!"

Both of the cops looked as if they were ready to tackle Kyle to the ground. Returning to his normal voice, the cop, who had just a moment ago looked like a rabid dog, asked calmly if I wanted to press charges against my brother. It was a strange feeling of power knowing that if I said yes, Kyle would be handcuffed and thrown in the back of the car for trying to help me out in the only way he knew how.

"Jesus. All I want is a fucking cup of coffee," I said.

The cops relaxed, got back in their car, and drove away.

"Hey, Kyle, you got a couple of bucks, man?"

"Yeah. Let's go," he said, and we started walking to the café.

I HAD NO IDEA what they had given me at the hospital. Mom told me they hadn't found any drugs in my system and had even taken a spinal tap in a last-ditch effort to figure out what was wrong. Whatever medication they had given me was wearing off quickly. I didn't feel sick so much as tired, and my back and rib cage were starting to kill me.

Kyle bought me a cup of coffee and a pack of cigarettes, but he refused to give me any money. I had to jump the turnstile to catch BART back to the city. I thought about going back to the hospital to get my wallet, but fatigue won over and I decided to go home and take a nap instead. Fortunately, my stuff was already in my room in a clear plastic bag. Going through the bag to get my wallet, I was disappointed to find that my favorite Pendleton shirt had been cut off with a pair of scissors, only an inch away from the buttons.

Under the shirt, I found a picture of me in a straitjacket, smiling straight at the camera with half of my beard shaved. Confused, I reached up to feel my face, and sure enough, one side of my beard felt noticeably longer than the other. *Why hadn't anyone—Jake, Mom, Kyle, John, the police—told me that I was walking around with half a beard?*

My back was now hurting so much that I decided to put off the nap and get high one more time. Too embarrassed to even buy drugs looking like this, I cleaned myself up and went out to score. That image of me smiling at the camera like a crazy person was still bothering the shit out of me. Luckily no one had been home to see me when I walked in, but who the fuck had taken that picture? I pondered it while I got high, then climbed up to my bed to doze off.

CONFUSED, ANGRY, and tired, I woke up for the second time in two days to a room full of people, but this time it was my room. I was up on my loft, so I couldn't see exactly who was there, but it sounded as if a convention were going on below me. Fucking assholes. Didn't they know I had no capacity to defend myself when I was waking up?

"Hey, Oran. Wake up." The voice was familiar, but I couldn't place it. "It's Jack, your father. We need to talk."

I sat up and looked down over the ledge to see Jack, Kyle, Mom, Jibz, Jake, Betsy, and the rest of my roommates staring up at me.

"Jesus fucking Christ. What are you doing here?" I said specifically to Jack. "Please . . . all of you, get the fuck out of my room . . . and stop digging around in there," I yelled at Jibz, who was methodically poking around in my trash can. She didn't listen to me. Luckily I had hidden the remainder of my dope in the back of my desk drawer.

"We're not going to leave because we all care about you, and we can't just stand by and watch you do this to yourself. We're here to help." It sounded like he had listened to a do-it-yourself intervention audiobook on his way up from Santa Barbara.

"If you really wanted to help, you would all get the fuck out of here so I can get some sleep. I'm fucking serious."

"We can't watch you do this to yourself," he repeated.

"Watch me do what? Sleep? Because that's what I'm doing," I said, lying back down.

"Okay. I don't have anywhere to be. I can wait here for as long as it takes," he said.

"Um . . . actually, I have to go to work," Jake said under his breath.

"Oran," my mom said. "This is ludicrous. We're not here to judge you. Jack flew out here because he's concerned. We all are. We'll sit here and wait around if we have to, but . . . . Jack, you tell him."

"I called Betty Ford, and unfortunately they're full, but they highly recommended a place out in Redwood City. And here's the deal: we're not going to leave you alone until you agree to come with us."

"How is that a deal? A deal would be that if I agree to go look at this place and I don't like it, you'll all leave me the fuck alone."

"Fine. Just look at the place. Okay?"

I thought about it for a little while and decided that the easiest way out of this mess was to go along with it. If I said yes, I could be back home in three hours, and it would give me some time to talk my way out of all this bullshit. If I said no, who knew how long they'd be hanging around.

"Okay. If you guys will just leave for a minute so I can put on some clothes, I'll go look at this fucking place with you."

They shuffled out and even closed the door behind them. I got out of bed already fully clothed and took a hit off the tinfoil I had hidden in my desk drawer. I was careful to take a small one since I was planning on being back in a few hours anyway and didn't have a dollar to my name.

THE ONLY RECOLLECTION I had of being in a car as a family was one time when we went to Disneyland. Jack had recently moved to L.A. from Massachusetts and agreed to meet us in Anaheim to celebrate Kyle's eighth birthday. We could not have picked a worse day. It was both Christmas break and the grand opening of Michael Jackson's *Captain EO*. The place was teeming with insane kids and annoyed parents. We waited on line for at least two and a half hours to see the fifteen-minute Michael Jackson movie where he turns all these mean and ugly space people into beautiful synchronized dancers by zapping them with some dance moves of his own.

I was pretty psyched after seeing that, but Jack, who had mostly been quiet all day, said, "Holy shit, I'm getting a vasectomy when I get home."

Maybe he thought we didn't know what he was talking about, but I couldn't believe he would say that after spending one day with us. One fucking day in the last three years. Happy birthday, Kyle.

Thinking about it now, I realized he may have been on to something. Not that I wanted to kill myself, but at that particular moment, in that car, driving to a fucking rehab with my mom, my dad, and my brother, it would have been nice to just not exist for a little while.

PULLING UP TO the rehab, they assured me repeatedly that they would be outside waiting in the car for me. I went in and talked to the intake counselor just to make it look as if I was giving it some consideration. I didn't even listen, but I nodded my head a few times to give her the impression that I was. She had all kinds of AA shit hanging on the walls, including a framed poster of the twelve steps, which I had never actually seen before. I couldn't help but notice the word *God* used throughout.

Fuck this. What did God have to do with me using heroin? I thanked the woman for her time, but told her I couldn't see this type of thing working for me.

Finding the car door locked, I knocked on the window. Kyle kind of jumped when he heard me, but he made no move to let me in.

"What the fuck? Open the door!" I continued to knock. Mom and I noticed at the same time that her door was unlocked. I made a grab for the handle but missed it as Jack, who had started the car, took off in a panic. They tried not to look at me as I ran after them for three blocks screaming profanity, except for Kyle who took a few quick glances out of the rear window until they finally lost me.

I sat down on the curb for a while, seething and trying to catch my breath while I tried to figure out what the fuck I was going to do. One thing was for sure—I was never going to talk to those motherfuckers again. Any of them. Fuming, I picked a direction and started walking, pretty sure I would find a Caltrans station sooner or later. I found one just as the last train was pulling up, and I got on and hid in the bathroom all the way back to San Francisco. From the train station, it was another two-mile walk back to my house. I was so pissed off that I was actually happy to see Jack's rental car parked back in front of the place. I had just spent two hours thinking about what I was going to tell those fuckers and had decided that short and sweet would be the best approach. Jack was a professional speaker, after all, and I didn't want to risk giving him the chance of saying anything that might trip me up in my attempt to let them have it.

They were sitting with my roommates in the living room.

"Fuck you, you, and you!" I screamed, pointing at Jack, my mom, and Kyle. "If you don't pay rent here, get the fuck out!"

"Hey, Oran, we're really—" Jack started to say, but I was prepared.

"Get the fuck out of my house. Now!" I screamed, before storming to my room. It was way too late for him to start in with this dad shit. It had been too late for twenty-four fucking years.

thirteen

In which the boy finds himself in trouble
with both sides of the law

I WAS ALMOST HOME from school when I saw Mr. Lutkenhouse step onto the corner with a bloody bandage taped to his face. I wanted to turn around . . . run . . . hide in a doorway, but I couldn't move. Luckily he turned right and kept walking without seeing me.

Mom was on the porch staring intently at a piece of paper she was holding. As I got closer I could hear her saying "What?" over and over again.

"Oh, Ory. I'm so sorry. I should have listened to you this morning," she said as I walked up the stairs. I don't think I had ever heard her say that in my life. I assumed she was admitting some responsibility for what had happened at school. "A lawyer just dropped this off for you," she said, handing me the paper. "It's a subpoena. You and Kyle are being sued for two hundred and fifty thousand dollars."

"Two hundred and fifty thousand dollars? For what?"

"Battery and assault," she explained.

"That can't be right," I said, looking at the paper. "First of all, *he* beat the shit out of me. Second of all, that was only two hours ago."

"Well . . . that's what it *says*."

"Did this lawyer have a goatee, a black suit, red tie, a bandage on his face?"

"Yeah, something was very weird about him. How did you know? Did he question you?"

"That wasn't a lawyer! That was the fucking guy! The teacher! Mr. Lutkenhouse!" I said, getting excited. "I told you he was an asshole, and you didn't fucking listen to me. He beats the shit out of me and now I'm getting sued? Jesus Christ, there were thirty . . . sixty fucking witnesses . . . what the fuck?" I was alternately crying, yelling, whining, and laughing, all of which seemed entirely appropriate.

We were still on the porch when another lawyer showed up to take a statement for the school district. I repeated my story for him, and my mom, who hadn't heard it yet, and we showed him the subpoena. The lawyer looked it over and told us we had nothing to worry about, that the school district would handle everything. Mom was well aware that we could have sued the shit out of them and won, but she was adamantly opposed to the legal system, though she never had a problem threatening people with it. For a few months the school district bent over backward to accommodate us; the superintendent even took me on private walks, and I found out he had been a professional magician for many years before he went into education. He divulged the secrets behind cutting people in half, making people float, and even told me some stories about the Magic Castle, a club shrouded in secrecy that only the best magicians in the world belonged to. He had a membership and invited me to go there with him, but once they realized we weren't going to sue, I never saw him again.

The day after the incident, my classmates treated me like a celebrity.

"Goddamn nigga. You fucked that teacher up. You see that motherfucker's face when he came back up here to get his shit? Blood dripping everywhere. I was like, 'Oh my God. My nigga Oran gave you a beatdown, bitch. Motherfucker deserved it, too. That was some insane shit, blood," Akbar said.

"Thanks, cuz," I said.

"What'd I say about calling me cuz?" he said after all that. "Nah. I'm just playin' wich you, nigga." It was the highest compliment I could have received.

I was let back into the basketball games, and even some of the junior high kids befriended me. Considering I hadn't suffered any serious damage, the whole thing seemed to have worked in my favor.

Almost all the kids came by my desk to shake my hand, and Carol came over and gave me a big hug. "I'm sorry" is all she said, but it meant a lot.

L IFE RETURNED to normal fairly quickly. Well, normal for me. Although I hadn't made it to that Coca-Cola audition, there were a zillion other auditions going on all the time. It seemed as if I went to every single one of them, but I never got a callback, probably because I was so stiff and awkward at these things.

My acting career wasn't panning out too well, so I decided to shift my attention back to juggling in order to enter the International Juggling Competitions, which were taking place in San Jose the next year. In preparation for that, I decided to enter a local competition that was held in Southern California. Every year on April Fools' Day, a few thousand jugglers would converge on Isla Vista, a little town next to Santa Barbara. This regional convention was started mainly in reaction to the stuffier, more corporate vibe of the international convention, which, to my knowledge, had never been held outside of the United States.

The one in Santa Barbara was started by a group called the Renegade Jugglers, which was a fitting name. They were a group of crazy pot-smoking, beer-drinking, womanizing (no small feat for a juggler), long-haired weirdos, who supported themselves by making juggling equipment. It was such a decadent environment that only two other kids signed up for the juniors competition. Convinced I had nothing to worry about, I didn't even bother practicing for it. Unfortunately it didn't go that well, but I tried to sound excited when I called Mom and told her I got the bronze medal.

"Wow, third place? That's wonderful, honey."

"Yeah, it was great."

"Good, because Judy Finelli has agreed to choreograph your routine for the international competition. Isn't that amazing?"

"Uh . . . Yeah. Cool," I said, but I wasn't looking forward to it. The other two kids were also competing in San Jose. Even if I had practiced, I still would have probably come in last.

Judy Finelli was the director of the Pickle Family Circus, another San Francisco one-ring circus, which had received a tremendous amount of respect for being one of the first circuses to trade in flashy tricks for a more artistic, political, and theatrical experience. We were hoping that getting her to choreograph my piece would provide an in for joining up with them.

A LONG WITH ALL my after-school activities, I had also taken a job as a paperboy. I had to be up by 6:00 A.M., and in true Berkeley fashion, I delivered my papers riding a unicycle rather than a bike.

Throwing newspapers was an easy job, plus it was great cover for writing graffiti. Nobody was out that early in the morning. Collecting money at the end of the month, however, was impossible. No one wanted to pay me for waking up at 6:00 A.M. to bring them the news. Mostly people just refused to answer the door, but if I happened to catch them mowing their lawn, or arriving home from work, they would tell me that they had canceled months ago or never ordered it to begin with.

I knocked on one door and was greeted by a juggler named Scott who was actually very successful.

"Oran? What are you doing here?" It was a shock to see him, as I didn't even know he lived in Berkeley.

"Scott? Hey, man, you owe sixteen dollars for your *Chronicle* subscription."

"You're kidding me, right? You're delivering papers? I'm sorry, but I can't pay you for that."

"Should I come back tomorrow?" I asked, disappointed he was giving me the same brush-off as everyone else. I had seen that guy collect a thousand dollars for one show at Pier 39.

"No. You shouldn't come back at all. You're too talented to be delivering papers; you could actually be making real money performing."

"Come on, man. I wake up at six in the morning to get you your paper, and you're not going to pay me?"

"How much do you make doing this?"

"I've only collected sixty bucks. Nobody, including you, wants to pay for their paper."

"Okay. I'll give you four times that if you stop doing this. It's depressing."

I should have taken the money, but who the fuck was he to tell me what I should do? I scratched Scott off my route. That motherfucker could go get his own paper.

The next house told me they would give me the money once I returned the Cadillac medallion I had stolen off their car.

"I have no idea what you're talking about," I answered, trying to cover up the Mercedes-Benz medallion I was wearing around my neck. I didn't even bother trying to collect from the house with the Rolls-Royce. They had already called the police to complain about their missing hood ornament.

―――――

I KEPT MY PAPER ROUTE, but that summer I dropped everything else to focus on the upcoming competition. I had come up with the clever idea of working my paperboy job into the routine when I heard a song by Midnight Star called "Headlines." It was a hip-hop song, with a robot singing the chorus: *Extra, extra, read all about it.* Judy Finelli choreographed the performance, with the help of Larry Dilahante, my jazz-, modern-, and interpretational-dance teacher. When the big day finally came, I could not believe that Scott, the bastard who wouldn't pay me for delivering his newspapers, was one of the judges. I could see him chuckling when I rode out on my unicycle wearing my *San Francisco Chronicle* bag. I rode around the stage juggling newspapers, which I then threw out to the audience.

I ended up doing much better this time, coming in second place after the older kid who had won in Santa Barbara. Although I thought his routine was terrible, I was content with my silver medal, until Scott found me backstage. "Hey, Oran, you were unbelievable. I take back everything I said about your paperboy job. Here . . ." he said, handing me sixteen dollars. "I'm sorry, but we had to give Robbie the gold."

I didn't understand what he was getting at. I just said, "That's okay. Thanks."

"What I'm trying to say is that this was his last year to compete in the juniors. You've got five more years. We just didn't have a choice."

What was wrong with this guy? I'm sure he thought he was giving me a compliment—just like when he had said I was too good to be delivering papers—but he may as well have punched me in the gut. I didn't give a fuck if it was Robbie's last year to compete. If I deserved the gold, I wanted the fucking gold. I had to endure people complimenting me for the rest of the night, many of them echoing what Scott had said. I tried to smile and say thanks, but I was pissed off.

I CONTINUED JUGGLING, but after that experience, I was disillusioned with the whole scene. Graffiti and shoplifting were taking over as my main interests, and I tried getting into drugs as well. The problem was that they didn't really agree with me—not the drugs that were available anyway.

Pot was really the only thing twelve-year-olds had access to. The first time I tried it, my friend Tony had stolen some from his dad, who was studying at the seminary to become a pastor. We hid in his basement and smoked the stuff. We sat there, waiting, but nothing happened. The second time was the same scenario, but that time I did feel it. It was the opposite of the cool, mellow vibe I had been expecting. Instead, I got paranoid and self-obsessed and decided I hated Tony. I was supposed to spend the night, but I couldn't handle being around him or his dad, who came down to the basement to hang out with us for a while. His dad was kind enough not to bring up Jesus or anything, but the pot was making me hate him too. After Tony's dad went to sleep, I decided I had to get the fuck out of there.

Sneaking into my own house made me so paranoid, it took me close to twenty minutes to get to my room. Whenever the stairs creaked or I made any noise, I would stand stock-still for a while, hoping it would sound as though the house had just creaked on its own, which it often did. When I finally made it to my bed and was just about to fall asleep, I heard a noise downstairs and spent the rest of the night wide-awake, terrified that stoned people were walking around the house.

I resolved to never do that shit again . . . until a week later when I hung out in Tony's basement and apparently forgot about the last time.

I WAS STILL HOPING to join the Pickle Family Circus, but instead of having me do a formal audition, they wanted me to hang around their compound in San Francisco to see if I would fit in. I started spending a few nights a week at the old Victorian mansion they had gutted and turned into their rehearsal space. There were two other kids around my age, Lorenzo and Gypsy Pickle, who were born into the circus. Although I got along with them well, I quickly became much better friends with a nineteen-year-old juggler named Andrew. Meeting him was like meeting a myth. I had never seen him juggle before, but everyone had been talking about him. Andrew had appeared out of nowhere a few years earlier and shocked the juggling community with a style no one had ever seen before. Not only did he live up to my expectations, he exceeded them. His arms moved at lightning-fast speeds around the three balls that appeared to hover amid the blur of his hands. Seeing him juggle didn't shed any light on what it was he was doing, but, unlike other jugglers who had developed their own styles, Andrew didn't mind being copied and would even show me what he was doing in slow motion.

Although Mom had never had a boyfriend to my knowledge, she had a habit of renting out our extra room to younger men who could change lightbulbs and be positive influences on Kyle and me. The last guy, Reggie, was a third-degree black belt in kung fu and had been our camp counselor for the last four years. She had to kick him out when it became evident he had no interest whatsoever in changing lightbulbs or acting as a positive male role model. Instead he hid in his room listening to Bob Marley while he smoked unbelievable amounts of pot.

Andrew ended up taking the extra room and had no issue with helping out around the house and mentoring me. At thirteen years old, he had run away from home and taught himself how to juggle to make a living. By sixteen, he had traveled all over the world as a juggler and learned seven languages, using a method of syllable association he had come up with himself. He claimed to have learned fluent Cantonese in four months. By nineteen, he spoke eleven languages, had written a book, and was reading *Beowulf* in Old English. He hadn't been to school since the sixth grade.

Juggling was just a means to an end for him, a way to support himself, travel the world, and learn more languages. Aside from that, he didn't seem to care much about it.

I didn't quite understand why he took such an interest in my life, until one day when he confessed his love for me.

"You can't repeat this to anyone. I have only told this to one other person, but the reason I ran away from home was that my sisters were molesting me. Because of that . . . well . . . I'm not attracted to women," he said. This was the first time I had heard of anyone being *turned* gay, but I didn't bring that up.

"What about Sky?" I asked, referring to his girlfriend, who was an amazingly beautiful trapeze artist.

"That whole thing is just a front. I mean, she doesn't know any of this, but it's an act." I didn't understand why he didn't just come out of the closet. A lot of the male figures in my life were gay—partly from growing up in the Bay Area and being involved in the performing arts, and partly because my mom still held a grudge against all straight men since one of them had left her with two kids.

"I don't get it," I said. "Why not just tell the truth? I mean, why are you telling me?" I must have sensed what was coming next because I felt a little uncomfortable.

"Because I'm in love with you—have been since we met, and I needed to say something about it," he answered.

I just stared at the floor for a while, trying to figure out what to say.

"Honestly, I haven't figured it out yet. If I'm straight or gay, I mean. I don't know what I want," I lied. Even as I was saying it, I couldn't figure why I didn't just tell him I liked girls. It seemed to work, though, since he never brought it up again.

Rather than putting a strain on our relationship, Andrew's confession seemed to put him in better spirits. He still gave me advice on everything from juggling to personal grooming. He even showed me how to shave for the first time, and I was long overdue. I had been bleaching my mustache since I was eleven because Mom thought that once I started shaving it would grow even faster and there would be no stopping it. At thirteen, I had two years' worth of facial hair, and was finding it harder and harder to explain to people why I had black hair but a blond mustache.

Andrew continued to act like an older brother until Kyle and I got arrested for stealing tapes at Tower Records.

I don't know if the security guard gave everyone the same lecture, but it was pretty effective. "When you guys walked in, I said to myself, 'now there's a couple of good kids.' I don't have children myself, but I was thinking what it would be like if I had a couple of good kids like that. That's what I was thinking about when you guys came in, because in this job I don't see too many good kids."

I was sufficiently humiliated by the whole thing.

Mom absolutely refused to come get us, and because it was a Friday night, we would have to spend the whole weekend in juvenile hall. The security guard decided he would keep us at the record store until they closed, just in case Mom changed her mind and picked us up. We sat with him for three hours behind the two-way mirror, watching for other shoplifters and praying to see Mom walk in. She never came, even after two more calls from the security guard, who kept telling her what a couple of good kids we were.

"I'm really not sure that juvenile hall is the right place for them," I heard him say.

Ten minutes before midnight, Andrew showed up with a note from our mom, asking the store to release custody of us to him. The guard took a couple of Polaroids, which he tacked to a wall next to hundreds of other pictures, and told us we were never allowed back. Andrew sent Kyle home in a cab and decided that he and I would walk. He lectured me for another hour about how, even when he was broke and homeless before he learned how to juggle, he had never stolen a thing from anyone. Stealing was the lowest thing a human being could do, and he wasn't even sure if he could be my friend anymore. Andrew was so disillusioned with me, he was going to have to think very hard about whether he could even stay in the same house with a thief. It was the worst walk home ever.

I was totally pissed off when I tried to steal a candy bar a few days later and wasn't able to go through with it. It had nothing to do with wanting to be a good kid, or realizing that stealing was bad; I was just too scared and nervous about getting caught. I was never able to shoplift again, which was all the more frustrating because I was always broke.

TO MAKE MATTERS worse, Mr. Lutkenhouse took his story to a journalism student at UC Berkeley, who wrote an article about it. I read the *Daily Cal* in order to keep up with what was becoming an increasingly nasty fight between the citizens of Berkeley and the university over the school's involvement with South Africa. I was stunned to come across an article about a poor teacher who had not only been beaten up by two malicious brothers but had also lost his job and was now working as a nude model in the university art department. This teacher's only aim in life was to help the kids, and we had destroyed his dream.

Our age didn't permit the journalism student to use our names, but she did mention that I could often be seen on campus doing my juggling act or on my unicycle delivering newspapers. She neglected to mention, however, that the only reason he became a teacher in the first place was that, after completing law school, he had repeatedly failed his bar exams. This had come to light during a cross-examination at one of the many depositions Kyle and I had attended.

I gave up performing at the university when a few people started heckling Kyle and me for being the kids who had attacked our teacher. A few days later, I was forced to give up my paper route, after being chased by four high school kids holding baseball bats. I recognized them as graffiti writers who had already come looking for me at my elementary school. When I heard someone yell, "There he is," and saw them heading toward me, I hopped off my unicycle and ran away as fast as I could. An older kid at school had warned me that they thought my tag was similar in style to their terminally ill friend's graffiti, but I didn't see any similarity. I used entirely different letters, for fuck's sake. Nonetheless, I started taking a different route to school and learned how to play foursquare instead of basketball as it offered a quicker escape route out of the schoolyard.

When I found myself with no income, an inability to steal, and a very real fear of leaving the house, Mom started looking into boarding schools.

fourteen

Sees our protagonist stand his ground
against a pack of fanatical well-wishers

OTHER THAN BETSY installing a padlock on her door, my trip to the hospital and subsequent family drama didn't seem to have a visible effect on my roommates. We all just did our best to pretend that nothing had happened. I still rehearsed with my bands and tinkered around in the recording studio, but I didn't have any money or work so I had to start selling shit. I never knew how much money my grandmother's trust was going to generate, but this month I had received only thirty-seven dollars. The first things to go were a whole bunch of old Schwinn cruisers I had bought at flea markets and fixed up over the years. Then it was records, and eventually I started selling off some of my nonessential recording gear.

I tried my best not to use, but I had horrible back pain from the fall, and my chest had been making a clicking sound like a grandfather clock ever since my trip to the hospital. The heroin didn't quiet the sound coming from my heart, but it took my mind off it.

A week later my definition of "nonessential" started to include some of my nicer microphones and other gear that had been off-limits only a few days earlier. Owning a recording studio had been my dream for a while, and I really didn't want to lose it.

I just needed to get a good week or so clean. Mom and I had started talking again only a few days after I had kicked her out of my place, and she agreed to let me try to kick at her house. I only lasted one day before sneaking out to get high. In a rare moment of clarity, I told her about it and asked her to drive me back to the rehab. I wasn't going to fall for all that God shit, but a few weeks away from everything would do me some good.

I filled out the paperwork, gave them my insurance info, and then went to meet with the head doctor, who interviewed me about my drug history. I didn't get very far into the interview when he got up and put his ear to the wall clock.

"Are you wearing a watch?" he asked me, looking confused.

"Yeah," I said, showing him my ten-dollar holographic Jesus watch, which I had bought in the Mission.

"Let me hear it," he said. I reached across the desk to hold it up to his ear.

"No, that's not it. What's that ticking?"

"Shit, you can hear that? My chest has been making that sound since I fell from my loft."

"What? It's been making that sound for a week? We got to get you to the hospital now. That's your fucking heart, man."

He didn't need to talk like that for me to figure out that he was perhaps a bit unorthodox as far as doctors went. His name was Barry, and he had long curly hair tied up in a ponytail. Instead of medical texts and anatomy charts, his office was filled with Buddhist art, and the bookshelves mostly contained texts on yoga, Eastern philosophy, and spirituality.

"Nah. It's fine. I'm sure it'll go away," I told him.

He stared at me as if I were crazy.

"Un-fucking-believable. I can hear your heart clicking from across the room and you're telling me—a trained doctor—that it's no big deal? Have you been to medical school?" he asked.

"No," I said, having a pretty good idea about what was coming next.

"Well, I have, and I am telling you that the sound coming from your heart—you know, the organ that keeps you alive by pumping blood through your system?—is in fact a very big deal."

Had we met under different circumstances I might have thought he was a pretty cool guy, but right then I decided he was a patronizing asshole and I didn't like him at all.

I WAS RIGHT ABOUT my heart. The specialist at the hospital told me I had a contusion—whatever that was—but that there was nothing to do about it except wait.

Barry had sent me to the hospital before finishing my intake evaluation, but decided that I should detox cold turkey in the hopes that it might scare me into staying clean.

"But I've kicked cold turkey before," I told him. What was my fucking insurance company paying these people for?

"Great. So you know exactly what to expect," he responded.

I DIDN'T NEED to look at the Feelings Chart they handed out at group therapy to know that I was fucking miserable. There were only about twenty patients, and in the morning we were divided into four groups for two hours. I sat hunched over, and rocked back and forth, shivering in silence, until the counselor, Jan (pronounced "yon"), asked, "So how are you feeling, Oran?" Despite the fact that Jan was clean and sober, he always looked as though he was about to nod off.

"Shitty," I answered.

Jan also had a habit of peppering his conversations with incredibly long pauses. Just when it seemed as if he'd forgotten all about me, he continued. "Shitty could mean a lot of things. Can you look at the chart and find a more accurate 'feeling' word?" he asked.

I looked at the Xerox of emoticons with different facial expressions and the feeling words underneath.

"I feel anxious, apologetic, bored, cautious, cold, frustra—" I was picking out the list of negative feelings alphabetically before Jan cut me off.

"Let's just start with the first one. Why do you feel anxious?"

"Maybe it's because I ended up in a fucking rehab, kicking heroin, and it's the last place I want to be right now. How the fuck am I supposed to feel?"

"I think that what you're feeling is absolutely appropriate. Have you ever heard of the disease model of addiction?"

I shook my head, bracing myself for what I was sure was going to be a load of bullshit.

"Would someone like to explain it to him?" he asked the group.

"The disease model," a middle-aged man in a suit and tie started, "is that addiction—just like cancer—is in fact an incurable terminal disease that wants us dead. Unlike cancer, though, the disease of addiction is in

153

our mind, and it tells us to do things that will keep the disease active rather than in remission."

"Did you follow that?" Jan asked.

I nodded, but in fact I had become distracted, trying to figure out why this guy had dressed up in a suit and tie for group therapy.

"Sure, that sounds like a nice little theory," I said as flippantly as possible, "but what would that have to do with anxiety?"

"Well, one way of looking at it is that your anxiety could be the disease talking to you, trying to make you uncomfortable, to get you to go back out there. Any junkie knows the best way to get rid of anxiety is heroin."

I nodded in agreement at that.

"Part of why we want you to identify your feelings is that, with practice, we can begin to differentiate our real feelings from the disease."

"Hmm. Have you ever kicked heroin?" I asked him, trying out Barry's technique.

"Many times," he answered.

"Then don't you think it's possible I could be feeling this way because I'm going through fucking opiate withdrawal?" I said as nastily as I could muster.

I didn't feel like talking anymore. Jan got the picture and moved on to the next patient, while I went back to rocking back and forth while I stared at the carpet.

I did feel some temporary relief whenever I defended myself against this AA shit. I hadn't even opened my little blue AA book yet, and already there was enough evidence to see that the whole thing was based on nonsense. *Disease model, my ass. How come I had managed to do heroin in the past and not get addicted? Was it contagious? How does it spread? Can they find it in a blood test?* I didn't buy it. I was just going through a rough spot.

The more I rocked back and forth thinking about it all, the more it became apparent that rehabs were the perfect setup to recruit people into what was clearly a cult. No one is more destitute than someone who has lost everything, and these suckers would believe anything if it promised them a way out. *Too bad for them, because once I start feeling better I'm getting the fuck out of here*, I decided.

THAT AFTERNOON I finished my intake session with Barry. "So, do you think you might be an addict?" he asked me when I was done telling him my drug history.

"I don't think so," I answered him honestly.

"Let's see," he said, looking at his notes. "A bottle of wine when you were seven, beer and pot at eleven. Mushrooms, acid, alcohol, pot, and speed, from thirteen to seventeen, then cocaine, speed, alcohol, and heroin from eighteen to twenty-four. Am I missing something? You came an inch away from losing your life to heroin last week," he said with that patronizing voice.

"That's absolute bullshit," I said. "You've taken what I said totally out of context. How does two beers when I was eleven constitute alcoholism? I told you I've tried mushrooms once, speed two or three times, I fucking hate pot, and aside from trying heroin a few times when I was younger, I've only been using it for about a year." I was pissed. "And I didn't almost lose my life to heroin. I fell off my fucking loft because of the Klonopin I took when I was trying to kick. You manipulated everything I told you."

"Are you crazy? What I have in front of me here is a clear progression into addiction, and you seem to have no appreciation for the fact that you almost died as a direct result of your using."

"I didn't almost die!" I said, noticing my voice increase in volume. "I fell six fucking feet. That hardly seems like a near-death experience."

Once again, Barry was looking at me as if I were an alien.

"You contused your heart, man. Do you hear me?" His voice was almost a whisper. "I'm a doctor, and I'm telling you it doesn't matter if you fell six inches. You are fucking lucky to be alive."

There was no use talking about it anymore. He was obviously being overdramatic just to scare me.

"I'll bring this to the staff meeting on Wednesday," he said, holding up his clipboard, "and we'll come up with a treatment plan for you."

"I wouldn't worry about it. I don't plan on being here too long," I said, hoping I had time for a cigarette before whatever I had to go sit through next. I was too sick to participate in much of anything, but they made me sit through all the bullshit anyway.

A FEW DAYS LATER I had my one-on-one therapy session with Jan. Despite his misguided attempts to lure me into AA, he seemed like an all right guy. If he was really clean, I was certainly intrigued by how he managed to seem as though he were high all the time. I desperately wanted to figure out that trick.

"Did you see Barry's intake diagnosis of you?" he asked as I sat down.

"No. You mean the thing he brought to the staff meeting?" He nodded and handed me the file.

It looked like any other medical chart, with different boxes filled in with my blood pressure and heart rate, but at the bottom, next to Diagnosis, it simply said "Terminal Assholism."

"Is this a fucking joke?" I asked. Barry had claimed to be a real doctor.

"That's what I thought, too, but it's not a joke. That's his official diagnosis. He was very serious about it," Jan said, also trying to be very serious. "What do you think about it?"

"Well, it's pretty funny actually, but honestly I had the same opinion of him. Maybe his isn't terminal, but he is a fucking asshole."

Jan smirked as I handed the chart back to him. "So you know you can never go back to the Mission, right? That your old life is over? If you want to stay clean, you're going to have to say good-bye to all that," he told me.

It was as if he had punched me in the gut. I had let my defenses down and my voice cracked as I tried to tell him that my music and my friends were my life, that I didn't have any reason to stay clean without them.

He seemed sympathetic, but his only concession was "at least during early sobriety, and by early sobriety I mean the first five years." I was too stunned by this suggestion to say anything, not that I had any plans of following it. "You know, I was in the record industry for twelve years, so I know what it's like," he continued. "That lifestyle is no place for someone trying to stay clean."

Maybe Jan knew what the industry was like, but I didn't. In the seven years I had been playing music, I don't think I had met one person in the record industry, and it didn't appear as if Jan had spent much time playing shows in front of ten people and sleeping on hardwood floors. I did heroin by myself in my room, and, except for that horrific Caroliner tour, I rarely had more than a couple of drinks when I performed. I was no closer to the lifestyle he was referring to than anyone who goes out to see music.

"What do you think about masturbation?" he asked, taking me off guard.

"What?" I couldn't imagine where he was going with that question.

"Do you like it, not like it? Does it make you feel ashamed?"

Since I couldn't tell how this possibly related to the AA stuff, I decided to be honest with him.

"Well, I do it, but . . . I certainly don't feel good about it," I admitted, feeling very uncomfortable.

"Good. Because I would know you were a liar if you said you didn't. But what I want to know is, why you would feel bad about it?" he asked. "Are you Catholic?"

"No."

"Well, give it some thought, and in the meantime keep doing it. We're strong believers in masturbation here. Addiction is a disease of self-hate. You have got to learn to love yourself if you want to get through this." His delivery was so deadpan I couldn't tell if he was joking. I conjured up a fake laugh, but the part about loving yourself turned my stomach. It sounded like my dad's *Chicken Soup* bullshit. I didn't want anything to do with it.

"I'm not joking," he said, as I got up to go to the afternoon yoga session. "Loving anyone else will get you kicked out of here."

There was one cute girl at the rehab, but I was such a pathetic, shivering, nauseated, cold-sweating, skin-crawling wreck that anyone who saw anything in me would have to be in even worse shape than I was, at least mentally. But I did intend to go set up my yoga mat behind her.

I T WAS DURING FAMILY session that I decided I had to get the fuck out of there soon. Mom, or rather Dr. Canfield, as she had introduced herself to the room, was going around the group giving everyone advice.

"You know, Ted has told me before that he would go to meetings and stay sober, and within days he comes home drunk. I just don't know why I should trust him this time," some woman was saying about her husband, a classic San Jose computer programmer, who hadn't uttered a word during my time there.

"Um, excuse me. Can I say something?" Mom asked Eileen, the facilitator. Before Eileen could answer, Mom looked at the woman and said, "Are you crazy? You need to leave that guy. If he's done it before, he's going to do it again. I mean, who would put up with that?" Mom punctuated this with one of her condescending laughs.

Kyle and I rolled our eyes at each other. That was just the beginning; she had something to say to everyone in the room. I wanted to walk out right then, but I was still too sick to trust myself. When it came my turn to speak, I announced my intention of leaving as soon as I felt better.

"Okay. Does anyone have any feelings about that," Eileen asked the group. At least ten hands shot up immediately.

"I wish you could see yourself from where I'm sitting. I wasted forty years of my life drinking, and you've got your whole life in front of you," said one of the patients.

"I came to my first rehab when I was your age, and I didn't listen to anyone either. Now look at me, this is my tenth rehab, and believe me it gets harder every time I come back. You don't have to go through what I did if you can hang on and give this a shot," another guy said.

"Look at your mom and brother. Look at them," added the previous guy's wife. "Can you imagine how devastated, how heartbroken they would be if they got a call that you were dead? I've been going to Al-Anon ever since Steve went to his first rehab, and I see it all the time: mothers who've lost their kids, husbands who've lost their wives. There's nothing like the look on someone's face who's lost a loved one to this disease. And that pain never goes away. Look at them. Could you live with that?"

It seemed inappropriate to point out that I would be dead at that point, so I just sat in silence, doing my best to tune out the rest of them.

When everyone was done, Eileen asked me if what I heard had changed my mind.

"No. I mean, thanks for all the concern, but seriously. If I wanted to go out and use, I would do it right now. That's why I'm staying until I get better. Believe me, I have no intention of ever using again."

People started talking all at once after that, until Eileen said, "Oran. We all care about you. So can you at least agree to stick around till the next family session?"

"Jesus Christ. If it means we can move on to the next person, I will agree to stay till next week," I answered.

It was a dumb thing to agree to. The following week, family session was spent solely discussing why I should stay at that place. They tried everything. People I had never seen before cried over my decision. More people testified that they had thrown away their chances of sobriety when they were young and were still struggling with addiction, and others told me I would die. Defending myself against all that was a drag to say the least. Luckily, I was over being dope sick and had finally gotten a few hours of sleep, which helped me get through it.

When it was finally over, Mom refused to give me a ride home. Fortunately, a landscaper-turned-speed freak from Gilroy had insisted that I borrow forty dollars from him when we had gone on a group outing to the grocery store.

"Don't worry about it, I can get home," I told my mom.

I said good-bye to a few people and walked to the train station.

fifteen

*Presents evidence that extracurricular
activities lead to communism*

MOM AND I VISITED three boarding schools, all of which pro-
moted various forms of alternative education in their brochures.
The first one we checked out was a Quaker school in California, which
looked appealing because it didn't use a grading system. One of the students took me on a tour, showing me the various places in the woods
where kids went to smoke pot and have sex. The tour ended when we
found a group of kids in a tree house who were passing a joint around. I
had a feeling that joining them was a bad idea, but not wanting to come
across as uncool, I took a hit when it was passed to me.

"What'd you think?" Mom asked during the two-and-a-half-hour
drive home.

"I want to see the other ones," I said, trying to hide my overwhelming anxiety and paranoia. Although it had a beautiful campus nestled in
the woods of central California, those kids in the tree house bummed me
out.

We then visited a school in Colorado. I spent the night on campus to
get a feel for the place, and somehow ended up in the backseat of a car
with three other kids, driving around the suburbs looking for a beer
truck. They found one stopped at a red light, and two of the kids jumped
out, lifted the roll gate, and grabbed a case of beer. I decided this time
that it was okay to be uncool since I had no intention of ever seeing them

again. They weren't having it, though, and I ended up drinking half a beer just to prove I wouldn't tell on them.

"What'd you do last night?" Mom asked when she came to pick me up the next morning.

"Played video games," I lied, hoping she would cross this one off the list for me.

"Yeah, I didn't really like that place," she said.

Our next stop was Sedona, Arizona, where I toured the most beautiful campus I had ever seen. Awe-inspiring red rocks surrounded the school on all four sides, and aside from one modern dormitory, nothing appeared to have been built after the 1960s. The white walls and red-tile roofs of the buildings gave the appearance of a Spanish villa. I knew this was the place before I even got out of the car, and I still felt the same way after going to a full day of classes with a kid named Eli, who volunteered to show me around.

There were a few hurdles to get over though. One was that tuition was sixteen thousand dollars a year, and the other was that I still had a year left of junior high. My grades didn't paint the picture of a kid who was smart enough to skip ahead, but Mom kept saying, "Don't worry, there are ways." I wasn't convinced, but somehow I got accepted, and they gave me thirteen thousand dollars in financial aid. It was cheaper than keeping me at home, especially after Jack agreed to pay for it.

I was happy to be getting out of Berkeley. I pictured my new school as an environment of enlightened kids who were socially conscious, politically active, creative, and misunderstood by the outside world but accepted and loved by one another.

That fantasy was smashed before I even got there. On the shuttle bus from the Phoenix airport to Sedona, a kid sitting next to me said, "I hate niggers." I had never heard anyone say that in my life and was so shocked I couldn't open my mouth for the rest of the trip.

I was hoping this was an isolated incident, but after getting my crappy stereo system in the mail, two other kids came into my room, without knocking, and told me to "turn off that nigger music." I turned it off, locked the door behind them, and turned it back on as loud as I could to cover up the racket they were making by pounding on the walls. I'd never thought of myself as having lived a sheltered life, but then again I had never really been subjected to the cruelty of white kids. A few days later almost all my music was gone. The only things left were an Art of Noise cassette, David Byrne and Brian Eno LPs, and my Beastie Boys record. I wanted to cry. Music had always been one of the only things that made

me feel human . . . that there were other people out there who understood me. Even though I would probably never meet them, it helped to
know they existed.

When I put on *Licensed to Ill* at a low volume, the same two guys, who
were now going by the nicknames Nipple and Head, appeared at the
door within minutes, saying, "What'd we tell you about playing that nigger music?"

"Fuck you . . . and anyway these guys are white," I said, showing
them the inside foldout of the Beastie Boys album.

"It's still nigger music," said Nipple, clutching me in a bear hug while
Head took the record. They were meatheads, and there was nothing I
could do to stop them. Having no use for the record jacket anymore, I
pinned it up on my wall. The cover was an illustration of a 747 crashing
into a red rock, and it seemed appropriately insignificant facing my roommate Aaron's life-size Yngwie Malmsteen poster. As usual, I didn't feel
like I fit in at all, but this time I had zero interest in making friends with
these assholes.

Aaron and I had actually been at Camp Winnarainbow together, and
I thought it would be a good idea to see if we could be roommates. He
sounded hesitant when I asked him, but he agreed to it. It turned out to
be a terrible idea. Aaron was a few years older than I was and seemed to
resent me. We had never even been friends at camp, and it became clear
that he didn't want to have anything to do with me at school either. He
was nice enough not to harass me too much in person, but I suspected he
had something to do with my music disappearing. A few times a week, I
would wake up in the middle of the night with my body being slammed
against the wall from my bed being flipped over. I never saw the culprits,
as they would be gone by the time I was able to crawl out from under the
bed, but Aaron was a logical suspect since he was never in his own bed at
the time. Without proof of his involvement or any experience in dealing
with this kind of shit, I would flip my bed back over and seethe myself
back to sleep. I was the youngest and smallest guy at the school, and
there wasn't a whole lot I could do about it.

That changed after an unfortunate incident over Parents Weekend.
Mom and Kyle flew out to visit me, and I learned firsthand how Aaron
felt about me when I was given the task of hanging out with my little
brother for three days. I begrudgingly took him to classes, and he even
spent the weekend in my dorm to consider the possibility of going there
himself.

The answer to that question was a definitive no when he woke up the second morning and found his ears full of toothpaste. Totally disoriented, he climbed off the bed and put on his sneakers, which had been filled with liquid laundry detergent. I couldn't remember ever being so angry as I led Kyle—humiliated and crying—to the shower. He tried to get the toothpaste out of his ears, while I washed the detergent out of his shoes. Kyle was pissed and spent the rest of the day walking around in wet sneakers, saying, "What?"

I blamed Aaron for that one and called him a fucking asshole. He didn't confirm or deny my appraisal of him, but he adamantly denied putting toothpaste in Kyle's ears.

"I tried to get them to stop, but there was nothing I could do," he said.

"Then who the fuck did it?" I screamed.

"I'm sorry, man. Really. I tried to get them to stop."

Aaron did sound extremely apologetic, and a few days later he made arrangements to find another room.

I N AN ATTEMPT to prove to the school that the thirteen thousand dollars they had given me in financial aid was a good investment, I volunteered to be the freshman representative in the student senate and joined the Model UN. Joining the senate seemed like a good idea at the time, but it didn't really work out the way I wanted it to. The other kids didn't hold us in very high regard, and we were all so ashamed of our involvement that we never associated with one another outside of our weekly half-hour meetings. The Model UN met only once because our teacher, Steve, was always leaving school for mysterious reasons.

Between class, work jobs, dorm jobs, sports, and study hall, we were left with only about four free hours a day, but that was four more free hours than I had ever had before. Feeling awkward, angry, and nervous around the other kids, I spent my extra time in the ceramics studio. In ceramics class, we were told that throwing pots was a kind of spiritual exercise—that centering the clay was an act of centering oneself—but it just made me frustrated. I was more at war with the clay than one with it. I spent four hours a day, and often ten hours on weekends, hunched over a spinning lump of clay that I couldn't center for the life of me. As difficult as it was, it allowed me to be by myself. My back hurt like hell whenever I stood up from the wheel, and when I closed my eyes—even to blink—all I could see was a slightly lopsided lump of brown mud spinning around in my head. But like the early days of my juggling career, throwing pots gave the impression that I was passionate and driven, rather than antisocial.

I started smoking cigarettes as a remedy for my back problems. My cravings were like an alarm clock that reminded me to stretch my body and take a walk every hour or so. Cigarettes however, quickly began eating up two-thirds of my fifteen-dollar-a-week allowance.

I HAD ALL BUT forgotten about the Model UN when I found a note in my mailbox saying that we would be meeting to prepare for our upcoming trip to the Model UN Convention in Tucson.

We met up at our teacher Steve's house. As always, he was dressed in military fatigues and a red beret. Over cookies and milk, he announced that, through some kind of back-room deal, he had arranged for us to represent Nicaragua at the upcoming convention. I was psyched because I had been to many United-States-out-of-Nicaragua protests back in Berkeley, and had seen more than a few documentaries about the conflict with my mom. Steve was also extremely excited and was in the middle of a speech about the evils of capitalism and the virtues of the Sandinistas when one of the students interrupted him.

"When is the convention?" a girl named Tara asked. This was her second year taking part.

"It's in a week," said Steve.

"So, don't we need to prepare? I mean, I've been there before and I don't even understand how it works."

"Don't worry about any of that. I've got a plan. You see, we're not going to play by the establishment's rules. Che didn't play by the rules, Lenin, Mao, Trotsky, Castro . . . They didn't play by the rules either. Revolutionaries, by definition, don't play by the rules, and that is the big lesson here. I'm willing to bet that, even though we're going to be the most important country there this year, the United States will use all of its power to keep us from being heard. The whole system is designed to keep the United States on top and everyone else in their place. So don't worry about that. I'm preparing you by giving you a history lesson in revolution."

———

I T WAS A LONG DRIVE to Tucson. For some reason, Steve owned a house there, and I had a restless night trying to sleep on his linoleum floor. I couldn't stop thinking about how insane we were going to come across to the other kids.

Steve had "prepared" us for the convention by teaching the ten of us a few communist slogans in Spanish and English, which we were to yell out at the convention whenever he gave us the signal. Nicaragua was bound to come up whether the United States tried to silence the issue or not, and yelling communist slogans and blowing whistles whenever the United States held the floor seemed like a recipe for trouble. I had a tendency to obsess on worst-case scenarios, but that morning, I found out I hadn't even come close to considering all the possibilities. Steve had gone out to run an errand and returned with a huge box of U.S. Army fatigues and green and black face paint. He hadn't mentioned anything about this when discussing what we were going to do to rile things up at the convention. Even though we were running late, he insisted we get into the fatigues before we left the house. When he started handing them out, I was shocked to find that a few of the outfits had Steve's last name embroidered on them. I exchanged uncomfortable looks with some of the other kids, but none of us had the nerve to ask about it. I didn't understand how Steve, an open communist, could be enlisted in the army, which at the time was conducting covert operations against the same people we were going to represent at the Model UN. It explained his mysterious disappearances from school on little or no notice, and why he owned a house in Tucson, which happened to be a few blocks away from the military base. I covered up his name and the U.S. Army patch with duct tape and did my best not to think about it.

In a way, I was relieved to be wearing a disguise, but the problem was that all the clothes were size Large, and we had to get creative with a spool of twine and a few safety pins he had lying around the house just to be able to walk around without tripping over ourselves. All that effort went to naught when he opened another box full of size-eleven combat boots. The absurdity of it was beyond comprehension. We looked as if we were in a *Little Rascals* film, where they had stolen some military uniforms in a cute but misguided attempt to enlist in the army—hardly the menacing communist rebels we were supposed to be. The face paint we dealt with on our way there.

Indeed, our late entrance to the convention center inspired far more laughter than fear. If anyone was afraid, it was us. When the speaker introduced us as the "Colorful Delegation of Nicaragua," we held up a queen-size bedsheet on which we had painted the words PATRIA LIBRE O MORIR, and just in case no one knew what that meant, we yelled "A free homeland or death!" as loud as we could to the thousand or so kids who had shown up to this thing.

Our first chance to blow whistles and yell slogans came when the U.S. representative was defending the SDI program to the Security Council. Following a commotion on the stage, the speaker announced, "The Union of Soviet Socialist Republics respectfully asks that the Nicaraguan delegation restrain themselves and allow the Americans to continue." We looked to Steve for guidance on how to deal with this unanticipated turn of events from an important ally.

"We'll keep quiet for now, but it's going to cost the Soviets," he told us.

At the next break, Steve conferred with the teacher from the Soviet school and came back to tell us he had secured three minutes of the Soviets' time allotment to make our case before the Security Council and that we could count on China for support as well.

"If that doesn't get us anywhere, we go back to the original plan. Tara, I want you to go up there and give them hell," Steve said.

Although some of what was being discussed by the Security Council was of interest to me, the jargon was so unbelievably dense that I couldn't pay attention to any of it. I was dozing off again when Tara was unexpectedly called to go speak on our behalf. As Steve had suggested earlier, the three minutes was just a token gesture by the Soviets to get us to stop yelling. After Tara made her case against the United States for illegal funding and supplying of arms to the Contras, the entire Security Council, including our supposed Soviet and Chinese allies, voted unanimously to move on.

"Remember the lesson. Playing by the rules doesn't work. Back to plan A," Steve said.

Plan A didn't work either. After three more outbursts, the United States passed a motion to throw us out if we caused any more disruptions. We didn't last another twenty minutes. Steve tried to argue, but he was outnumbered by the ten other teachers, who escorted us to the parking lot.

"Great work, everybody," Steve told us on our way to the van. "I think we learned a lot today. The system is set up to serve the powerful. That said, we can take a vote on whether to try and force our way back in tomorrow, or just spend the day in Tucson. If they do let us back in, we are going to have to be good little boys and girls, or they will throw us out. So, all in favor of boycotting the Model UN for serving no purpose other than being a mouthpiece for America's imperialist policies, say aye."

"Aye," we said in unison. We stopped at a McDonald's drive-through on the way back to his house.

sixteen

In which the young man is caught in a
torrential downpour of fecal matter and
encounters pure evil in the form of a rock

O N THE TRAIN FROM Redwood City back to San Francisco, I tried hiding in the bathroom again, but that trick only worked once. When the conductor knocked on the door, I reluctantly came out and gave him three dollars. Even though I had no intention of using heroin ever again, forty dollars wasn't a lot of money and I wasn't sure when or how I would get more. That rehab was such a bummer that if kicking cold turkey wasn't enough to scare me into staying clean, the thought of going back there was. My relapse prevention plan was simple: don't fucking do it. I still had a tremendous amount of back pain, but otherwise I felt fine.

After ten days in Redwood City, I had never been so happy to see my roommates, and, despite all that had gone on in the last couple of weeks, they seemed happy to see me as well. I hung out with them in the kitchen as long as I could, but I hadn't really had more than a few nights' sleep since I had left. Exhausted, but feeling pretty good about myself, I crawled into bed.

And then the monsoon came. Shortly after falling asleep, I awoke to what sounded like a full-blown tropical downpour in my room. Turning on the light, I found that the sewage main from upstairs had exploded right above our bedrooms. If being showered with sewage wasn't bad enough, this sewage came from the residency hotel above us, whose tenants included all manner of drug addicts, prostitutes, and other unwholesome types. My roommate Jake packed up what he needed and left then and there. Eli and Beth were in Japan, and Simon, our new roommate who had only been living at our place for a week, went back to his room and pretended nothing happened. That left Betsy and me to gather as many trash cans, buckets, pots, and pans as we could find to try and catch the sewage coming from the ceiling. When we had run out of containers, I went back to my room, grabbed a raincoat, and started hauling trash cans full of water to the back door. Betsy armed herself with an umbrella and joined me, but it was a lost cause. The trash cans were filling up with thirty gallons of sewage every fifteen minutes, and they were only catching a third of what was coming down. Leaks were nothing new to us—at least three times a week we discovered small drips coming from the hotel—but we had never seen anything like this. As usual, I ran upstairs to tell the landlord what was going on. He came down, took one look, and without saying a word, turned around and left. We didn't hear from him for four days. He probably thought that any sane person would pack up their bags and leave. When he finally realized that we weren't sane, he posted an eviction notice on our door.

I had never experienced this kind of exhaustion, and my back was in excruciating pain from emptying the sewage-filled trash cans twenty-four hours a day. Shit storm or not, I needed to get some rest. I hadn't had more than a few nights of sleep in the last two weeks. Delirious and in pain, but proud of myself for having stayed clean this long, I limped outside to get some heroin just one last time.

WHO KNOWS WHAT would have happened if I had held out a little longer. When I woke up the next morning, what had sounded like the Niagara Falls had miraculously quieted down to the volume of a peaceful babbling brook. By the end of the day, the leaks had all but disappeared. I was totally broke, but the three roommates who were left pooled their rent money to hire a plumber to patch up the pipes. Jake had moved his stuff next door to a friend's house on day one, and Eli and Beth, fresh back from Japan, had come in on day two with a shopping cart and wheeled all their shit over to a storage space. Simon, the new guy, went about the unenviable task of finding a lawyer to fight the eviction and countersue. I think he knew I was ready to kick his ass out for hiding in his room the whole time that Betsy and I wallowed around in the sewage. Mick, another new guy, was the only one of us with a decent job. He hadn't done much in the way of helping during the disaster either, but we needed at least one responsible guy around, and I actually liked him. We all agreed it was time to stop paying rent.

I had been running on fumes for so long now that when everything quieted down, every muscle in my body was screaming in pain. It had been one of those first nights of sleep that actually made everything worse. No matter how good my intentions may have been about staying clean, any junkie knows that when there is dope left, it's going to get used. I still didn't think of myself as a junkie, though, so when I smoked the rest of it that morning, I was once again completely dumbfounded as to how I let myself do it again. That set off the same goddamned cycle I had already been through at least five times by now.

My recording equipment had made it through the flood undamaged, but with six inches of raw sewage covering the basement floor, there was no way I could bring clients down there. I had no choice but to start selling shit, until Simon got me some work running a mixing board for a company that ran events over at the Hilton. It wasn't a bad gig, since it paid well and they fed you, but after nodding out for the third or fourth time when I was supposed to have been cueing in some music, they never asked me back.

I CALLED UP the rehab a week later and told them I needed to come back in.

"You guys were right, I'm definitely an addict," I told Barry when I got back to Redwood City. "But there has to be another way besides AA." I had convinced myself that I would try to play along, until I saw those goddamned steps on the wall again.

"I'm sure there are a million other ways, but it's the only one we know about that has consistent results. And it's the only thing that has worked for any of us," he responded.

Barry decided to take it easy on me this time and emptied a vial of a synthetic opiate called buprenorphine under my tongue. It was supposed to ease my withdrawal symptoms, but it didn't seem to help.

Since I couldn't play along with the AA stuff, I decided the next best thing was to just try to keep quiet and not argue so much. It was tough. People kept talking about spirituality, God, and higher powers, and they wouldn't leave me alone about it. As much as I didn't want to make any waves, I was unable to keep my opinions to myself.

"Oran, you have been unusually silent today. How do you feel about what we've been discussing?" Jan asked during group.

"Believe me, you don't want to know what I think about it," I said, thinking of all the religious and spiritual nutcases I had encountered over the years.

"Actually, I do very much want to hear what you think," he said, closing his eyes and going into one of his simulated nod-outs.

"I think it's all a load of shit." I tried to control myself, but the best I could do was pause long enough for Jan to accept my answer and move on to someone else. Instead he asked me to elaborate. "Well, first of all, it just makes no sense to me how the fuck anyone could believe in any of that shit when there is absolutely no fucking evidence of God ever having existed. Second, on a personal level, I have never seen anyone's belief in God benefit them or anyone else, and third, on a much greater scale, religion has been and continues to be the cause of a huge percentage of all the fighting throughout history and now. I don't want anything to do with it." I felt as if what I was saying was so obvious it didn't even warrant mentioning.

"Fair enough, but we're not talking about religion; we're talking about spirituality and a god of your understanding. Could be anything you want," Jan said. He still had his eyes closed and was tapping his fingers together almost in a prayer position.

"Maybe there's a difference to you, but where I grew up it's the same exact shit. I knew a guy who lived on our block who used to meditate six hours a day, but he was always yelling at me and my brother just to fucking yell at us. Then, after he died of cancer, we found out he had been beating his kids. Sorry, but spirituality didn't seem to help that guy or anyone around him too much. Shall I go on? Because I've got plenty more stories where that came from," I said.

"No. That's fine. I just really want you to give some thought to this idea that it can be anything. Even the doorknob or the light switch. Some people use the ocean. Whatever. The main thing is it can't be you, and it should be loving and nonjudgmental," he said, finally opening his eyes to look at me.

"You've got to be kidding me. That light switch is loving and nonjudgmental?" I asked.

"If not, then find something that is."

I WAS DISAPPOINTED to find that my yoga spot behind the cute girl was taken by a new guy. He was about my age and looked like your everyday suburban, blond football-player type except for the yarmulke pinned to his head. He was so white that I decided he must be an albino, but when he approached me after yoga, I noticed he had blue eyes. The only albino I had ever met before had pink eyes.

"You kickin' dope, man?" he asked me outside at the smoking area.

"Yeah, I'm actually starting to feel better, though," I said.

"Me, too," he said. I gave him a closer look.

"You look fine to me," I said.

"I mean, I'm kicking dope, too. Or I will be in a few hours. I had to finish everything before I let my parents bring me here. But yeah, I feel fucking great right now."

"Are you adopted or something?"

"Oh, you mean this?" he asked, touching his head. "No, I'm not adopted. I converted when I was thirteen. My best friend was Jewish, and I just really got into it. My parents are still Catholic. Are you Jewish?"

"My mom is, but she converted to anti-Semite when she was thirteen." It was a stupid joke of mine that no one else ever seemed to get. "I was never raised with any of it," I explained.

"That still makes you Jewish. You're lucky. I had to go to Hebrew school to become one."

We both laughed.

"Where do you live?" he asked me.

"Sixteenth and Mission. Fucking right in the middle of it," I answered.

"Holy shit, so you were doing speedballs? Me, too," he said, getting really excited. "I used to be able to quit doing heroin whenever I wanted to, but since I started doing those, I haven't been able to stop. That's how I ended up here."

In the Mission, it was virtually impossible to just buy dope. The heroin always came in a balloon with a separate bag of cocaine since most people mixed them together and did speedballs.

"Nah. I don't fuck with that shit. I just did heroin," I told him.

"Are you serious? What the hell did you do with all the cokes?" He was clearly agitated.

"I've never understood why anyone would do speedballs. Shooting heroin and coke at the same time doesn't make any sense," I said, lighting another cigarette.

"No. You're right, it doesn't make any sense at all, but, man . . . It's fucking unbelievable."

People on the street were always telling me how great it was, but I had never been convinced. This guy was making a very strong case for trying it, and my anxiety level was shooting through the roof.

"But what did you do with the cokes?" he asked again.

"I traded most of them in for dope, but I probably still have fifty of them sitting in my room."

I could see his brain ticking, like maybe he wasn't done after all and he hadn't even started kicking yet.

That night I couldn't stop thinking about my conversation with the new kid. Barry had given me my last dose of buprenorphine the day before, so theoretically the opiate blockers should have left my system by then. Even though I wasn't feeling that bad physically, I was extremely agitated. Back at the residence—an unassuming suburban duplex we were bused back and forth from—I couldn't fucking sit still. I was done kicking, my back felt better, and I'd even been getting a little sleep, yet all I could think about was getting high. When I went inside to take a piss, I noticed that someone had left her purse on the couch. I took sixty bucks out of it and, grabbing my bag, climbed out the window and ran to the train station as fast as I could.

I had never experienced such an extreme urge to get high before, not without being sick anyway. The train ride back was excruciating, and the anxiety was so overpowering I couldn't even wait for the bus to show up. I walked about a mile from the train station before a bus came by. Not wanting to run into my roommates and explain to them yet again why I was back after only ten days, I opened the door as quietly as I could and went straight down to the basement. I didn't have an explanation for them anyway.

I had bought a syringe and a couple of balloons on my way home, and I knew I had a spoon still hidden down in the basement somewhere. This time I emptied the little bag of coke into it as well and cooked it up with some bottled water I had taken from the rehab. As antsy as I was, I was still afraid of injecting cocaine and decided that, just in case I had a heart attack or something, I should do it out by the stairs. That way someone would find me quicker than if I did it inside the studio. Nervous with anticipation, I put the needle in my arm and pushed down on the plunger.

My first thought as I clutched at my chest and fell to my knees was that I had done too much. I could *taste* the cocaine as my heart, which felt as if it wanted to jump out of my chest, pumped the shit through my body. The euphoria was so overpowering that I could no longer connect to any sense of fear. When the initial rush subsided, I found myself on all fours with my hands and knees in a puddle of vomit. As soon as I caught my breath and managed to stand up, I fixed myself another shot without any hesitation. Then another. Too afraid to retrieve the coke from my room and risk being seen by my housemates, I snuck outside and spent the remainder of my sixty dollars and injected those. Eventually I fell asleep in my recording studio, which because I had the foresight to seal it up with plastic, had made it through the shit storm unscathed.

After that night, there was no such thing as essential recording gear. The only thing that mattered was that I fall down, clutch at my heart, and vomit. I kept pretending to myself and everyone else that I was fine, but the charade was wearing thin. I was losing weight rapidly—punching out new holes in my belt every couple of weeks—as well as my sanity, from a combination of too many drugs, too much lying, and an inability to remember what lies I told which people. My roommates, who were dismayed that I had left rehab again, must have known what was going on, but there wasn't much they could do.

The thing about cocaine is that in the beginning of a run, five or ten bucks' worth would make me fall to my knees and puke, but six days later I could be spending up to five hundred dollars a day, shooting up every five minutes just to stay awake. I had to stay awake to peek out of the keyhole in my door and record the conversations of my roommates plotting to catch me using. I could hear them talking about it all the time, but my tape recorder wasn't able to pick it up for some reason.

I became so paranoid that I only left the house when absolutely necessary. To sell more shit, to buy more drugs, and occasionally to work some random job to get money to buy more drugs. When I did run into people, I tried my best to convince them that I was just stressed out from dealing with the flood, the lawsuit, my breakup with Heather—anything but the truth.

A FEW PEOPLE WHO weren't fully aware of what was going on took pity on me and gave me random jobs here and there. I restored pianos for a guy in Oakland, and bar-backed at a couple of neighborhood establishments. I even took a job at a leather-goods factory, making cock rings and dildo harnesses, which turned out to be dangerous work for a junkie. My job was to feed leather strips into an industrial sewing machine, cut the strips into eight-inch sections, attach some buttons, and voilà . . . a cock ring.

Making a hundred of these a day was monotonous work, and it was easy to nod off, especially when I was sewing. Usually I woke up right before my hand reached the needle, but when I woke up and saw three Mexican women looking at me in horror, I knew I was in trouble. I couldn't feel a thing, but when I looked at the machine, I saw that my thumb had gone right through the double-stitcher and had been sewn onto a strip of leather that was only two steps away from becoming a cock ring. I was bleeding profusely, and even though I didn't feel it, I knew it was supposed to hurt. I put on a show of tremendous pain while one of the women ran to go get help. My boss was able to stop the bleeding with some bandages, but if I had nodded off while stamping out patterns for the dildo harnesses, that machine might have taken my hand.

None of these jobs were able to support my habit, so in the hopes of stretching my money a little further, I got on methadone and started buying crack instead of powder cocaine.

Someone on the street had told me you could inject crack by breaking it down in lemon juice. He was right, but it was a ten-minute process, and ten minutes was sometimes too long—long enough to fall asleep and wake up eighteen hours later with the pattern from my computer keyboard pressed into my face. So I started smoking a little of it while I waited for the rest to dissolve. Then I started smoking it all the time and spent even more money. I hardly ever had problems with buying heroin, but the crack dealers were not to be trusted. They were always selling me bits of soap, drywall, even cat litter. Those guys had no fucking morals.

M OST OF MY FRIENDS had stopped talking to me at this point. It started with Jibz after I agreed to record our band, the Roofies, and got her to pay me in advance. I planned to use the money to get my tape machine out of the pawnshop, but it never happened. I spent it on drugs, and when it came time to record, there was nothing to record with. The studio had dwindled down to almost nothing. I tried to tell her, Eli, and the rest of the band I was sorry and I would pay them back, but that wasn't enough for them. Jibz decided that unless I agreed to pay them back and get random drug tests, they were going to kick me out of the band. It surprised me, as I never really cared too much about that band anyway. I told them to fuck off, and stormed out, strangely relieved that I had one less obligation to think about.

A week later, before Optimist International practice, Eli surprised me as I was coming out of the bathroom after shooting a particularly good speedball. My tolerance was so high that really getting a good shot was rare, and this was a rare one. My heart was still beating like crazy as Eli asked me, "Were you shooting up in there?"

"No. I was taking a shit," I answered with as straight a face as possible. Taking shits had become very rare as well, which was an unfortunate side effect of heroin.

"I just don't know what to believe anymore. I could have sworn you were using again, but then whenever I talk to you, you do a good job of convincing me that I'm wrong," he said. I was kind of proud of myself for being that convincing moments after puking into the toilet, but Eli continued. "So I've decided that since you're such a good liar, I just can't talk to you at all anymore."

His words stung, but I was still trying to combat the rush from the cocaine and couldn't come up with an argument against his line of reasoning. I had to concede that it made a certain amount of sense.

"Okay. Do you mind telling Sean?" I asked him as if it were no big deal. I wanted to get out of there before I started crying. This band *was* important to me, and Eli and Sean were important to me. Normally I would have argued or apologized, and tried to convince him I was fine, but I didn't have it in me. I left him in the kitchen and walked to my room without any obligations left.

E LI MUST HAVE told my last two close friends, Jake and Betsy, that he thought I was using again, because that night they staged a last-ditch intervention. They suggested that I accept that I was a junkie but, instead of quitting, I just try to cut down to a reasonable amount, get my life back on track, and try not to beat myself up so much about the whole thing. It sounded like a good idea to me, and I agreed that I would give it a shot, which made it all the more confusing at five that morning, when I found myself on Jake's roof, clearly planning on breaking into his house. I tried to tell myself to stop. I had twenty bucks in my pocket, the pawnshops opened in three hours, and I still had that Fender Champ I could sell. But it was as if I were watching one of those shitty teen horror movies where you're yelling at the screen, telling the girl not to go down to the basement, but there's nothing you can do. Just like that poor girl, I couldn't yell at myself loudly enough to turn around as I watched myself bend the security bars and squeeze my hundred-and-twenty-pound body through the window.

I looked around and noticed a bunch of sleeping bags scattered around the floor and saw Jake's sister looking up at me from one of them. Without answering her, I walked straight to the front door and let myself back out. What the hell had I been thinking?

Once again I woke up with people in my fucking room. Jake and Mick were standing in my doorway. Jake started by asking me if I had broken into his house the night before.

"Yes," I answered.

"Okay, buddy," he said. "I hate the fact that I'm doing this, but I already filed a police report, and if you don't leave town in one week, I'm pressing charges."

I could see Mick fuming. As soon as Jake was done, he exploded. "One week? Fuck that! Where's my camcorder, motherfucker? You're getting the fuck out of here right now, you lying, stealing piece of shit. Get up, motherfucker! I'll teach you to fucking steal from me, you piece of shit."

I had come across Mick's camcorder a few weeks earlier while I was in his room looking for records to sell. I figured I could pawn it and get it back to him before he ever noticed it was missing. In a terrible twist of fate, he looked for the fucking thing that same night. So far, I had spent at least two hours helping Mick look for his camcorder while telling him, "It's got to be here someplace. Are you sure it's not in your room?" At least I'd managed to get it back from the pawnshop a couple days earlier. My hope was that he would find the camcorder behind his records, and think he misplaced it, but unfortunately it hadn't worked out that way.

"Get up, motherfucker!" he kept yelling at me. "You're out of here!"

Jake tried to diffuse the situation by convincing Mick to leave me alone for a minute and let him talk to me. I was in shock. Everything had come to a head, and I couldn't see any way out of it, especially with Mick out in the hall still yelling at me.

I got up, told Jake I was sorry, and then led the way to Mick's room. I showed him where the camcorder was, but it didn't stop him from yelling at me. All I could do was hang my head in shame, as I walked out the door to spend my last twenty bucks in the hopes of getting at least another few hours of not giving a shit before I started thinking about what the fuck I was going to do.

Mick followed me all the way to the street, screaming "You're out of here, motherfucker!"

I came back to the house ten minutes later, and my key didn't work. There was no way they could have changed the lock that quickly. I pounded on the windows to no avail, and realized they must have done it while I had been asleep. *Someone has to come out eventually, I'll just jam my foot in the door and force my fucking way in*, I thought as I paced back and forth, starting to feel sick. It was a bad situation, but I couldn't blame them for changing the locks on me. I deserved it. All the same, I was standing on the street shivering and I needed to get into the fucking house. I decided to call the cops, tell them the truth, and see if there were any legal rights I could take advantage of.

"Your name's on the lease?" the emergency operator asked me.

"Yeah," I said.

"Okay. Just sit tight and I'll have a car there in two minutes," she said, hanging up.

It didn't even take two minutes. The police car was pulling up pretty much at the same time I hung up the phone. I couldn't count how many times I had called the cops to report a fight or someone passed out in front of our door, even a drive-by, where the bullet had literally ended up in a brick wall six inches from my head. Most of the time, it would take them up to forty-five minutes to show up, if at all.

"You the guy who called?" the cop asked me as I approached the car.

I nodded to him.

"What's going on?"

"Well . . ." I hesitated. "Let me be honest. I've been having a problem with heroin, my roommates have noticed some of their stuff has gone missing, and I just came back to the house to find the lock has been changed."

"You've been stealing your roommates' stuff?" he asked me. I nodded again. "Okay, we'll take it from here," he said as he and his partner walked over to the door.

"This is the police! Open up!" they said while pounding their Maglites on the piece of plywood we had used to replace one of the windowpanes. There was no movement in the house. I peeked through the crack and could see them standing back by the kitchen.

The cop had a look through the door, too, and yelled, "Hey. You with the blond hair. I can see you. Open up now."

That got Mick to come to the door.

"Listen," the cop said after hearing Mick's side of the story. "Nobody wants to live with a junkie, but the law is the law. His name's on the lease, and yours isn't. If you don't like it, the only thing you can do is move out. Now give me a copy of the key." The cop went to the door, tried the key, and handed it to me.

"You should really stop using that stuff," he told me on his way out.

BEFORE GOING back to my room to get high, I apologized to Mick and told him I would be gone soon. He just ignored me. I didn't know where I was going to go. The only solution I could come up with was to call my friend Aaron and see if I could kick on his couch. Our friendship had gone through many ups and downs since we had been roommates at boarding school, but I could always count on him if I was in trouble. Going to Aaron's house didn't fulfill Jake's requirement of getting out of town, but it was all I could come up with.

As always, I was determined to really clean up my act. Then I found a few thousand dollars lying on Aaron's dresser the next day. It was money he had been saving for a trip to Thailand, but I figured he wouldn't miss two hundred bucks.

"Why does it look like someone's been rifling through my shit?" he asked me when he got home from work.

"I don't know." I was laid out on his couch pretending to be sick.

"How much money did you take?" he asked, ignoring my answer. I gave up the act of being sick and told him I took two hundred bucks.

"It seems like it was more than that," he said.

"Man. I swear I just took two hundred. Count it."

"I would, but I don't know exactly how much was there. Come on, let's go."

"Where are we going?" I asked him.

"I don't know. I'll take you anywhere you want to go, but you better figure it out soon."

First he gave me a ride home. I packed a bag and gave him my Fender amp—which I never got the chance to sell—as collateral for the money I stole. From there, he drove me all the way to Santa Cruz to a rehab our friend Sam had just successfully completed. By now I had absolutely no faith that it would work for me, but what the fuck else was I going to do?

seventeen

*In which a journey to the outlands finds
our protagonist in the back of a cop car
sniffing a curious white powder*

ONE OF THE MAIN selling points of my new boarding school in
Arizona was its field trips program. The program offered trips to
the Hopi and Navajo Indian reservations, to Baja, California, or to work
with charity organizations in Tucson, but freshmen were required to go
on the Mexico trip. We drove to a small town in northern Mexico, and I
was dropped off in front of an adobe hut that I was told I would be staying at for the next three weeks. I said my good-byes to the remaining
kids in the van and watched them drive away on the dirt road, sending
up a cloud of dust. My heart sank at the sight of it. I didn't really know
any Spanish and my host, a middle-aged man named Oscar, didn't speak
much English. I picked up my bags and made a gesture to imply that I
wanted to bring them inside, but he made a motion that I interpreted as
"wait."

"*¿Donde está el baño?*" I asked him. He motioned for me to leave my
bags where they were and led me behind the hut to an outhouse. A
woman out back was carrying water buckets from a well, up a ladder, and
finally to a large metal tank on the roof of the hut.

"*Mi esposa,*" he said. "The water is for *la ducha.*"

I shrugged my shoulders to indicate that I had no idea what he was
talking about. He ran his hands through his hair and pantomimed rubbing soap over his body.

"Ah. A shower," I said.

"*Sí*. Showard," he repeated to himself.

I held my breath before going into the outhouse. When I came out, the woman was lighting up a pile of wood under the tank to heat up the water.

"Showard!" Oscar yelled to his wife as we walked back to the front door.

Again I picked up my bags to bring them inside, and again he motioned for me to leave them. When we entered the house, I understood why. Oscar introduced me to his two kids, his parents, and his wife's parents, all of whom were living in the one-room hut. How the fuck did this place get approved by the school if there was no place for me to stay? The four old folks were making eye movements toward a free chair, so I sat down. We just sat there and stared at one another while Oscar's wife, who had come back in, hung a sheet in front of a raised platform covered with a piece of sheet metal.

"Showard," Oscar said again before disappearing behind the sheet. His wife left the house again. I just sat there absorbed in my discomfort, wishing I had followed the school's advice to cut off my dreadlocks, while these four ancient Mexicans studied me in silence. I was jarred out of it by Oscar yelling "*Ahora!*" at the top of his lungs. That was followed by the sound of water hitting sheet metal. When he yelled, "*Bien!*" the water stopped. A few minutes later the same routine was repeated.

When he was dressed, I followed him outside and up to the roof, where he opened and closed the water tank for his wife and then the kids. I was dreading the prospect of having to go through this production myself, and I was still totally confused as to why my bags were still out on the front porch. After about five attempts, I succeeded in asking him where I would be staying.

"My nephew, he take care of you. But don't tell him the money."

"What money?" I asked.

"From *la escuela*. I says to him I brought you here so I could speak the *inglés*. *¿Sí?* You speak the Espanish, and I speak the *inglés*, yes?"

"*Sí*," I said.

"*Más importante*. Don't tell *la escuela* you stay with my nephew, okay, or they will not give me the rest of the money, yes? He is good kid, but only nineteen years old."

"*Sí*," I repeated, but I wasn't so sure. The whole setup bummed me out. The school had told me I was staying with the head of the city council, which I had assumed meant somewhat modern living conditions. I had never seen anything like that shower situation, and while I was aware that there were people in the world living eight to a room, I had never experienced it, nor did I want to.

As I took in the view from the roof, it appeared that this was the biggest house on the block, and the only one with anything resembling the contraption Oscar was operating.

"My nephew's house mucho better."

W E WERE STILL on the roof when a police car skidded to a stop with the sirens blaring right in front of the house.

"*Vámonos,*" Oscar said, darting for the ladder.

As I climbed down after him I felt a surge of adrenaline, an involuntary reaction I had to sirens and cop cars. Even as a kid, I felt guilty of wrongdoing every time I saw a police officer, or any authority figure for that matter. We were required to watch *Midnight Express* before going to Mexico, so my fear of authority had become absolute terror. *I should have cut my hair*, I was thinking when I was close enough to the ground to jump off the ladder.

Instead of running away, though, Oscar ran straight for the car. A huge policeman got out wearing aviator glasses, and Oscar introduced me to his nephew, Raul. Raul nearly broke my fingers when he excitedly shook my hand. He seemed too smiley for someone who had to share his room for three weeks with an American kid he'd never met, but it gave me a good view of his one silver and one gold front teeth. It was hard to understand why Oscar had made such a mad dash from the roof when Raul had showed up, until his wife came outside yelling at an incomprehensible speed, holding up their naked daughter, who was covered in soap and crying because she got shampoo in her eyes while waiting for the rinse cycle.

"*Ay, chinga,*" he said under his breath. He ran back to work the shower, yelling *hasta mañana* to us.

I carried my bags to the car, and got in, before getting another surge of adrenaline when Raul turned on the siren and peeled out, sending up a huge cloud of dirt. A few seconds later, he slammed on the brakes and skidded to a stop on the next block. *Was he responding to a call? Did he forget to do something at Oscar's house? What the fuck was going on?*

"*Mi casa,*" he said, turning off the siren. I looked out the back window through the dust cloud that was still hovering in front of Oscar's house, less than two hundred feet back. I could even see Oscar waving at us from the roof as I unloaded my bags. These people were crazy, but there was no way out. Nowhere to go and no one to call. There wasn't even a phone to call anyone with. The best I could hope for was to get through the next ten days until my Spanish teacher, Carmen, came to check in on me, at which point I would start crying and tell her that I was living with a crazy nineteen-year-old cop, and that the city council guy—if in fact this town even had a council—was only in it for the money. She would scold them, apologize to me, and place me with a nicer family. Raul spoke zero English, and I had absolutely nothing to say to him. At least he did have a TV and a bathroom with a shower you could control all by yourself. We watched Mexican soap operas and ate quesadillas until he went to work. Raul worked nights, so I hoped that, like my night nurse roommate at The Farm, I wouldn't ever see him. He freaked me out with his gold teeth, aviator glasses, and creepy grin.

O SCAR HAD NOT mentioned that *hasta mañana* meant he would be shaking me awake before the sun was even up.

"What the fuck?" I mumbled, totally disoriented and blinded by the single twenty-five-watt bulb in the room. When my eyes adjusted, I found myself looking up at Oscar. I could hear a few roosters calling out in the distance, but no humans should have been awake at this hour.

"*¿Café?*" he said, holding out a thermos to me. I took the thermos as he continued, "Goot mordning, señor. *Arriba*. We have mucho work to do." I took a few sips of coffee, which was surprisingly good, and got dressed while he waited for me on the porch.

No one had told me about any work, but then again, nobody really told me anything.

"What kind of work do you do?" I asked Oscar while we walked through the silent town to wherever it was we were walking to. "Carmen told me you were on the city council."

"Ah . . . Carmen," he said in a faraway voice. "I want to sex her."

"What?" I couldn't help but start laughing. She was around fifty years old and married to the headmaster.

"She's too old for me," I said.

"No too old. Esperienced," he said with a sigh. "Professor Carmen. She know many things."

I was still laughing, but I really didn't want to think about it.

"*¿Carmen es de España, no?*"

"*Sí, pero,* she told me you were on the city council."

"Yes. That is what I say to her so I can sex her. I always want to sex with an Espanish señora."

"So, you made that up so you could *have* sex with her?" I said, stressing the word he had previously left out. Something about "sexing" her made the idea of sleeping with Carmen way worse than if he had simply said he wanted to fuck her. I thought about correcting him, but I figured there would be plenty of time for that.

"No, no, no . . ." He got slightly defensive. "*Es la verdad.* I am on the council, but look around you. Where is the city? We only meet a few hours in the month. We have nothing to talk of."

I looked around at the dirt roads, the little huts, and the chickens and goats running around the yards. Oscar had a point. What could they possibly talk about, other than maybe telling Raul he didn't always have to speed around with the siren on? It was probably very similar to our monthly student council meetings, which rarely lasted more than fifteen minutes.

Unlike Oscar, though, I wasn't under the illusion that being on the council was going to get me laid. Pretending I was a "good kid" might have made an impression on the administration, but it seemed to inspire a fair amount of mistrust and awkwardness in the other students, none of whom seemed to hold "good kids" in very high regard. That probably had something to do with my decision to grow dreadlocks and listen to Bob Marley, who along with Jimi Hendrix, were the only two black musicians I could listen to without those assholes coming in to my room and taking my records.

"Oh, *mi esposa,* she ask me what is wrong with you hair."

"I have a disease with my hair." I came up with this excuse before the trip. The school had made a big deal about telling all the vegetarians to use this technique when declining meat, and I decided to use it for my hair as well. There had been more than a few incidents of families kicking students out of their houses for being vegetarians, but not since they had come up with the disease explanation.

"Ah. I am very sorry." He led me into an empty dirt lot. "*Aquí.* This is where we build *casa* for my mother." The dawn sky provided just enough light to see a wheelbarrow and a pallet stacked with fifty-pound bags of cement.

"We?" I asked.

"*Sí.* You and me." The prospect of Oscar, a short roundish middle-aged guy, and me, a scrawny hundred-and-fifteen-pound thirteen-year-old, building a house was comical, but he seemed serious.

"Don't worry. *No es problema. Vámonos, hijo.* Let's start. Three weeks, we make big house."

We got to work with only a wheelbarrow and a shovel. We emptied three bags of cement into a five-foot pit we had dug into the lot, and, using the wheelbarrow and two five-gallon buckets, got water from a spigot down the street. My job was to mix cement, while Oscar ran around with a tape measure, marking off spots with the endless amounts of litter that had been strewn about the lot. Every once in a while he would step back and gaze at this mess, remeasure something, and move a candy wrapper or a beer can a few inches here or there.

"*Ven aquí,*" he called to me while intently studying the trash he had rearranged.

"*Mira.* See the Negro Modelo, that is the southwest corner, that plastic bag is the northwest one . . ."

"The green one or the white one?" I asked.

"The white one. The green is for *la puerta y,* that Tecate *es por la otra* corner, and this Tecate is the front door. See it? What do you think?"

"*Bien,*" I said, lacking the language skills to ask him what the hell he was thinking. This outline of beer cans and candy wrappers was at least six times the size of his other house.

"So you've built a house before?" I asked, because it really didn't seem as if he knew what he was doing.

"*Es muy facil,*" he said. "Like your game Legos. After this you can go build a house in America *no problema.*" I initially attributed his inability to answer questions as a language barrier, but I was becoming less sure about that.

"But you have built one before. Yes?"

"You will see. Very easy."

I took his answer as a no.

"*Vámonos.* The cement is ready."

We filled the wheelbarrow with cement and rolled it over to what I had thought was a ladder lying on top of a tarp. On closer inspection it looked more like a twelve-foot-tall bookshelf made out of two-by-six-foot pieces of wood. He started shoveling cement on top of it till the wheelbarrow was empty, and I went back to get more. By now it was afternoon and the sun was beating down hard on us. We filled the bookcase with cement and Oscar said, "We go now for *siesta.*" The best thing I had heard all day.

We walked back to his house, where his wife had lunch ready for us. I had been planning on making the switch from being a vegetarian to a meat eater until I saw whatever it was she was serving.

"*Lo siento*, I cannot eat meat. It's my disease. Meat makes me sick," I had to tell them.

"Ah. Same as your hair?" he asked.

"*Sí. Es muy terrible*," I said. I wasn't sure if *terrible* was a real word or one of the English words I often added an extra syllable to in order to make it sound Spanish. It sounded right, but I rubbed my stomach and made a sick face to make sure.

He explained this to his wife, who muttered *pobrecito*. Her expression even changed for a fraction of a second from her severely stern look to something resembling pity. She fed me some quesadillas, and I was sent to Raul's house to take a much-needed nap.

When we got back to the lot, Oscar grabbed two pieces of the crumbling sidewalk and started banging on the cement that had hardened in the "bookcase." He directed me to do the same, and I followed his example, moving up and down the twelve-foot thing, banging on the concrete until he directed me to lift the bookcase while he continued pounding on it. After lifting, shaking, and a lot more banging, we had twenty cinder blocks, which Oscar started arranging in a straight line next to the sidewalk. He only made it a third of the distance between the Negro Modelo can and the Tecate can before running out of bricks. It didn't take a high level of math skill to realize that building a house this way wasn't going to happen in three weeks. Oscar looked slightly dejected, staring at the paltry beginnings of his new home, but he recovered quickly, exclaiming, "*Está bien*. I will return," before leaving me to mix three more bags of cement.

I had already filled the mold when he came back with more two-by-sixes, a saw, and a hammer. I mixed more cement while he built two more molds. By the end of the day, we had almost a hundred blocks.

T HE IDEA THAT I was somehow being taken advantage of was not lost on me. Even in Mexico I figured Oscar was probably violating child-labor laws. Not only was I not getting paid for my work, Oscar was actually making money off me from the school.

I didn't dwell on it because Oscar was actually a fun guy to hang out with, and he bought me unlimited bottles of Coca-Cola, which for some reason tasted a zillion times better in Mexico than back home. His comments about Carmen were getting more and more graphic, and I took a guilty pleasure in listening to his fantasies involving my fifty-year-old Spanish teacher. I couldn't stand his broken English, however, when it came to telling me what he wanted to do to her.

"You want to fuck her," I explained to him.

"*¿Qué?*"

"*En inglés*, you say 'I want to fuck her,' not 'I want to *sex* her.'"

"Ah, yes. I want to fuck Carmen *en* her *panocha*."

"Oh, man. That sounds terrible. *¿Que significa panocha?*" I was pretty sure I already knew the answer.

"I don't know how you say *en inglés*. You know, *panocha*?" he said, pointing at his crotch. "You and I . . . *muchachos*, we have *verga*. *Carmen y las muchachas* has *panocha*. *¿Comprendes?* How you say *panocha en inglés?*"

I didn't know what to tell him. While I could stare at pictures of them for hours, I was repulsed by every English word there was for them. Vagina just sounded terrible to me as a word. Pussy sounded okay but went against my feminist upbringing because it was also used to describe men as weak sissy boys. I had been called a pussy many times. And the C word was so bad I don't think I'd ever used it, and I wasn't about to start now. Lately, I had taken to using the word *pudendum*, which I had seen used in a performance by the San Francisco Mime Troupe. I thought it was a funny word, and it didn't have any negative connotations that I knew of. But aside from me, I'd only ever heard it used that one time. Because Oscar wanted to learn English, I settled on "vagina."

"Vahina?"

"VA-GI-NA," I said slowly.

"*Bueno.* I ask Carmen to show me her vahina when she visits?"

"No, no, no. Try 'pussy.'" The whole conversation was making me feel very uncomfortable.

"Pushy?"

"Oh, man. Just use panocha. Carmen will understand."

THE FIRST WEEK went by like a blur. I was not used to physical labor and was exhausted all the time. Exhaustion was nothing new, but this was different. At school I was always tired because I tossed and turned all night, rehashing every conversation and situation I had encountered during the day, often beating myself up about some stupid shit I had said or trying to come up with clever comebacks. After working on the house though, it was actually nice to lie down and feel as though I were sinking into a pool of cement. There was no internal dialogue or resentments to keep me awake. By the end of the week, we had four walls standing about three feet high.

S ITTING ON RAUL'S porch on Friday night, I could hear the town start to come alive. Conversations, arguments, the smell of food, and that fucking siren were all drifting through the air. I was reading a collection of short stories by Paul Bowles that centered around various tourists traveling to strange lands and finding themselves in the most unlikely situations. The story I was reading was about a guy who was in Morocco for his honeymoon. He left the hotel one day in a simple quest to buy some milk, and by the end, was wandering around the desert wearing a full body suit made out of the bottoms of tin cans, the sharp sides facing in. I could hear the police siren getting closer and was interrupted from the book by Raul skidding to a stop in front of the house.

I looked up to wave hello and saw two other guys in the car with him. Raul turned off the siren to tell me to get in the car.

"*¿Por que?*" I asked, not wanting to have anything to do with these guys. He said something to the guy in the passenger seat, who translated for him.

"Raul, he asks if you want to be policeman for one night."

Maybe I was wrong, but I had always been under the impression that a lot of cops out there thought us regular people looked up to them. I figured that since they had always wanted to be policemen, they assumed everyone else did, too. People who didn't like cops were clearly jealous of them. We just didn't have what it took.

I had nowhere to be and nothing to do and was unable to come up with an excuse not to get in the car. I got in the backseat and was introduced to Chino, who was either Chinese or just happened to have high cheekbones—I couldn't understand their explanation of his name, or why they laughed so hard about it—and Charlie, the guy who spoke a little English. Before I could even close the door, Raul was peeling out and had turned the siren back on. He fishtailed into a left turn, speeding into the center of town, where he did a few donuts at the roundabout before shooting on to another road and skidding to a stop in front of a liquor store.

I wanted out of that car immediately. Maybe there was something wrong with me, but I just never got a thrill from that kind of thing like other people seemed to get. Roller coasters, fireworks, horror movies, driving fast in police cars . . . I had more than enough anxiety just sitting alone in my room. I sure as hell didn't need to go out and look for it.

Raul handed me some money and Charlie told me to go into the store and buy four *botellas grandes*.

"You have to go. I'm only thirteen," I said.

"*Está bien*. They do not care. Four of the big ones, in the brown bottle."

I didn't ask him why he wanted four. I didn't even think about it. When I got back to the car, Raul opened one of the bottles and passed it back to me.

I couldn't help but think about the book I had been reading before these guys had shown up. It dawned on me that each one of those stories started to get ugly after the main character started drinking, smoked some kif (whatever that was), or followed a twelve-year-old boy somewhere he shouldn't have. I drank the beer anyway. I needed something to calm my nerves so I drank it fast. Raul was driving slowly for the first time so that Chino, who was in the back next to me, could focus on the task of peeling the tinfoil off a chewing gum wrapper. I didn't know why he was doing it, but there must have been a good reason if it got Raul to slow down.

"How come you no drink the *cerveza*?" Charlie asked me. I held up the bottle and turned it over to show him I was done. "*Ay chinga. ¡Raul! Vámonos al mercado cabrón. Ordan nececita más cerveza.*" Instantly the lights and siren went on as Raul slammed on the brakes, skidding into a U-turn. Chino started yelling up a storm.

"*¡Chinga tu madre!*" he yelled at Raul, holding up two broken pieces of his chewing gum wrapper. "*Despacio, por favor.*" He threw the bits of paper out the window and pulled out two more sticks of gum. He offered me a piece after he took it out of the wrapper. When I declined, he threw it out of the window as well.

I bought four more beers, and Raul started heading out into the country. "*Mira*," Chino said, showing me how to peel the tinfoil off the paper.

"What is he doing?" I finally asked Charlie.

"He is making, how do you say . . . you know, *Papel por la . . .*" he held up his thumb and forefinger to his lips and inhaled deeply as if he were smoking a joint. I understood what he meant, but he held his breath for a while longer anyway before breaking into a fit of fake coughing.

"They think no *papel* is going to stop us from smoking the *mota*? Nothing can stop us." If "they" meant the police, then "they" was sitting right next to him with no intention of stopping him from doing anything. This time Chino was successful.

"Now ju try," he said, handing me a wrapper. I gave it a try but ended up ripping right through it. He handed me three more sticks of gum to practice on and started rolling a joint.

If there was ever a time I felt serious peer pressure to smoke pot, this was it. I couldn't imagine a worse situation to get high than in a cop car in the middle of the desert in northern Mexico. I should have told Raul back at the house that I was allergic to cop cars, that the lights gave me seizures, that I was molested in one, something, anything. How did this happen?

I tried taking as small a hit as I could, but within moments I went straight into that self-absorbed place in my head that pot always took me to. This time was different, though, because the alcohol was making it hard to hold on to any one thought for too long. It was more of a free-floating sense of anxiety and paranoia than the everyone's-out-to-destroy-me vibe I usually got. The combination also nauseated me. Raul had now left the highway for the open desert, and we were bumping around all over the place.

"*Alto*," I yelled at Raul, but it was too late. I started puking out the window before he had a chance to stop. They all burst out laughing. I couldn't take it anymore. I had to get out of that fucking car, but as soon as I did, Raul did his classic peel out, leaving me there in the middle of nowhere.

I was too fucked up to care, and too fucked up to stand, so I just sat down, trying to stop my head from spinning as I watched them drive away. They didn't go too far, just sped around, swerving left and right in an apparent attempt to flip over. Then I watched them jump the car over a hill a few times before coming back to get me.

"*Vámonos.* We go back now," Charlie yelled down at me. I stood up and felt much better, having puked up all the alcohol.

"*Una más para Ordan*," Raul said, stepping on the gas.

I put on my seat belt and clenched my stomach muscles as we sped toward the hill.

"Raul say he take you to Moscar now, but you can't say him what happened. *¿Sí?*" Charlie said as we were getting back to the town.

"*¿Moscar. Que es Moscar?*" I asked.

"Oscar. We call him Moscar. It means, you know bzzzzzzzzz . . ." He pretended he was watching something flying around the car, and then slapped Chino on the top of his head.

"*Chinga tu madre, pinche puto cabrón,*" Chino said, trying to hit him back.

"Fly?" I asked after the two of them settled down.

"*Sí.* Fly," he said, taking a bag of white powder from Raul. He dipped a key into the bag and held it out to me. I shook my head, but he insisted. "*Es muy poquito.* You need it to help Moscar. I promise, you won't even feel it. If you don't, Moscar will know you are *borracho*, and we are all in trouble."

It was so tiny, just a white spot on the tip of a key. I sniffed it up and felt instantly sober. Too sober really. I started smiling at the absurdity of it. It was a lot easier to smile now that I had made it safely back. How did this shit happen to me? I didn't ask for any of it. Not that I was complaining, but how many thirteen-year-olds had gotten drunk, smoked pot, and sniffed cocaine in the back of a police car?

R AUL HAD DROPPED me off on the other side of the roundabout, and I had to step over more than a few passed-out Mexicans on my way to Oscar.

"*Hola, Moscar,*" I said as I approached him on the sidewalk in the town square.

"*Ay chinga.* You are *borracho*," he said, obviously annoyed.

"Who me?" I didn't feel drunk, but I couldn't stop grinning. The whole night had been too much.

"Yes, you. I try to make my nephew into good kid, but *yo no sé. Es muy malo* because Carmen is coming to check on us *en la mañana.*"

Fuck. I had forgotten about that.

"We no worry about that now. *Ahora* we have work to do," he said, walking over to one of the guys who was passed out in the gutter. "*Mira.* I grab the arms like this," he said, squatting down to get a grip on the guy, "and you grab his legs."

We carried him on to the sidewalk.

"What's wrong with them?" I asked. It was obvious they were drunk, but there were so many of them it was hard to believe.

"*Es muy peligroso.* Every weekend twenty, thirty *muchachos* go to sleep right *en la calle. Es un milagro* no one has died yet with Raul driving around like he does. Raul *está loco.* These are *mi amigos.* I no want them to get hurt. *Juan! Arriba hombre!*" he yelled at one of them.

There was no response, so we laid him down next to the last guy. A few of them started kicking and yelling, but for the most part it was like carrying sacks of potatoes. There were a lot of them, though, and the cocaine was wearing off. I kept apologizing as I started to lose my grip more often. With one guy, I didn't clear the sidewalk and could hear his tailbone hit the curb. I felt horrible about it, but it didn't even wake him up. We moved about fifteen more of them out of harm's way, but the drunks kept coming.

"*Vámonos*. There is nothing more we can do," Oscar said. "You know I like the *cerveza*, too, but I no understand these men. They are good *hombres*, but every weekend here they are. I drink one maybe two beers, that's enough for me." He was shaking his head in confusion. "*Mañana*, we says to Carmen you drank some *agua* by mistake, and are no feeling good, *bien*? She no show me her *panocha* if she thinks I get you *borracho*," he laughed. "*¿Comprendes?*"

"*Si. Comprendo*," I said, trying to stay upright. That cocaine was amazing while it lasted, but, holy shit, I just wanted to sit down for a minute.

"*Ay chinga*," Oscar said as I started to lie down in the middle of the road.

T HE NEXT DAY Carmen came and left without incident. We had been told that every year more than half the students did get dysentery from drinking the tap water, so it was a believable excuse. I had been drinking tap water all week and couldn't figure out why I didn't get it. Maybe it had something to do with living in Guatemala when we were kids.

But who knows what Mom did to us. One time I had gone on a hike at camp, and all of the other kids were completely covered in rashes from poison oak. One kid was blind from rubbing it in his eyes, but I didn't show a single sign of it. I told Mom about it when I got back home and she said, "Of course, honey. When you were six months old, I fed you poison oak and poison ivy. The Native Americans used to do it to all their babies." The American Indians also supposedly threw their babies in the water at six months old to teach them how to swim. The only reason I knew about that was because she had a newspaper clipping on the wall that showed a picture of me at six months, all by myself in an Olympic-size pool.

I had a terrible hangover though, and I absolutely refused to get back in the cop car when Raul and his two buddies showed up later that evening.

"*No, gracias. Mi estomago no es bien*," I said.

"You will feel much better if you have a *cerveza. Vámonos cabrón*."

"No. Really I can't, plus Moscar is not too happy about last night."

"*Ay chinga.* You tell him?"

"No. He could tell."

"*Bien.* Maybe we come by later and see if you are feeling better."

I sat on Raul's stoop for a while, feeling shitty for a few more hours until Oscar came by on his way to the square.

"*Hola*, Ordan! I hoped to find you here. I was afraid you went off with my *loco* nephew again. *Vámonos*, it is time we go help *mi amigos*."

"I stay here. No feel so good." It was weird to hear myself speaking in broken English. I guess I thought it would help him understand me.

"You feel better after you eat something. *Vámonos, amigo*."

I reluctantly got up and followed Oscar to a hot dog vendor in the square.

"I can't eat those," I told him, looking at rows of greasy hot dogs wrapped in bacon. Goddamn, they looked good.

"*Está bien.* I won't tell *mi esposa*. You think I don't know you just don't want to eat her food? Every year es the same thing, until I bring you guys here. You think I want to eat that stuff she cooks? I wish I knew of this 'disease' you American kids have before I married her. I would have it, too."

"Okay," I said after I saw the vendor put one in a bun and completely smother it in guacamole. It was possibly the best thing I had ever tasted, and it only cost the equivalent of a quarter. I ate three of them in a row.

"See, I knew you would feel better. Let's go to work." He walked over to the nearest drunk guy. It was the same shit as the night before. We couldn't seem to get them off the street as quickly as they fell down, and despite the fact that there were a fair amount of other people walking around, Oscar and I were the only ones getting these guys off the road.

"What do you do when you don't have an American kid to help you with this?" I asked him.

"I do the same thing, *pero* they wake up in a lot more pain. When I no have help, I have to drag them over here by their feet."

It seemed very sad to me, but it was comforting to know there was at least one guy who cared. I was actually proud to be helping him.

"Really the only reason I do this is because it makes me feel better," he explained on the walk home. "If I do nothing, I have very bad dreams. I don't mind, though. I do a good thing, I feel good. I do a bad thing, I feel ... ah, it depends on what bad thing. *Carmen, por ejemplo,* I want very much to do that bad thing."

S UNDAYS IN MEXICO were perhaps the most boring thing I had ever experienced. There was nothing happening there any day of the week, but at least there were always people walking around. On Sunday, everyone was either at church or hiding in their houses so as not to be seen not going to church.

Oscar was the exception. Despite being born and raised in this small Catholic town, he didn't believe in *Jesucristo,* nor did he give a damn what anyone thought of that. Not only did he get away with being an atheist, but he was revered by everyone because he was the only guy who helped the drunks or escorted old ladies across the street. If there were leftovers at dinner, he would always make a plate and take it to someone who needed it. It was kind of problematic when it came to working on the house. If some old person happened to be walking by and happened to be carrying a bag—any size bag—Oscar would drop everything to run over and help the person carry it home only to come back and curse up a storm upon finding his block set at some crazy angle. It happened so many times he had to teach me first how to knock the misplaced blocks out with a sledgehammer, and then how to lay new ones since, undoubtedly, another old person was going to walk by at some point. Laying blocks was a welcome relief from the monotony of making them.

Oscar claimed to love Sundays because it was the only day he had off from helping everyone. We were sitting in his backyard drinking coffee. "Let those Catholic people do their job for once. Someone else can help those damn old people. Today, I no help nobody!" he said triumphantly.

"Let me see that," he said, pointing to the sketchbook I was doodling in. Most of my drawings involved penises at the time, but I handed it to him anyway, curious what he would make of it. A loose sheet fell out as I passed it to him. He picked it up and examined it.

"*¿Qué es?*" he asked, showing it to me.

"It's called an Exquisite Corpse. You fold the paper three or four times, and one person draws the head, another one the middle, and someone else gets the feet," I explained. The one he was holding had been done in a Chinese restaurant in Flagstaff, where, for seventy-five cents, they would give you a pitcher of coffee with unlimited refills. Since I never had more than a few dollars at any time, I would often sit there for five or six hours, drawing and getting completely jacked up on coffee, so far the only drug I truly liked. "*¿Comprende?*" I asked Oscar.

"*Si*. Let's do one *ahora*," he said, ripping a blank sheet out of the book and handing it to me. "You go first," he told me.

I folded the paper into halves and drew a character, extending the lines of the waist a little bit over the crease to show Oscar where to start. It took him almost twenty minutes of intense focus before he opened it up so we could see the whole thing. It was very disturbing because most of my drawings unintentionally came out as self-portraits, and this one was no exception. Underneath the unmistakable drawing of me was a pair of crudely drawn legs spread wide open, with an even cruder depiction of a vagina. He had written the words *Panocha de Carmen* next to his sketch.

"*Muy bien*," I said. "I will show this to Carmen when she asks me what I learned in Mexico."

Oscar lunged for the drawing, but I was too quick for him. There was no way I was going to give up this drawing. Dodging past him, I ran out into the street and hid the drawing in a bush to pick it up later.

I went back to see if I could get him to do another one, but he was already on it.

"Now I do the top," he said, hunched over the paper.

He eventually handed it to me, and I drew a pair of pants and shoes. When I was done, I opened it up to find almost the same exact drawing of Carmen's *panocha*, only this time it was sitting on top of a pair of pants. He was too quick for me this time and snatched the picture while I was still pondering how amazing it was. He stuffed it in his pocket.

"You no get this one. This is mine."

"Even if I show Carmen the other one?" I threatened.

"I no care. I tell her you did it. Who is she going to believe? You, or Señor Oscar from the city council? *Vámonos*, we go work on *la casa*."

WE HAD ANOTHER blurry week of grueling heat and grueling work. It was starting to look as though we might finish the house before it was time to go. I couldn't believe that we might actually pull it off, until I saw him building a dirt ramp up to the ceiling.

"*¿Que es?*" I asked him.

"Stairs to second floor," he answered. As impressive as it looked already, I wanted to be able to show Carmen and the other kids that I had helped build a whole house with nothing but cement and a level. I wanted to feel as though I had finished something.

"You have another gringo coming to work for free?"

"No. I finish myself. I didn't expect to get this much done anyway, so now I say myself, 'why I make *casa* only for *mi madre*? I tired of living with all those people.' Now I build second floor for *mi esposa* and her family. Ay, they make me *loco*. Then I have other house for myself. *¿Sí?*"

"That place? How are you going to take a shower by yourself?" I asked.

"If I am by myself, I no need shower. I no need nothing. I stay there and smell bad, and think about Carmen's *panocha*. Es good life, no?"

"*Sí*. Sounds great," I answered, but I had spent enough time with him to know he would never leave his wife and stop taking showers. He couldn't do the wrong thing if his life depended on it. All day I would listen to him bitch and moan about this or that old person whom he couldn't stand, but the moment he saw one of these people crossing the street he would run over, grab their elbow, and ask them how they were doing, always making sure they didn't trip over the curb. It was the opposite of bad habits. Instead of compulsively shoplifting or masturbating, like I did, Oscar was a compulsive helper.

M Y TRIP WAS nearing an end, and the last thing I wanted to do was spend my final night in Mexico with Raul and his buddies, but getting drunk did seem like a good idea. After I laid my last block on the house I would never see finished, I wandered around until I found the store that had sold me beers that night. The clerk didn't even look at me, as if, by not seeing me, he couldn't be responsible for selling beer to a minor. Since my only fear of the cops was that they were going to ask me to get in the car for a joyride, I didn't even bother trying to hide my beer. I did try to stay aware of where I was in relation to the siren that could be heard crossing back and forth through the town.

I went to the square and sat down on the curb and watched the town come alive as hundreds of people started to show up. Some of the passersby would nod at me, say hello, or raise their own bottle, and I would raise mine back and say, "*Salud*." It was still so hot and I was so zoned out from working all day that I drank the beer a little too quickly again.

While I was on my second one a kid a little older than myself decided he wanted to practice his English on me. I was feeling the effects of the beer, and I welcomed the company. After the preliminary "Where are you from?" "How do you like Mexico?" and "Can I stay at your house when I visit?" questions, I asked him why everyone was so dressed up. He was looking pretty sharp himself, so he seemed like the right guy to ask.

"It is the richest girl in town's *quinceañera*."

"Quince-what?" I asked him.

"You no have *quinceañera*? It is very big deal in Mexico. How do you say?" He was thinking hard. "Fifteen birsday," it came to him. "You want to go?"

"Why not?" I answered, "but, *primero yo necesito un mas cerveza*." It was amazing how much easier it was to speak Spanish when I was drunk.

"They have all the free cerveza and tequila you could drink over there. I already tell you; this girl is rich."

Things got hazy very quickly. There was a live band that seemed to know only three songs: "Low Rider," "La Bamba," and "Tequila." Somehow I ended up dancing with the birthday girl, who was as cute as she was rich. She was wearing what looked like a full-on wedding dress and a tiara.

"*¿Que significa 'La Bamba'?*" I asked her. "What's it about?"

"*Nada. No tiene sentido.*"

"*No comprendo.*" Alcohol may have helped me speak Spanish, but it did nothing in the way of helping me understand it. These people, all of them, spoke so fucking fast.

"No es Espanish," she attempted.

Holy shit, she was cute, and I was drunk. I had never kissed a girl in my life, and for the first time, the urgency to do so outweighed every other excuse I usually used. Since it was my last night in Mexico, none of my excuses worked anyway—all of them had to do with the possibility of getting rejected and having to see the girl the next day, or worse yet, not getting rejected and having to see her the next day.

Without thinking, I leaned in for a kiss. She turned her head, and I pecked her on the cheek. She was giggling, though.

"*Mi padre está acá,*" she said, nodding in the direction of a group of guys decked out in alligator-skin boots and huge cowboy hats. I tried to connect to the part of myself that should have been very afraid of these people . . . the voice that would have normally told me to get the fuck out of there, but I couldn't.

"*Vámonos*," she said, leading me through the crowded dance floor and out to the square. "What is wrong with your hair?"

"My hair? *Yo tengo un problemo con mi pelo.*" I decided telling her I had a disease was counterproductive to what I was trying to accomplish.

"*Me gusta*," she said, leaning into me.

T HE BAND HAD JUST finished playing "Tequila" for the nth time when, Maria, I think her name was, pushed me away and said, "*Mierda. Me voy.*" She turned around and ran away as fast as her high heels and wedding dress would allow her.

I waited a few minutes before going back in and found her dancing in the middle of the room with her father. The crowd had circled around them and was clapping in time to the music and cheering them on. I made my way to the bar for another free margarita and just kind of lurked around, waiting for another opportunity to hang out with her. She kept glancing at me, but she now had to dance with what seemed like every single guy in the whole town. It was uncomfortable to watch the first girl I had ever kissed dancing with all these young cowboys, which led me to drink more. Starting to feel nauseated, I made my way onto the dance floor and interrupted her long enough to say good-bye.

I was surprised that she actually gave me a hug, and whispered again, "*Me gusta.*"

"*Yo tambien*," I replied, before turning around to leave.

I walked home, still nauseated from the alcohol and trying to figure out why I felt so sad. Maybe it was because I liked it here, and I was leaving the next day, and I wanted to hang out with Oscar and finish building that house, and eat more of those hot dogs, and make out with Maria, and get her out of that crazy dress. Maybe we could get married, and I could buy some cement, and build my own house. I stumbled over to the curb and started puking.

"*Ay chinga*. Where have you been?"

I wiped my mouth off with my shirtsleeve, and looked up at Oscar, who must have been on his way home. "I had to carry all of my friends by myself. I need to find another gringo, unless *mañana* you say Carmen you no want to leave. Yes?" He helped me up and we started walking home. "You can live in the small casa, and I move into big house with me esposa, except for when Carmen visits. Then I get small house, and you have my wife. *¿Bien?*"

"*Si*." I knew he was joking, but I was definitely sad about leaving. "*Es la verdad*. I like it here," I said.

"*Ay hijo*, you talk crazy; nobody like it here. This place has nothing, and *las mujeres son muy feas* . . . ugly and *estupid*. You are *borracho y loco*."

I may have been drunk and crazy, and Maria may have been stupid (it's hard to tell when you can't speak to each other), but goddamn she was beautiful.

eighteen

*By what low road he arrived at his
father's house*

IN SANTA CRUZ I made it through the twenty-eight-day program,
only because the rehab was so big that it was easy to slip through the
cracks. They wanted your money, and then they wanted you out, to make
room for the endless stream of drug addicts who went through the revolv-
ing door of that place.

I was too scared to move back to San Francisco, partly because I was
nervous as hell that I wouldn't last a day without relapsing, and also
because some detective from the SFPD kept trying to get in touch with
me about the breaking-and-entering charges Jake had pressed. The
rehab suggested I go into a sober-living environment (SLE), as they
called it. I agreed and convinced my grandma's trust to give me seven
hundred dollars to buy a '61 Buick Special I had seen for sale on the side
of the road, telling them I needed it to get to meetings. The transmission
didn't go into reverse, but the owner convinced me it would only take ten
minutes to fix. I believed him for no other reason than it was the coolest
car I had ever seen.

The SLE was a little house on a cliff overlooking the Pacific Ocean
where I shared a room with five other guys. There was nothing to do at
the house, so I spent my days reading books at a café, and at night I went
to AA meetings as a requirement for staying at the house. The boredom
was excruciating, and I missed my friends terribly. It felt as though I were

just biding my time until they accepted me back. The only friend I had made in Santa Cruz was an eighteen-year-old girl named Annie who had also been at the rehab and now lived across the hall from me in a room she shared with seven other girls.

Once in a while, Aaron, Eli, or Jake (who eventually dropped the breaking-and-entering charges) would drive out to check up on me, and after a few months of telling them that I was doing well, the Roofies invited me to come back to San Francisco to play a few tracks on the new album they were recording. The truth, however, was that I had started drinking occasionally, and I was now driving back to the Mission a couple of times a week to buy dope and was on the verge of getting hooked again.

I managed to keep my drinking and drug use a secret until I got back to Santa Cruz from the recording session and the owner of the SLE asked me if I had used any substances while I was away.

"If you just come out and tell us, it will save us the forty dollars for a urine test," he said. Since I didn't want anyone to find out I was back on heroin, I told him I drank a few beers.

"Thanks for being honest," he said, "but we still have to kick you out of the house."

The first offense usually resulted in having to leave the house for seventy-two hours, long enough to get the substance out of your system and pass a drug test, but I didn't know how I was going to manage to stay clean that long.

"Fuck. What should I do?" I asked him. "Do you know of anywhere I can go for the next three days?"

"I don't know. You could maybe check yourself into a detox, or a hotel, but we also heard that you got together with Annie."

I never thought that Annie and I would hook up, but a few weeks earlier we had been sitting in the living room watching TV when she just came over and started making out with me. She must have been bored too. She made Santa Cruz bearable for a few weeks, until she relapsed and went back to the rehab for her fifth time.

"Well, normally we would just kick you out for seventy-two hours," Roger said, "but because of Annie I'm afraid we can't let you come back."

It was late at night, and I had nowhere to go. I had nothing to lose, so I asked him if I could take the forty bucks I had just saved him on the piss test and use it for a hotel. He must have felt sorry for me because he reached into his pocket and gave me a twenty.

The extra money didn't solve my problem. I sure as hell wasn't going to spend it on a hotel, but where the fuck was I going to go? I had burned every bridge I could think of, and after ripping off my bandmates, breaking into Jake's house, selling my roommates' stuff, stealing money from Aaron, and almost getting Kyle arrested, I was out of people to ask for help. I couldn't blame them. No matter how much I wanted to do the right thing, the urge to get high eventually outweighed anything else. Mom was on some sort of tough-love trip, and I could even see her calling the cops on me again if I showed up, so going to her house was definitely out.

The only thing I could think of was to head back to San Francisco and get more drugs. While driving back to the city, I thought about what my next move was going to be and came up with the idea of going to my dad's house. *If that motherfucker is capable of feeling even the slightest bit of guilt*, which I wasn't 100 percent certain of, *he has to take me in.*

To make sure I actually made it to my dad's house in Santa Barbara, I decided I had to spend all my money—the worry being that, if I still had any cash on me, I would change my mind before I got there and drive back to San Francisco for more dope. It was the kind of logic that only a drug addict could come up with, because I simply didn't trust myself unless I was broke.

With the extra twenty I had scammed off the owner of the house in Santa Cruz and the money left over from the trust, I had close to three hundred dollars on me. When I got back to the Mission, it took me less than ten minutes to spend two hundred and sixty of it on a bunch of balloons, a fair amount of crack, three syringes, a pipe, and a bottle of water. Hoping forty dollars for gas would get me to Santa Barbara, I filled up the tank and headed south on the 101.

I started smoking crack the moment I hit the freeway and was immediately overcome with a terrible case of paranoia. Before going to the rehab, I thought I was the only one who imagined SWAT teams and helicopters were after me, but it turned out to be so common that everyone just laughed about it. It annoyed me that my paranoia was so clichéd, but when I was high, I would swear to God that those fuckers were following me and it was just a matter of time before they landed on the roof of my car. I guess it was preferable to the story I heard in rehab about little monkeys that lived in your car's air-conditioning vents and spent their time conspiring to kill you so they could steal your closely guarded cocaine. I liked monkeys as much as the next guy, but invisible homicidal crack-smoking monkeys scared me even more than the cops.

Regardless of the paranoia, my choices were to keep smoking crack or fall asleep at the wheel. I kept overdoing it, though, and had to pull over every fifty miles to come down with more heroin, which would require me to smoke more crack to stay awake.

By the time I got to Santa Barbara, the coke wasn't working for more than five minutes at a time, my tank was on empty, and it was four in the morning. But the real problem was that I had no idea where I was going. I knew my dad lived in an extremely wealthy neighborhood called Hope Ranch, but even if I found it, I didn't know his address. I didn't even have his home phone number, since I only ever talked to his secretaries. His work number was easy, though. 1-800-4-ESTEEM is a hard number to forget, but it was a three-day weekend and I knew that nobody would be at the office anyway.

My plan was to drive around Hope Ranch until I recognized my dad's street. Crescent Something? Something Heights? Via Del Someshit? It didn't matter, because the plan went to hell a few miles into the city limits when my car ran out of gas. I had forgotten all about it. I pulled over. I had no money, no phone number, and no address. Coming up with a new plan was more than I could manage, so I leaned my head against the window and went to sleep.

Startled awake by the tapping sound of metal on glass, I opened my eyes to a cop shining his Maglite at my face. I was so high I could hardly hold my head up, and the car was full of drugs, broken crack pipes, bent spoons, and syringes, all hidden in various rips in the thirty-eight-year-old upholstery. This really looked like the end of the road for me. I rolled down the window and tried to compose myself.

"What's going on?" he said, scanning the inside of the car. "I pulled over 'cause I figured this was an abandoned vehicle. I didn't expect to find anyone in here." He was probably a few years younger than me, twenty-two or twenty-three.

"Yeah, sorry, sir. I ran out of gas and decided to wait till it got light to find a station."

"Man," he said, shaking his head. "If you had rolled to a stop twenty feet farther, you would have seen the Shell sign just beyond that overpass."

I tried to look surprised, but it wouldn't have made much of a difference unless they happened to be giving gas away for free.

"Where are you going?" he asked.

Wondering if he had already seen any paraphernalia with his flashlight, I answered him as best I could. "I'm trying to get to my dad's house. He lives here in Santa Barbara. Hope Ranch, I think it's called."

"Well, you sure got close. That's the exit right there." He pointed to the next exit, which couldn't have been more than a hundred feet away. I couldn't believe how close I had come, and here I was about to get arrested as soon as he searched the car.

"Come on, let's get you some gas, I'll give you a ride over there."

I have never understood my luck with cops. Obviously, being white helps, but I had plenty of white friends who went to jail for minor offenses like jaywalking, putting up posters, or riding their bikes on the sidewalk. My interactions with the police always involved actual crimes, such as drinking and driving, narcotic possession, being under the influence, and breaking and entering, and I had never once been to jail. I was lucky. As much as I hated the police, they seemed to like me fine. Assuming that I was off the hook again, I started to relax until I saw him bend down to take a look at my license plate. I had owned the car for only a month, and hadn't made it to the DMV to get it registered.

"Something's weird about those tags. I'm going to have to call your plates in," he told me.

"What do you mean? What's weird about them?" I asked.

"I don't know. They're just not right. Sorry, but I have to call it in."

He walked back to his car and left me standing there.

The funny thing about my paranoia was that whenever a cop did pull me over, I instantly snapped out of it. I had been lying about my drug use to people for so long that I had become pretty good at acting sober, even when it was all I could do to not lie down on the ground and go back to sleep. A few minutes later, he came back to give me the bad news.

"I thought something was weird about those tags. Those stickers were stolen. This thing hasn't been registered in over two years," he explained. "I know it's a bummer, man, but I've got to call the tow truck."

Again I wondered why the cops were always so friendly to me. Apologizing and calling me "man." While we waited for the tow truck, he asked me, "What year is that Buick, anyway?"

"It's a '61 Special," I answered.

"No shit. The one with an aluminum engine?"

"Yeah. How'd you know that? I didn't even know they made aluminum engines until I got this thing."

"They only made them for one year, and only for that car. Hardly any of them left. Goddamn, I bet that thing hauls ass."

"Yeah, it's fast as hell, but the reverse is shot. I've called a few places, and they said there was no way I could a find a new transmission for this thing," I explained.

"Oh, man, there's this place up in the hills where we used to go to take acid and mushrooms. It's a huge junkyard up in Carpenteria. This old hippie owns it, so he never minded us running around up there, but I'm sure you could find a transmission for that thing at his place."

"Yeah? How much do you think one would cost?" I asked.

"It'd probably be expensive but worth it. That's a beautiful car. You should go check out his place anyway. You'd like it up there."

Then he started to go into more elaborate detail about his acid experiences. "Man, it's so incredible when the sun's coming up over the hills and everything's purple and pink and lavender. You wouldn't believe it, man."

"Sounds nice," I said, not knowing what to make of this whole situation.

"Yeah. Too bad I can't do that anymore."

"Yeah, too bad," I agreed. I didn't know what else to say. Like most people, I get extremely nervous talking to the police, and this guy was just one decision away from searching my car and introducing me to jail life. As much as I loved telling people I had my first acid trip with Jerry Garcia's daughter, I just wasn't comfortable trading acid stories with an officer of the law.

The tow truck showed up and ended that conversation. As the driver was hitching up my car, I asked the officer what I should do about my things. Even with him standing right next to me, I was hoping to retrieve at least some of my heroin. I knew I would be getting sick soon.

"Just leave your stuff in there. Your things will be safe at the pound. That way you'll come down to get your car back." It was sad watching my new car drive down the freeway without me, especially with all my drugs still in it. I didn't even give any thought to what I was going to do next.

"Hey," the officer called to me, "get in the car, and I'll give you a ride to your dad's house."

I got in the car even though I had no idea where his house was.

"So, where's he live?"

"Actually," I said, "I'm not really sure. I'm pretty sure it's in Hope Ranch, but I've only been there a couple of times so I can't remember where exactly. I think his street had something to do with apples." Apple Crescent? Avenida del Manzanas?

"Okay, we'll just drive around and see if anything looks familiar."

Again I wondered why this guy was being so nice. *What if I had been a Mexican with a broken taillight? Maybe he was just a nice guy.*

"Does any of this look familiar yet?" he asked.

"Yeah, I'm pretty sure you take a right somewhere at the end of this lake."

"What does your dad do that he can afford to live in Hope Ranch?" He must have known I was in bad shape, and just didn't want to know exactly what kind, because this was the first personal question he asked me, even though he had found me nodded out on the side of the freeway.

"My dad writes those *Chicken Soup for the Soul* books."

"Oh . . . I've heard of that. I've never read it, but I think I've seen that book in my parents' bathroom," he said, veering right at the end of the lake.

"I haven't read it either, but that sounds about right."

We kept driving around while I pointed out familiar landmarks, sometimes changing my mind and backtracking until the scenery looked familiar again. It was hard because the suburbs all look the same to me. The cop didn't seem to mind at all. I guess there wasn't too much crime going on in Santa Barbara at five in the morning. Eventually we ran into a street called Via Manzanita.

"This must be it," I said.

"Which house is it?"

"I'm not sure. That one, maybe," I said, pointing to the first house I saw. "I think I recognize that gate."

"Let's check it out."

We drove all the way up the long driveway to the front door before I realized it wasn't the right house.

"That's okay. We'll try the next one," he said.

He seemed to enjoy seeing all these multimillion-dollar estates. Even when I said a certain house didn't look familiar, he would say, "Let's just check it out anyway, just to make sure."

Hope Ranch is one of those communities with its own private police force, so he probably hadn't seen too much of it. We entered at least seven or eight more properties before we found my dad's house. The last time I had been there the driveway was full of luxury cars, but today there was only a neglected Dodge Caravan.

I was sure the cop was going to want to meet my dad or someone who could vouch for me before just leaving me at some mansion in the middle of the most exclusive neighborhood in Santa Barbara, but he just dropped me off and wished me good luck. I thanked him for everything and he left.

The first thing I did was try all the doors to the house, all nine of them. The front door, the back door, the exercise-room doors, the kitchen door, the door to the pool, the sliding glass door to the guest room, the laundry door, and the maid's door were all locked. Next I tried the cabana, the office building, my dad's office, and the garage, and finally I walked down the path to the horse stables and checked the apartment above the barn. Everything was locked up tight.

"Where is everyone?" I asked one of the horses, before heading back to the house. The last time I had been here, there were so many employees running around he just left the place wide open. The only reason I could see him locking up the whole compound was if it was going to be empty for a while. It was now about six in the morning and I was so tired from being up for two days straight, completely wasted on drugs, driving eight hours, and chumming it up with the police that all I wanted to do was sleep. I walked back to the house, went to the pool, lay down on a lawn chair, and nodded out. Someone would show up eventually.

nineteen

On how he came to eat a bit of paper that
is said to open minds

BOARDING SCHOOL WAS full of drugs, and I found that, for the most part, long hair and tie-dyed shirts meant that you were a hippie as the term related to drug use only. Even though the majority of the student body looked just like the activists and hippies I had grown up around, they had very little in common other than their dress code and sometimes their record collections. None of them seemed to give a shit about anything other than smoking pot, which was so common you could smell it at almost any hour of the day, wafting from various areas of the campus.

In the interest of trying to connect with the other kids, I would take a hit if a joint or pipe was ever passed to me, but most of the time the other kids ignored me. I might not have been the least cool kid in school, but I was pretty close. And I still looked to be about two years younger than my age of thirteen. Add to that the fact that I had absolutely no money and very little to offer personality-wise, and there just wasn't much reason to give me drugs. Whenever I did manage to get a hit off a joint being passed around, the environment and the people would disappear, and I would be all alone listening to my thoughts, which didn't have anything nice to say about me or anyone else. I would then go straight to my room and wait out the high with my head under a pillow. Of course, I always smoked again at the next opportunity. My real interest, though, was in getting ahold of some acid, which was also extremely popular but kept much more under wraps.

On a weekend trip to Flagstaff, I had bought a book called *The Electric Kool-Aid Acid Test* for fifty cents. I wanted very much to take LSD and have my mind opened up like Ken Kesey and the Merry Pranksters, but the problem was no one would give it to me. Aiden, the school drug dealer, would have sold me a hit for ten bucks, but I would have had to quit smoking for a week to afford it. Waiting for a benevolent older kid to give me some proved fruitless, so when I got back to Berkeley for the summer, I went over to the Hog Farm, a big house where Wavy Gravy and about twenty other old hippies lived, to see if I could get a backstage pass to a Grateful Dead concert at the Greek Theatre. The last time I had asked they gave me one in exchange for volunteering to watch the kids. I must not have done a very good job, because this time they told me they didn't have any passes left. Period.

"I can teach the kids juggling, or whatever needs to be done," I told Wavy's wife, Jahanera.

"Sorry. There just aren't any passes left."

I didn't believe her, but there was nothing I could do.

The problem was that I didn't have money for a ticket. I'd been working as a busboy at a restaurant in Jack London Square until one of the regular clients said she would no longer eat there if I didn't cut off my dreadlocks. I was becoming sick of them, too, but getting fired over it gave me a new resolve to keep them. I got very self-righteous about the whole thing, but really I just didn't want to work. It was a pain in the ass, and some days I would only make five or ten dollars in tips. I went back to folding newspapers at five in the morning, which gave me just enough money for cigarettes and coffee.

Even if I did have the money for a ticket, I wouldn't have bought one. I didn't like the Grateful Dead at all, and frankly, I felt it was beneath me to hang out in the audience with the fans. The only reason to go was to hang out backstage, eat free ice cream, and play the arcade games they always brought on tour with them. In a last-ditch effort, I called Trixie, a girl I had met at camp the previous summer. I didn't know her that well, but it was rumored that she had a crush on me, and I knew she couldn't run out of passes since she was Jerry Garcia's daughter.

Trixie sounded excited to hear from me, but unfortunately I just wasn't interested in her that way. I felt a little guilty when I picked up my ticket at will-call. I found her backstage, though, and after a little catching up, I asked her if she had ever taken acid.

"No," she said.

"Really? I figured all you guys had done it before," I said, referring to the children of famous hippies.

"Not me. You want to do it?" she asked.

"Yeah. I just read this book. Your dad is in it, by the way . . . but yeah. I think I'm ready to try it."

"Okay. Let's try it," she said.

I couldn't believe my luck. Taking acid for the first time with Jerry Garcia's daughter was a way better story than doing it at school, although the desert would have probably been a more conducive atmosphere than being stuck in an amphitheater with ten thousand people.

Trixie led the way out to the soccer field, which in Berkeley served as the makeshift parking-lot scene. We walked around until we passed a hippie saying "doses" under his breath. Neither of us knew what we were doing, and Trixie gave me twenty dollars to give to the guy. I knew Aiden was a scam artist, but I had no idea how much of one until this guy handed me a grayish piece of paper with twenty hits of acid on it. At a dollar a hit, I could have made a fortune back at school and run Aiden out of business.

We took one each and wandered around the soccer field, which was really just a big flea market for hallucinogenic drugs, tie-dyed shirts, and paraphernalia, while we waited for the acid to take effect.

Nothing happened, though. Dejected and feeling ripped off, we walked back to the amphitheater. I wanted to go backstage, but it wasn't often that Trixie got to hang out in the audience and see her dad play, so we went up to the lawn area. It was there that things started to get weird.

The first thing I noticed was that the band didn't sound half bad. They actually sounded really good, which was strange since I had heard this shit a million times before. Despite my dislike for them, I knew most of the words to their songs simply from singing them so many times at summer camp. But I had never heard the songs played like this. It seemed as if every note had some hidden meaning that I wanted to unlock. But the notes were coming so fast, it proved hard. Or maybe the meaning was actually coded into a series of notes. I couldn't figure it out exactly, but whatever they were trying to tell me was very deep.

The people around us were twirling around in circles or bouncing up and down on one foot, moving their hands around in what seemed like a sign-language translation of something impossible to describe with words. I chose to lie on the grass and dug my hands into the dirt so I would have something to grab onto if I started floating away. I didn't understand how these other people could hop up and down or twirl around as they did without falling over. It was all I could do to keep myself horizontal. Unable to maneuver through three-dimensional space, we stayed in the same spot till the show was over, and there were fewer obstacles between our destination and us. The audience was long gone and the crew was starting to clean up the unbelievable mess that was left before Trixie and I got it together to make our way backstage to meet up with her dad. I had been so consumed by my own thoughts that it had never occurred to me to ask Trixie what she was going through. She seemed happy, though, when she introduced me to her parents.

I shook Jerry Garcia's hand and said "nice to meet you," even though I had met him, shaken his hand, and said the same exact thing at least twice before. What really sent my acid trip in a whole other direction was when Trixie introduced me to her mom. She must have been in her mid-forties at the time, but when Trixie said, "This is my mom, Mountain Girl," her mom instantly morphed from an old hippie into the eighteen-year-old Merry Prankster from *The Electric Kool-Aid Acid Test*. I had finished reading it only a few days earlier and had fallen in love with the Mountain Girl character in the book. I had no idea she was Trixie's mom.

"No way," I said, totally overwhelmed by it all. "I just finished reading *The Acid Test*." She gave me what appeared to be a polite smile but didn't respond. I couldn't come up with anything to add, so I stood around awkwardly until Mountain Girl asked Trixie if she was ready to go, and the three of them walked off together. They looked like a happy little family.

Even though Trixie and I hadn't talked a whole lot, I felt very alone the moment she left. I hung around the backstage area in the hopes of running into someone I knew, until it dawned on me that running into people was the last thing I wanted. What had I ever had to say to these people anyway?

"Hey, how have you been?"
"Good. How have you been?"
"Pretty good. What's been going on?"
"Not much. How about you?"
"Same."

S INCE I HAD NO interest in finding out how seeing my mom might affect what was turning out to be a somewhat negative acid trip, I decided not to go home. Instead, I wandered aimlessly around Berkeley, analyzing everything in the universe and what my place in it was. Eventually, when the sky started taking on a blue tinge, I walked back toward my house.

Mom was more then a little shocked to find me wide-awake and cleaning my room when she came to wake me up at eight in the morning. I had moved from my room in the attic to the seven-by-ten-foot addition on the back porch, so there wasn't a whole lot to clean. Even so, it was always a mess. By the time I got home, though, the world looked so ugly to me that, for the first time in my life, I started to collect my dirty clothes, organize my tapes, dust, and even clean the windows without the threat of being grounded, or not eating dinner, or whatever Mom could come up with. Cleaning helped take my mind off the unbelievably sad state of affairs I had concluded the world was in.

"You're up? Whoa, what's going on in here?" she asked. One look at Mom told me that she knew exactly what was going on. My mind was still reeling and had come up with the idea that the only reason I would ever be up so early cleaning was because I had taken acid, and she was just trying to get me to tell her.

"Oh come on, Mom. You know," I said.

"Know what?" she asked.

"You've done it. You know exactly what."

"Hey, Ory. Are you okay? Really, I have no clue what you're talking about."

"Acid," I said, and gave her a moment to pretend to figure it out.

"Acid what? Seriously, I have no idea what you're talking about, but if it gets you to clean your room . . ."

"I took acid last night," I said a moment before registering that she really didn't know what the hell I was talking about. This was possibly the first time in my life that I had seen Mom confused. Not confused about what I had told her, but confused about what she should do. It was momentary, though, and when she regained her composure, she said, "Okay. Are your bags packed?"

I nodded.

"Then I'm going to get ready, and we can discuss it in the car. Okay?"

We had a big day ahead of us. First, I had to go to a wedding with her. Then I was to get on a plane with Jack to go to a summer camp in Southern California. He was in town giving one of his self-improvement talks to a captive audience of teachers, who I'm sure would have much rather been enjoying their time off. Although I was over the hump, I was still catching visuals from the LSD and felt like a total wreck.

I really hadn't thought about how Mom would react to my admission since she had done so much of the stuff herself. We were on our way to a wedding that would be a who's who of the early '60s psychedelic movement. Not the Merry Pranksters, but the academic faction who had PhDs and were working as psychiatrists before hippies even existed. The groom was an old colleague of my mom's who had been involved in Timothy Leary's LSD experiments at Harvard.

There was a good chance that Timothy Leary would be there, but my mood had really turned sour, and I no longer cared about meeting any more of these people. I just wanted to stay in the car and hide from the world.

"Seriously, you're only fourteen years old. What were you thinking?" she asked me once we were in the car.

"But you've told me so many stories about it," I tried to defend myself.

"Ory, I . . . We were conducting academic experiments with well-known doctors and professors in an attempt to see what kind of impact these drugs would have as they related to psychotherapy and personal growth. No one knew anything about LSD back then. You just turned fourteen years old, and this is a very different time period from the 1960s."

I was intentionally tuning her out until she brought up Jack.

". . . and it's totally unfair for you to ask me not to tell Jack about this. He is your father."

"What! Since when have you ever felt the need to tell Jack anything? Now all of a sudden he's my father?"

"Okay. I won't tell him today because I realize how awkward that could make things, but I have to tell him."

"That's fine. I just really don't want to deal with it today," I said.

The wedding was in a redwood forest on top of a beautiful mountain overlooking the ocean, and all I could think about was how ugly everything was. Mom wouldn't let me stay in the car, but I was spared from having to talk to anyone because we were late in meeting up with Jack.

By the time I met Jack at the airport I'd mostly come down from the acid but was tired and in a foul mood. Seeing him was always awkward, because I had no idea how fathers and sons were supposed to relate to one another, but today felt way more uncomfortable than usual. He didn't have any experience either, but had spent the last thirteen years instructing teachers about instilling self-esteem in their students and teaching parents how to love their kids. Supposedly he was pretty good at it.

Agitated, irritable, and cranky, I reluctantly returned his hug. Making up a lie about recovering from a recent bout of insomnia, I closed my eyes and pretended to sleep the moment we got to our seats on the plane. I did the same thing during the drive to his house in L.A.

twenty

Recounts a daring heist from the police
and a subsequent visit to the psych ward

"HELLO . . . CAN I help you?" I heard a voice say. I opened my eyes and looked around, trying to figure out where I was.

"Uh . . . hi. I'm sorry, what was that?" I asked a woman who was standing on the other side of the pool at Jack's house.

"Can I help you with something?" she said, looking as though she was just about to dial 911 on the phone she was holding.

"Hi, I'm Jack's son" was all I could come up with for an answer.

"Okay . . . and?"

I was hoping that was all I would have to say, but she wanted more. "Well, I'm kind of in a situation. I ran out of gas on the freeway, and the cops towed my car, and . . . and this was the only thing I could think of to do."

"And you say you're Jack's son? What's your name?" she asked.

"Oran."

"Okay, Warren. Just stay there. I'll be back in a minute."

"It's Oran . . . with an O," I called to her as she walked away.

It was more than a few minutes because I was asleep again when she finally came back.

"Hey, Oran. Are you awake?"

I opened my eyes.

"My name is Jennifer. I'm your dad's personal assistant. I just spoke to your father, and the problem is that he's in Hawaii, but he said you could stay down in the barn until he gets back. I'm going to take you grocery shopping, and I'll check in on you until he gets back. Okay?"

"Okay," I said, standing up to follow her.

THE GOOD THING about crack, if there is such a thing, is that the exhaustion after a three-day binge is so severe that you actually get to sleep for a few days before having to experience the nastiness of heroin withdrawal wide-awake.

Jennifer helped me get set up in the barn—which was actually a pretty nice one-bedroom apartment above the horse stables—and I was able to eat and sleep for the first few days until the heroin withdrawal kicked in worse than ever. Fortunately somebody had left the barn stocked with about five unopened bottles of alcohol, and when Jennifer showed up on day three, I was wide-awake and shitfaced from the bottle of Jack Daniel's I had been working on since I had woken up. It wasn't my intention to get plastered by nine thirty in the morning, but I had woken up so goddamn sick that I needed something, anything, to take the edge off.

"How's it going . . . you doing okay down here? Need anything?" I was sitting on the top of the stairway, smoking a cigarette from the carton she had bought for me.

"Nope. I'm absolutely fine," I said, wearing a weird alcohol-induced grin that didn't fit my circumstances at all.

"I had a feeling that leaving all that booze in there was a bad idea," she said.

"What are you talking about?" I asked, taking another sip of a Jack and Coke.

"I don't know who you're trying to fool, but if you think I don't know what's going on, you're—"

"Oh, now I get it. You talked to Jack. Ha. I wonder what he had to say. That guy has no fucking idea what I'm going through right now."

"I don't need to talk to anyone to see what's going on. I found you passed out by the pool, broke, with only the clothes on your back. It's fairly obvious, don't you think? But you're right. How could your dad have any idea what you're going through? He's never been through it."

"Yeah, right, and you have? I doubt that very much."

"As a matter of fact, I have. Ten years ago I showed up at my parents' house, same as you: broke, no job, no friends. I had lost everything to alcohol, but I haven't had to take a drink since," she said.

"I'm sorry to hear that, but I'm actually going through something different."

"Are you keeping up this charade so I won't tell your dad? I mean, how many people are drunk by ten in the morning?"

"All right . . . fuck it then . . . you want to know what's going on? I'm drunk because I'm kicking dope. I'm not an alcoholic."

She stared at me with incomprehension, and I realized I should have kept my mouth shut. These Santa Barbara people probably didn't come across too many junkies, and I'm sure they didn't want us in their town.

"Shit. I'm sorry I told you. Listen . . . don't worry about me. This is my problem," I said.

"Wow. You're a serious piece of work. Anyway, the only reason I came by was to tell you I'm going to a meeting tonight, and you're welcome to come along if you want."

"What? An AA meeting?"

"Yup."

"Thanks, but I don't think so. I'm *really* not an alcoholic."

"Oh man," she mumbled to herself. "So, can I take the booze out of here then?"

"Why? I just told you I'm not an alcoholic."

"God, you're impossible, but call me if you change your mind about the meeting or just want to talk."

I spent the next two days finishing off the alcohol before taking Jennifer up on her offer to go to a meeting. I was losing my mind in the barn, and I was nervous about having to confront Jack the next day. I wasn't looking forward to another "loving father to the rescue" trip like the one he had pulled back in San Francisco, but I suspected that, without the audience he had last time, it would be a different routine. The only thing I was sure of was that it would be awkward.

S O I HAVE to admit. This puts me in an awkward situation," Jack said the next day, after I explained how I ended up there. We were in his office and I was bundled up under a couple of blankets, still shivering cold from the withdrawal. He was standing in front of the huge bay window that looked out over the horse corrals.

"I don't usually find myself in this position, but I really don't know what to do. I mean, I've never dealt with someone kicking heroin, and I don't know anything about it. It seems to me that you should be someplace where they have experience dealing with this kind of thing," he continued.

"I see your point, but I've been through it before, and it's already been four days, so I think if I just stay in the barn for a little while longer I should be fine."

"Well, I'll be honest, it's hard to see you like this, and Inga just moved in with her kids."

I didn't know much about his new girlfriend, but I had heard there was some drama.

"We're both going through divorces right now, and having someone . . ." He paused, trying to choose his words carefully.

"Kicking heroin at the house doesn't look good," I finished for him. There was no denying how strange it must have been for my ten-year-old half-brother, Christopher, whom I had only met a few times, to see me in this condition—not to mention Inga's kids, who were not at all happy about being there in the first place. It would only be a matter of time before news of the creepy dope-sick guy lurking around the house reached their father.

"Even for four or five more days?" I asked anyway.

"And then what?"

Having no answer, I just shook my head. It was clear that Jack was very gently trying his best to get me out of there without kicking me out. As much as I wanted to be angry with him for it, I couldn't blame him. My main focus was trying to put off any decision making till I could go get what was left of my heroin out of the police lot. I desperately needed to get my dope out of there, and I was worried that if I didn't get there soon, someone else would find it and I'd be in a whole different kind of trouble. Jack wanted me to make a decision now, and I could tell we weren't going anywhere until I gave him one.

"Okay. I guess I should probably check in somewhere," I said.

"Well, I already did some research," he said, confirming my suspicion that he was just holding out for me to come to the conclusion myself. He pulled out a legal pad with a bunch of phone numbers on it. "There are a few rehabs in the area. But I think the best thing would be for you to detox at the hospital and then figure out what to do next," he said.

"Okay, but seriously . . . I need to get my stuff out of the car before I check in anywhere."

"Great. Let's go, then."

We drove to the police impound lot, and I explained to them that I couldn't afford to get my car back, but that I needed to get my belongings out.

"Too bad. Because that's one nice car," one of the cops said.

I was paranoid that they'd already searched it and were just waiting for me to come back, but I had no choice but to go through with this. I asked Jack if he could get whatever was in the trunk, while I went up front to clear out all my drugs and paraphernalia. Everything appeared to be just as I left it, but I didn't trust these cops. Maybe it was a bigger offense if they caught you holding the stuff than if they found it in your car? Maybe they needed a search warrant and it was easier to wait until I showed up? Shit, they could probably even get me on distribution, since my dope was in individual bags.

Whatever the case, the only thing to do now was try to get as much of the evidence out of there as possible. I went through all my hiding places and took the five balloons of dope I had left, one syringe, and a spoon and slid them into the lining of my jacket. Everything else—needles, spoons, glass pipes, Brillo pads, and cotton balls—I threw into my messenger bag. Then I swept off the remnants of crack that were stuck in the crevices of the seat cushions and ground them into the carpet. I was still expecting to be arrested when we drove up to the gate, but the guard waved us through.

A wave of relief hit me for about two seconds, until Jack asked me if I needed to stop for anything before going to the hospital.

"What? We're going straight there?" I asked, as if this were the first time I'd heard of this.

"Yeah. Remember? That was the plan."

I knew full well that that was the plan, but now that I had the dope in my possession the plan had changed.

"I thought we were going back to the house first. That fucking cop wouldn't even let me take my clothes with me, and I've been wearing the same shit for a week now. I thought I could at least take a shower and change, before God knows how long, when I get to the hospital." I didn't have to pretend to be on the verge of tears, as I was about to start crying anyway.

Back at the house, I practically ran to the bathroom and turned the shower on while I fixed myself half a bag of heroin. In only a few seconds, an unbelievable warmth replaced the freezing cold that had been coming from my bones, and lying on the carpet in the fetal position for the past five days seemed like a distant dream. Less urgently, I opened the rest of the balloons and flushed all the little bags of coke down the toilet. I secured the heroin in my jacket lining with the syringe and spoon. Then I wrapped the rest of the paraphernalia in a wad of paper towels and threw it in the trash, hoping no one would find it. Ten minutes later, I was showered, shaved, and wearing different—if not necessarily clean—clothes for the first time in a week.

"Well, you certainly look a lot better," Jack said when I walked into the kitchen, reminding me that I was still supposed to be in the thralls of dope sickness.

"Thanks. The shower helped. I still feel like fucking shit, though." I hated acting dope sick. It was never easy to act awkward and uncomfortable while keeping in mind that my normal method for dealing with discomfort was to act cool and uninterested. It was a complex role to play, but I had the advantage of playing it in front of someone who didn't really know me that well.

"I can't even imagine," he said sincerely.

T HE DETOX WARD at the hospital turned out to be the psych ward. After I was thoroughly searched, which was normal, they took away my shoelaces and replaced them with two large rubber bands.

"One of the patients tried to strangle herself with her laces," the nurse explained.

"Wow, but why do you need mine?"

"Well, about an hour later she stole someone else's and tried again."

"Jesus Christ."

"Anything else we should know about?" the nurse asked after I had turned over my razor, toothbrush, matches, lighter, and the keys to my fucking Buick. I offered her my cigarettes as well, if only to seem cooperative.

"You're going to want to hold on to those," she said. "Just find one of us to light them for you."

"That's everything then," I said, thankful they hadn't patted me down and found my dope and the extra pack of cigarettes I had hid in my jacket. Even I was aware of how insane it was that I was checking into a detox/psych ward with drugs on me, but I couldn't bring myself to throw away perfectly good heroin, no matter the circumstances.

"Okay then. Go to the window over there, and the nurse will give you your meds. Then I'll show you to your room."

I shuffled over to the window—the rubber bands did a very poor job of keeping my shoes on—and took a large assortment of pills without asking what they were giving me.

"Don't worry," the nurse said as I was struggling to wash it down with water from the smallest Dixie cup I had ever seen in my life. "You're going to sleep tonight. That's for sure."

"Thanks. I can't fucking wait," I answered, suddenly overcome with a strong urge to just lie down right there in front of the window.

A LL RIGHT, you're finally awake. I was worried that maybe we'd overdone it with the meds. You've been out for fourteen hours."

I was lying in a bed, looking up at the doctor who had checked me in the previous night.

"So, how are you feeling today?" he asked.

I didn't know how I felt, but I used my stock "I feel like shit" answer I always used with doctors who were responsible for doling out the drugs. "That was the first sleep I've had in four days." I didn't want him thinking I had been out so long as a result of too much medication.

"Don't worry, we don't believe in making people suffer here. I've found that method ineffective," he said, handing me a cup of pills.

"Me, too," I agreed.

"So listen. Just take it easy for now, and when you feel up to it, we have various group activities going on all the time. You might feel better if you get up and participate."

I wasn't alone in the room. There was another kid—who must have been eighteen or so—sitting on his bed, staring straight into outer space. I watched him stare at the wall for close to an hour. *What the fuck happened to him?* I asked myself until my bladder was about to explode and I got up to go to the bathroom.

There were no locks on the doors, which was to be expected. I wasn't worried about my roommate, as he was completely occupied at the moment, but there was a door leading to another room, making what I was about to do more risky. I turned on the shower and fixed myself a shot as quickly as possible, then got in the shower and injected it, using one of the rubber bands from my shoes as a tourniquet. When I came back out, my roommate was still sitting in the same position.

I wanted to avoid my room as much as possible, which only turned out to be a few minutes. When I walked out to the ward, one of the nurses guided me to a circle of people talking about their feelings. No sooner had I sat down than whatever drugs the doctor had given me started taking effect on top of the heroin. I was determined to stay, but when I started sliding off my chair, I knew it was only a matter of time before I ended up on the floor. I excused myself and used every ounce of strength I could muster to walk the thirty feet back to my room.

T HIS TIME I woke up to a nurse telling me I had a phone call.
"Huh? Nobody knows I'm here."

"Someone does, and she's waiting for you." God, it was a struggle to get up.

"You can use that one on the wall," she said, after I had followed her out to the hall. I had a bad feeling about this, but I picked up the phone.

"Hello?" I asked.

"Ory? Finally. God, they've had me on hold forever." Oh, fuck. How did she get my number?

"How did you find me?" I asked my mom. I had explicitly told Jack not to tell her I was here.

"I found out from Jack after calling every one of your friends, who had no idea where you were. Everyone's worried about you. I called Jack just to let him know you were missing and I was shocked when he told me you were there."

"Uh-huh." I was pissed at Jack for telling her.

"How do you think that made me feel?" she asked.

"SO YOU'RE CALLING ME AT THE FUCKING HOSPITAL TO GIVE ME A GUILT TRIP? FUCK YOU!" I had snapped and there was nothing I could do to turn it off. "DID YOU EVER THINK THAT MIGHT BE THE REASON I DIDN'T TELL YOU WHERE I WAS? THAT MAYBE I ALREADY FEEL SHITTY ENOUGH WITHOUT YOU TRYING TO MAKE ME FEEL EVEN SHITTIER?" I had to pause for a breath of air.

"Hey, Oran. That's not fair. I am not trying to give you a guilt trip, but what'd you expect me to do? You think I'm not going through a hard time too? Do you have any idea what it's like for me to watch you go through this?" She was surprisingly calm. I noticed two orderlies walking toward me down the hall, but I didn't think anything of it.

"SEE, THERE YOU GO AGAIN BLAMING ME FOR YOUR HARD TIME. IT'S ALWAYS THE SAME FUCKING SHIT. THIS IS EXACTLY WHY I DIDN'T TELL YOU WHERE I WAS. I CAN'T FUCKING DEAL WITH IT ANYMORE. MY WHOLE FUCKING

LIFE HAS BEEN . . . ." Then one of the orderlies had me in a bear hug, while the other one ripped the jack out of the phone.

He held me until the other guy had taken the phone from my hand and then he let go.

"You okay, man?" the orderly who grabbed me asked. I was a little bewildered by the suddenness of what had happened, but actually I felt fine, even thankful that these guys had intervened. It was the first time I had felt like someone had seen the truth about my mom.

"Yeah. I'm fine. Sorry. That was my mom," I answered as if that would explain everything.

"Your mom? Holy shit, man, I ain't never heard no one talk to their mom like that," he said. "Well, let's go talk to the nurse. She didn't know what was going on. Thought you was in a fight or something."

We walked around the corner to the nurses' desk.

"What was that all about?" the nurse asked.

"He was on the phone with his mom."

"His mom?" She looked surprised.

"Yeah, sorry. She wasn't supposed to know I was here," I said.

"Your mom? Well, we better make sure that doesn't happen again," she said, picking up the phone. "Hello. I need a block on any incoming calls from . . . . What's her name?" she asked me, holding the phone away from her mouth. I gave her Mom's name, which she repeated to the operator before hanging up. "That ought to do it then. I think you scared the whole ward, certainly scared me. By the way, if you want to eat, dinner ends in ten minutes."

FUCKING HOSPITAL FOOD. I hadn't eaten in so long, yet it was still a struggle to force down the piece of toast, the cold tomato soup, and the cube of bright red Jell-O that was on my tray. Noticing a bunch of people filing out of a door holding cigarettes, I gave up on the Jell-O and followed them out to a patio, which was walled off with chain-link fencing. A nurse lit all our cigarettes, and, while I was smoking, a girl somewhere around my age approached me to ask if I had an extra cigarette.

As I handed her one, I noticed what looked like shoelace marks around her neck.

"So what are you getting off of?" she asked me.

"Heroin. How did you know I was in here for drugs?" I asked her.

" 'Cause you're not wearing a gown. That's how you can tell the druggies from the psychos."

I looked around the patio to get a sense of how many psychos surrounded me. The druggies were outnumbered four to one.

"So I take it you're the reason they took my shoelaces?" I said, unsure if it would be taken as a joke or set off another suicide attempt.

"Those fucking bastards took everything from me. Not just my shoelaces . . . all my clothes, even my bra and underwear. Now I have to walk around looking like one of these psychos."

I didn't bring up the fact that strangling yourself with a shoelace was clearly psychotic behavior.

"How does that help someone who has just lost their kid and is trying to *build* self-esteem, not lose it? All they do is try to make you feel shittier to justify keeping you here, so they can take more of your goddamn money," she said, getting completely worked up. In a change of tone, she asked, "Heroin, huh? I'm here for speed."

"Speed? Where are your clothes, then?" I asked.

"Oh, they took them yesterday when I supposedly tried to kill myself. They're supposed to be these professionals and they couldn't see I was just trying to scare my ex-husband? Fucking bastards. Do they know how degrading it is to walk around dressed like one of these nuts?" She said it loud enough for the nurse to hear. The nurse ignored her, but the other gown wearers were starting to give her nasty looks.

"You believe me though, right? That I'm not one of these crazy people?" Again she was talking a little louder than I thought she should have. I didn't know what to say. I was never good at these on-the-spot situations.

"Honestly? Well, I only met you two minutes ago."

"True. I'm in a psych ward, but you can tell that I'm just angry, right? Not crazy like the rest of them. Who wouldn't be angry the way I've been treated? In fact, I would be crazy if I *wasn't* angry. They took my daughter away from me." With that she broke into tears. I stood there uncomfortably for a while. "I needed the money. I was broke, and Gary wasn't paying his child support. What'd he expect me to do? I only did it once," she sobbed.

"Canfield . . . Oran?" The nurse with the lighter called to me just in time. I wasn't sure I wanted to know what it was she had done just once. "Time to get your meds."

"Uh. I guess I have to go," I said, but the girl didn't respond. She just stood there crying. I wasn't safe anywhere in this place.

The nurse walked me through the door and said, "You looked like you needed some help. I would stay away from that one. She's a bit crazy," which seemed an odd thing for her to say. It seemed to me that everyone here was more than just a bit crazy, they were totally fucking nuts. "We'll find you when it's really time to take your meds," she said.

I shuffled back to my room and was relieved to find my roommate lying down, staring at the ceiling. I did the same until a nurse came in with my medication.

"Thanks," I said and quickly nodded off.

Again, I was woken up by the doctor. "So how are we today?"

"What? I have no idea how we are, but I feel like shit." My eyes were trying to adjust to the sunlight.

"Really? Because based on what you told us during your intake, we're giving you more than enough medication. You should be quite comfortable."

"That's the thing. I think I might be a little too comfortable. I feel like a fucking zombie. I've been mostly asleep for two days. I may regret saying this, but I think it might be too much," I said, neglecting to mention that I had been doing heroin on top of whatever else they had me on.

"I've been at this for twenty years, and I'll never understand you heroin addicts. When you guys are out on the street, you'll stick anything that some stranger tells you is dope in your veins, but when a trained doctor gives you something, you don't want to have anything to do with it."

"Yeah? And?"

"So we're going to stick to the regimen as planned for now, and we'll start tapering you down tomorrow. Okay?"

"Uh," I hesitated, but I was too medicated to come up with an argument.

"Good, and I would try to check out some of the groups today. You might hear something."

"From these people? I doubt it, but I'll give it a shot."

"There you go. Just give it a shot. You never know, right?"

I did know, but I gave him a noncommittal nod in the hope that he would leave.

After getting high in the bathroom again, I went out on the patio. I found an unoccupied corner to smoke my cigarette in peace, but the girl from the day before found me and interrupted my isolation.

"Hey. Sorry about yesterday. You must think I'm crazy."

"I'm here, too," I said, neither confirming nor denying her.

"Anyway, I just wanted to explain—so you don't think I'm crazy—

that all this started when my ex-husband saw me acting in a porn movie. It was stupid, but I was broke and it was just a onetime thing. Anyway, he flipped out and used it as evidence to get my daughter back from me, and that's when I started doing too much speed."

It was a strange explanation for not being crazy. I had never met a porn star, though. I didn't actually know whether being in one movie qualified someone to be a porn "star," but suddenly I found her a lot more interesting.

"Yeah, that's terrible. I mean, you said he wasn't paying child support, right? What did he expect you to do?" *Jesus. What the hell was I saying to this girl? Not receiving child support seemed like the worst excuse to have sex with a stranger for money—especially on camera.*

"Exactly. What's the big deal? I don't know how I could tell, but I knew you would understand," she said, stepping a little closer to me.

Because I will say the stupidest shit in the world to avoid awkwardness, I thought to myself.

"It's too bad we're stuck in this hospital," she said, edging even closer.

"Oh, the doctor told me to check out one of these groups," I said, uncomfortable with where my thoughts were going. "I should probably go."

"I'll go with you," she volunteered.

There were three groups sitting in circles when we went back into the ward. We found one with two chairs available and sat down as people were introducing themselves. Two of the other patients got up and left when we showed up. It wasn't long before I understood why.

"Hi, I'm Oran," I said when it came around to me.

"Do you mind telling the group why you're here?" the counselor leading the group asked.

"I'm kicking heroin."

"Okay. Very good. Anything else?"

"No."

"Good."

"I'm Stacy and I'm here because my ex—"

"Thanks, Stacy, but I only asked Oran because he's new to the group."

"Now, who wants to start?" she asked, staring directly at me.

"I will," Stacy said.

The other patients rolled their eyes and shifted uncomfortably in their seats.

"Actually, I was hoping to hear from Oran, since he hasn't been with us. Oran, would you like to start?"

"No, thanks. I'm still pretty foggy. I thought I would just listen today." I had learned in the other rehabs that this was the right way to decline because it implied a sort of silent participation.

"Anyone else want to start then?"

"See what I mean?" Stacy turned to me, but she was obviously talking to the counselor. "They don't want me to get better. Every time I try to help myself, they try to shut me out." Then she turned and stared straight at the counselor. "It's because they know my parents' insurance is covering this and you want to keep me here as long as you can."

"Stacy. We've been through this over and over again, and you know that's not what's going on."

"Oh yeah? Well then, tell me again because I don't understand why else you guys would keep me here when I'm about to lose my daughter to that fucking asshole. Do you even know why I was in that movie? Because that bastard . . ."

"Yes. Everyone knows why you were in the movie, Stacy," she said condescendingly. "And you know as well as I do that that has nothing to do with why you're here. The reason you're still here is that when someone tries to take their own life, we are required by the State of California to hold them until we see evidence that they are no longer a threat to themselves or others."

"Oh, that's great. Now tell me how losing my daughter is going to give me a reason to live. I'll die without her." She started crying.

"What are you implying by that?" the counselor asked, totally unfazed by this display of emotion.

"See what I mean?" Stacy said, turning toward me.

"You can't even open your mouth without them interpreting it as suicidal. It's fucking evil!" she screamed, turning her attention back to the group. "I bet that bastard's paying you to keep me here till after the court date. Is that what he's doing? I should have just kept my mouth shut like this guy . . . You'll probably release him right away! From now on I'm not saying anything!"

"That sounds like a great idea, Stacy. Let's move on," the counselor said without even taking a pause. "Brian, how are you today?"

"Fine," said the guy sitting next to Stacy. Brian was wearing a robe, indicating he had a *real* problem.

"That's great, Brian. Can you tell me what 'fine' feels like?" she asked.

"Like okay," he said.

"That's a very good start. Now can you elaborate on 'okay'?"

"Jesus Christ," Stacy interrupted. "He said he was fine. How come when someone's fine you try to get them to talk, but when someone isn't at all fine you just want to shut them up? It's so obvious you're just trying to get him to say something that you can use to keep him here longer."

"This isn't helping your case, Stacy."

"Since there's obviously nothing I can say to help my case, I might as well tell the truth. . . . . . What? Are you afraid the other patients are going to get wise to your plan, too? I'm going to tell everyone. Then see what happens."

". . . And that's more important than seeing your daughter?"

"You fucking bitch! You have no right to bring her into this!" she yelled hysterically.

"Okay, group. Stacy and I are going to have a chat in my office, and I hope to see the rest of you this afternoon. That will be all."

I SAT IN THE CIRCLE awhile longer by myself, staring into space, wondering how the hell I had ended up here. It was almost as if Stacy had held up a mirror for me. Did I sound that crazy at my first rehab? I, too, had been convinced that I was right, and no one had come up with a single argument that didn't reinforce my various theories about AA, rehabs, and God all being a huge conspiracy to get people into their cult. Even when someone said something vaguely sensible, I thought, *These people will say anything to get me to join up with their bullshit.* Although I still wasn't convinced that I was wrong about them or nearly as crazy as Stacy, I did see a glimpse of my own paranoia through her, and it scared me. I needed to get the hell out of there now. I only had one more day before I would no longer be faking withdrawal. I'd be going through it for real. I struggled out of the chair to look for the doctor.

twenty-one

*In which he is saved from untimely death
and avoids broccoli and zucchini through
his own resourcefulness*

I NEVER THOUGHT I would look forward to school, but after the worst summer ever, I couldn't wait to go back to Arizona. I had been fired from a job and kicked out of summer camp for smoking cigarettes, and Mom and I did nothing but scream at each other once I got back to Berkeley and had to face the consequences of admitting I took acid. For the first time in my life, Mom started treating me like a kid, and our interactions often escalated into yelling matches within twenty seconds. She wanted me to tell her where I was going whenever I left the house. Whom I was going with. What I was going to do, and when I was going to be home. Stuff normal kids had to deal with their whole lives, but, as far as I was concerned, it was too late to all of a sudden start treating me like a fourteen-year-old.

High school didn't end up being much better. We came back to a new headmaster, various new teachers, a crop of new kids, and a staggering number of new rules. The only good thing about this, if there was one, was that it was easier to make friends under the new regime because nothing brings people together like a common enemy. The common enemy was Bill, the new headmaster. Bill had no business whatsoever at our hippie school. He had come from a stuffy East Coast prep school and, at our first assembly, went on and on about the life lessons he had learned playing rugby and how it was his honor to pass these virtues on to us. He then explained that the tie he was wearing was given to him by his former headmaster as he lay on his deathbed and told Bill he was passing the mantle on to him.

Bill was hell-bent on purging the school of its bad apples, but enrollment was already down. The costs of losing more kids were being passed on to us in the form of fewer activities, crappier food, and a new air of paranoia as supposedly people called "finks" were walking around, collecting data on everyone and reporting straight to Bill.

O NE OF THE NEW rules Bill instituted was that we were no longer allowed to smoke on campus. The campus itself was huge, and the nearest place to smoke was behind the girls' dorm, which was built only twenty feet from the barbed-wire fence that separated the campus from what was officially state property. Any other direction and it would have been a fifteen-minute walk to get off the grounds, plus this new smoking rule was my only excuse to go anywhere near the girls' dorms. The dorm had a big courtyard that we walked through in order to go to Cow Pie, a huge rock formation/smoking patio that looked exactly like its name.

Shortly after returning from working at an orphanage in Oaxaca—my field trip that year—my friend Matt and I were having a cigarette during lunch break, and on our way back we staged a ridiculous fake fight in the girls' courtyard. I hardly ever used my circus skills, but I had been teaching Matt how to fall without getting hurt, and how to slap his thigh, and turn his head when I took a swing at him to make it look like he was being punched, and other slapstick tricks. Although neither of us would admit it, we were probably hoping to get some attention from the girls, and the fight escalated to where Matt was throwing me against the wall and kicking me when I was down. He then picked me up and gently threw me against a big window that looked out onto the courtyard from one of the girls' rooms. We had a crowd of about five girls watching who didn't know what to make of it all, and when I bounced off the window they seemed a little freaked out. We both started laughing.

"Wow, that was a good one. Let's try that one again," I said.

This girl Caroline who Matt had a crush on walked in just then and Matt said, "Hey Caroline, you got to see this. It will freak you out." He grabbed me by the collar and . . .

Climbing out of the window, I found everyone staring at me in total silence while Matt, who was sitting on the ground next to me, held his head in his hands mumbling, "oh no," over and over. I looked down and noticed an eight-inch gash on my chest and a flap of skin hanging down to my waist. It looked like an anatomy drawing from a textbook, as if the muscles around my rib cage had been woven on a loom.

Feeling something wet dripping down my fingers, I looked at my hand and saw a two-inch gouge in my wrist, all the way down to the bone. The gash in my side had been kind of fascinating, but the cut in my wrist and the blood squirting from it brought me back to earth. I figured I only had a few minutes left to live, and I decided to spend them running around in circles yelling, "Fuck! Fuck! Fuck! Fuck! Fuck!" until this girl named Anna appeared out of nowhere, grabbed on to my wrist with her hand, and pressed herself against my chest wound.

Anna was a bit of an anomaly. While almost everyone else dressed in cutoff jeans, tie-dyes, and Birkenstocks, she always wore these amazing matching outfits. That day it was a white one-piece tennis suit with a white sash for a belt, white socks, and a pair of white Keds. All the other kids were standing around dumbstruck until Anna started barking orders at them.

"Matt! Run to the infirmary and tell the nurse what happened. Let her know we're coming, and tell her to stay there. Caroline, go get John. He's down in the music room. Tell him to meet us at the infirmary with a van. And Sarah, I need you to untie my belt."

Anna wrapped her sash around my wrist as tight as she could, then grabbed onto it again, squeezing hard. With her other hand she reached around my waist and pulled her body against mine, applying pressure on my chest.

"Good. You're going to be okay, but we need to get to the infirmary. You ready?"

I wasn't so sure I was going to be okay, but I nodded and we awkwardly set out to find the nurse.

We ran into her, hurrying down the path holding a fistful of Band-Aids. At this point Anna must have looked much worse off than I did, with her white tennis suit completely covered in blood.

"Oh dear. Let me see what happened," the nurse said, trying to peel open a Band-Aid.

"Don't let go of me," I said.

"Those aren't going to help right now," Anna said. "Go back and get your car started in case John doesn't show up."

"But I need to see what happened," the nurse said again.

"I'm not letting go of him. Get your car, or go find John," Anna said with such authority that the nurse actually turned around and ran away. "Don't worry. I'm not letting go of you,"

"Thanks," I said, continuing our slow walk.

When we got to the infirmary, John and Matt were already there with the van. We got in and John took off before the doors were even closed, only to slam on the brakes a moment later. The nurse was chasing after us with more Band-Aids and a bottle of iodine, which she handed to John. Anna, who had maintained incredible composure until this point, screamed at her, "You're not helping! John, go!" He took off for good this time.

John was driving as fast as he could, and I finally started feeling the pain as the van started bouncing all over the dirt roads. When I wasn't wincing in pain from bouncing up and down, I was morbidly reflecting on what I had accomplished in my short time on earth. *Not bad for a fourteen-year-old,* I thought, but Anna still hadn't loosened her grip on me, and I could feel her breath on my neck. As much as I was trying not to think about it, I couldn't get around the fact that I still hadn't done the one thing I wanted to do more than anything else in the whole world. It seemed totally wrong to be thinking about sex at a time like this, but I wasn't ready to die. Not yet.

I even started crying about it, which caused Anna to start whispering to me that everything was going to be all right. "I've got you. I'm not letting go," she said, but this only made my dilemma seem even sadder.

WHEN I REGAINED consciousness after being sewn back together, I found out that I had cut two tendons and a nerve, had broken my wrist in the same place for the third time, and had an eight-inch open wound on my chest.

"The bad news is that you'll be in that cast for the next six months and will most likely permanently lose some of your muscles while the nerve grows back," the doctor told me after the operation. "The good news is that you're lucky to be alive. You missed your artery by a centimeter."

I WASN'T FEELING too lucky. Everything I did relied on that hand: ceramics, painting, guitar, writing, masturbation. On top of that, my ceramics teacher, Jeff, warned me that Bill was trying to figure out a way to kick me out.

"For what?" I asked, as if I wasn't already going through enough hell.

"He says you were on drugs."

"You've got to be kidding me. I was just messing around with Matt."

"Don't tell me. Tell him."

It was ludicrous, but sure enough I was called into Bill's office.

"So, what happened with Matt? Why don't you tell me the real story," Bill said.

When I told him what happened, he said, "Yeah, I know that part. But before that, you guys were smoking pot, so I have to suspend you. I know you're going through a lot, so I'm willing to just let you take the rest of the semester off to recover instead of an official suspension."

I couldn't believe what I was hearing. "First of all, I have no idea what you're talking about with this pot thing. I was smoking a cigarette, and as far as I know there's no rule about getting thrown through windows. At least there wasn't a few days ago." I had only smoked pot once at the beginning of the year, and there was no way someone could have seen me getting high.

"Why do you insist on making everything difficult? I'm offering you a reasonable way out of this. Why don't you take it?"

"Because I have nothing to get out of. I have no idea where you get your information or whether you're just assuming I was high, but I wasn't. How can you suspend me for something you have no proof of?"

"I know for a fact that you smoke pot, and I can get proof if I need it. But again, it would make things easier if you just went home to recover."

All of a sudden my mouth just started stringing words together on its own, like the time I had gotten into it with Mr. Lutkenhouse. As scared as I was, I said, "It was that fucking doctor. What the fuck? He told me that was confidential information. This is total bullshit." The anesthesiologist had asked me a whole bunch of questions about drugs before he shot me up with Demerol.

"Where'd you learn to talk like that?"

"It doesn't matter where I learned it, unless you've got a new rule I don't know about. I can't believe that fucking guy. But how can you get proof if it's confidential?"

"It's not. You're a minor."

"Good, then when you get the paperwork you'll see that I told him the last time I smoked pot was three months ago, which was during summer break."

"Really? That's not what he said."

"I don't care what he said. Look at the file."

"Okay, I will. If you're lying, I'll do my best to kick you out. If I can't find proof, you can stay, but we're going to give you random drug tests. That's the deal."

"No. What happened had nothing to with drugs, and to prove it, I'll make you a deal. You can test me once. If I was high, it'll still be in my system. You can't punish me for something I didn't do."

"Who taught you to talk to authority like this? When I was a kid, I would have been slapped around if I acted this way."

"I'm glad I'm not you," I said, storming out.

B ILL'S TERM AS headmaster was a dark period in the school's history. He'd kicked so many students out, and enrollment for the next year was only half what it had been when I started. We weren't told whether he was fired or if he resigned, but we all celebrated when we saw a moving truck in front of Bill's house. A few days later he drove away without even saying good-bye.

B ACK IN BERKELEY for summer vacation, I was in desperate need of a job. Coffee and cigarettes cost money. Food was also an issue if I didn't want to eat my mom's nightly meal of boiled broccoli and zucchini with soy sauce. Not only had she been cooking the same exact thing for as long as I could remember, but she had also recently changed the rules so that if Kyle or I didn't help her make the weekly batch on Sunday nights, we weren't allowed to have any the whole week.

It may have been a valid rule, but the consequences of not helping her outweighed the benefits as long as I had a dollar to go to the Chinese restaurant around the corner. If she had enough broccoli and zucchini left on Friday or Saturday I could usually get some out of her whether I had helped or not, since the shit was so soggy and old by then it was almost inedible. Wednesday and Thursday were out of the question since that was when it had reached her favorite consistency. Other than a bloody rare steak once a year to get her folic acid, she had survived for at least the last fourteen years almost exclusively on zucchini and broccoli.

I needed money, and getting a job spared me both from having to help her make the same dinner we'd been eating for years and, more important, having to eat it. I went through the want ads calling about any jobs I thought might hire a fourteen-year-old. The only place to call me back was a silk-screen company down in Emeryville who needed someone to fold shirts for ten dollars an hour.

The manager, Brigitte, showed me around the place and told me that my job was to fold the shirts as they came out of these gigantic heat-setting machines. It seemed easy enough, but I wasn't aware that I would be working on all three of the heat setters. The machines were fed by a motley-looking cast of punk rockers who were printing the shirts way faster than I was able to fold them. All day long I ran back and forth, folding as many as I could in one area before the boxes that were set out to catch the others overflowed and started spilling onto the floor. The work was great physical therapy for my hand, which was still healing from my accident at school. But, as the doctor warned me, a few of my muscles had atrophied and would never recover.

Just when I was getting the hang of the job, the company ordered two robotic screen-printing machines, which were able to pump out fifteen shirts a minute each. Once the printers got a handle on how to work the new machines, it was necessary to time my cigarette breaks with the rest of the crew since I could no longer leave my job unattended for more than a minute at a time. Everyone who worked there seemed to be in a band, and I felt left out as they talked about the punk-rock scene.

"What bands are you guys in?" I asked them in an attempt to be included. These guys did not seem like the friendliest lot, and although I was sure I would hate their music, sitting around in awkward silence was bumming me out.

"My band is called Neurosis, and Malcome is in Christ On Parade," this guy Scott said. I'd never heard of Neurosis, but I saw Christ On Parade flyers everywhere I went. Scott seemed like a nice enough guy, but it bothered me that he had *S-K-I-N* tattooed across his knuckles. I didn't know much about the punk scene, but I knew that skinheads were violent, nationalistic, racist, evil motherfuckers. He looked menacing, but he just didn't seem like the type. Plus, he had hair.

"Neurosis?" I repeated. "Okay. I'll check it out," I told him. I was making more money than ever, and most of it went toward records.

"You don't have to buy it," Scott said. "I'll bring you a tape tomorrow, and you can let me know what you think. By the way, are you available to work nights or weekends? John and I have some big orders coming up, and we can pay you cash."

"Sure," I answered.

"Cool. We'll use you tomorrow night."

I HAD ALWAYS wondered why I was always the only person to leave
at five o'clock while everyone else kept working. After five, Scott and
John got to use the place for their own business, and the next night I
stayed an extra four hours, folding Operation Ivy and Green Day shirts.
When I got home, I listened to Scott's tape. It was a lot darker and more
musical than what I thought of as punk rock. I actually liked it.

I started staying late with them more often and was psyched when
Scott asked me if I wanted to roadie for Neurosis's next show. It was at
the Women's Building in San Francisco, and I didn't do much besides
carry an amp in. I was supposed to sell merch for them, as well, but only
about ten people showed up.

"What's up with that tattoo?" I asked Scott while one of the other
bands was playing. We were outside smoking.

"I was a skinhead when I was your age. Proud of America and the
Constitution . . . . I guess I believed in what the flag used to stand for, but
now I'm fucking working twelve hours a day and living in a fucking squat.
I'm not trying to defend myself. I mean, I was just a teenager . . . but you
should read the Constitution sometime. Those guys were pretty fucking
radical at the time and would probably try to start another revolution if
they saw the miserable state of this country now."

To me the Constitution represented oppression, intolerance, slavery,
imperialism, and unbelievable stupidity. Scott was the first person who
had ever told me otherwise.

O N MONDAY SCOTT showed up to work with bruises all over his
body and two black eyes. His nose and mouth were swollen.

"What the fuck happened to you?" I asked him during our cigarette
break.

"I was drunk and started talking shit to a pack of skinheads," he
said.

"Jesus Christ. What did you say to deserve that?"

"I called them a bunch of Nazi shitheads. I may have been a skin, but
I was never a fucking racist."

"Fuck, man. I'm sorry they got you."

"This is nothing. They were bound to get me at some point. When I
get drunk, I can't control myself. And anyway, Malcom and I managed to
get a few good punches in before they beat the shit out of me. If they
didn't travel in packs, I would be the one beating the shit out of them,"

Scott told me. I considered myself a pacifist, but if there was anyone who I fantasized about beating up, it was those guys.

After that, I looked up to Scott even more and was super excited when he invited me to go see a band called G. G. Allin and the Murder Junkies. That weekend I ended up getting such a bad case of the flu that I couldn't make it to the show. Nobody showed up to work on Monday but Brigitte and I. Brigitte didn't have all the details, but Scott and Malcom, along with the rest of the printers, were in the hospital, or at home recovering after the same pack of skinheads forced their way into the G. G. Allin show and started beating everyone up. Meanwhile, G. G. Allin had decided to light himself and the stage on fire. I couldn't decide whether I had missed out or gotten lucky.

THE MONOTONY of folding shirts made the summer pass quickly. Right before going back to school, though, I experienced my second psychedelic experience. It was at a reggae festival in Mendocino when I took mushrooms for the first time. Although they were far less intense than the acid, the mushrooms ended up having a much more profound impact on my life. Maybe I was just having a bad trip, but all these free-thinking, nonconformist, mud-covered hippies looked exactly the same as one another. In all but a few instances, the girls twirled around in circles and the guys hopped around on one foot, doing weird shit with their hands. These hippies suddenly looked about as straitlaced to me as a guy in a suit working at the bank.

When I got home, I threw away my tie-dyed shirts, my Birkenstocks, and my Guatemalan vest and went to the Salvation Army with an overwhelming urge to cover my body in polyester and say good-bye to my hippie roots for good.

twenty-two

Is long, but holds the reader's interest
through a series of comical interludes

JACK PICKED ME up from the hospital.

"Hi, Jack," I said, opening the door to his Lexus.

"Don't say that in an airplane," he said with a laugh. "So how are you feeling? All better?"

"I feel okay," I said, but I was starting to panic since I had just used the last of my dope earlier in the day. I wasn't about to tell him I had been shooting up in the bathroom at the detox ward, though.

"Well, Inga made up a list of twenty-eight-day programs for us to check out when we get home, but I'm glad you're feeling better."

"I was thinking. What if I just stay in the barn for a little while, maybe go to a therapist, and see what happens? This rehab thing just isn't for me," I said.

"Okay. You're welcome to stay in the barn, but you've got to come up with something to do with your time. You ever think about getting back into ceramics? I know someone who has a studio you could probably use."

"Sure, that sounds like a good idea." I didn't care one way or the other about ceramics, but if it kept me out of rehab . . .

As far as they knew I was all better, but I started going into withdrawal only a few hours after getting back to his house. That night, after everyone went to sleep, I took my dad's old minivan and drove all the way to San Francisco to score drugs. Somehow, I made it back before they noticed I was gone, and a few nights later I did it again. My money was coming from the petty-cash box in the office, which always seemed to have a few hundred bucks in it. Although I looked everywhere, I never found where my dad kept the real money. On my third drug run to San Francisco, I got too high to drive back and ended up spending the night at a rest stop. When I got back to Santa Barbara the next afternoon, Inga had already set up an appointment for me to look at a rehab forty-five minutes away, in Oxnard.

WHILE I TOURED the treatment center, I began to realize that, no matter what it had going for it—success rates, famous clients, volleyball, acupuncture, mud baths—it was still a fucking rehab. At least this place looked like it would be easy to keep to myself and fall through the cracks. I also didn't fail to notice the one cute girl who seemed to be at all these rehabs. She sat by herself on the smoking patio, dressed all in black. I don't know how much she influenced my decision, but ten minutes later I was out in the parking lot hugging Jack and Inga good-bye.

SO TELL ME again how much you've been using?" the intake doctor asked me.

"Well, I was kicking for about six days, and then I've been using a bag a day for the past seven or eight," I answered.

"Great. So it shouldn't be too bad. You'll just be a little uncomfortable for a few days and be through with it."

"What do you mean? I feel terrible . . . can't sleep—" I cut myself off. My voice was going up in pitch, and I didn't want to sound too needy. This was known as "drug-seeking behavior" in the rehab world.

"Lack of sleep never killed anybody, but don't worry. We'll give you something for that. I just think that if you go cold turkey right now, it will be easier in the long run. We want to get you participating as soon as possible."

"But if I felt better, I could start participating right away, you know what I mean?" I could hear the whiny tone of my voice.

"We have found that participation is really only useful when the patient is 'present,' so the goal is to get you there as quickly as possible.

I **HID IN MY ROOM** until dinner and then sat outside smoking cigarettes. I watched people come and go, some laughing and telling jokes,
some on the brink of tears, some with a blank look of shock on their
faces. The cute girl came out and sat on the grass next to a volleyball
court, which was being used as a giant litter box by three stray cats. She
sat by herself, deep in thought about God knows what, and I sat deep in
thought about her.

She was obviously young, obviously fucked up, and, although I didn't
really trust my judgment as I was kicking dope, beautiful. I wasn't usually into blondes, but she was an exception. I sat out there and chain-
smoked until it was time to get in line for my sleeping pills.

"What's this?" I asked the nurse, curious about what looked like a
little container of pancake syrup from McDonald's.

"That's chloral hydrate. Otherwise known as a Mickey."

"A Mickey?"

"You know in those old movies when they slipped you a Mickey?"

I had always wondered what a Mickey was. If it could knock out Sam
Spade, it must be good enough for me. Except that it wasn't, and I went
to the nurses' station every hour to prove it. They said they couldn't do
anything about it unless the doctor prescribed more. I tossed and turned
all night, unless a nurse came by in the morning and took me to the psychiatrist's office.

"Good morning, Mr. Canfield. Have a seat," the psychiatrist said.

"Yeah, hi. They told me I would be meeting with you later this
week."

"This isn't an official meeting. I just need to check out something on
your chart here to figure out if you're in the right place."

"This is a rehab, right?" I asked.

"Yes, but we run another facility across the street for psychological
issues. Anyway, on your chart it says that you hear voices in your head?"

"Um. Yeah?" I said tentatively, unsure where this was heading.

"Is that a yes?"

I nodded.

"Well, that's what's got me a little concerned. Can you tell me what
these voices say?"

"Oh, you know, the regular shit," I said, figuring that a psychiatrist
working with addicts would know exactly what I was talking about. But
he shook his head and motioned for me to continue. "The normal stuff,
like, 'you're a piece of shit . . . what the fuck were you thinking . . . you're

an idiot . . . you fucked up again . . . look at you, back in another rehab . . . when are you going to get your shit together, you fucking moron . . . ' That kind of shit," I said. His intense stare was unnerving. "I thought everyone talked to themselves like that."

"Well, yeah, but my question is *who* tells you these things?"

Then I understood.

"You mean like a talking dog or something? No . . . it's just me . . . I mean, my own voice."

"Oh." He closed the folder. "Your voice? Yeah, we all have that. Sorry to bother you, I just needed to make sure. If it were a talking dog, then, yes, we'd have to send you across the street. Okay, I'll see you when you're feeling a little better."

THE ONLY ADVANTAGE to being sick was that I got to sit outside and smoke for the first four days while everyone else was in group therapy. During breaks, a few people approached me, but I wasn't very talkative and was more interested in listening to other people's conversations than having my own. I noticed, for example, that the women mostly talked about how they were going to avoid getting shitfaced at airport bars, and I listened to a group of three muscle-bound guys telling some of the crudest anal sex jokes I had ever heard in my life. They didn't even sound like jokes as much as threats, and as far as I could tell, they were straight.

The one who did most of the talking was in his late forties and had an unbelievably thick Boston accent. The other two seemed like relatively normal young kids aside from the fact that they were around six-and-half-feet tall and muscle-bound. "So this guy keeps coming into the bar just so's he can heckle me, and finally after like a month I says to him, 'Oh yeah. You think I can't score, eh? How 'bout you bend over and I take a shot at your ass, you lousy bastad. What do you say to that?' I says, getting my stick off the wall." The other guys were doubled over laughing. "When I turn around, he's gone . . . full beer just sitting on the bar. I never seen that fuck again."

I had no idea what the hell these guys were talking about, but I was scared just listening to them.

All I did was smoke and watch and listen until they told me I had to start going to the groups. The first one met at nine in the morning. All the clients sat in a circle, but none of the staff were present—I figured it was so they could get an extra hour of sleep. I was somewhat horrified when the guy from Boston, apparently in charge of the meeting, started reading from a laminated printout.

"Herro everbody. I'm brank, an I'm an alcohoric." He was slurring so bad I figured he must have been drunk or heavily medicated. I could barely understand him.

"Seth, that 'blank' is where your name is supposed to go," his friend whispered to him.

"Wha? Oh . . . thorry ith's my firsth thime. Okay . . . I'm Theth and I feer good thoday," he said, turning to his friend. Maybe he was gay after all.

"Doug. I feel good." Doug turned to the next person.

"Good morning. I'm Sandra, and I feel pretty good."

And so on down the line. Almost everybody, including me, said they felt good. There were about twenty-five of us, and I didn't really pay any attention till it came around to the cute girl, whose name was Dawn. *Goddamn, she was cute. Clearly fucked up, but shit, weren't we all?* Finally, it got back to Seth, who started reading from the printout again.

"I'm Theth an I'm . . . wai I arready read thath parth," he said, studying the sheet very closely. "Parth a the recobery prothess isth to identhify our feeringths . . . Thethus Christh!" he yelled, throwing the sheet of paper on the floor. He then reached into his mouth and, to my amazement, pulled out a whole set of teeth.

"There. Much better," he said, smiling at the group. "I'm still not used to having teeth." Little metal rods were sticking out of his gums. Nobody laughed except for his friend Doug. I think we were all in a bit of shock from the whole thing.

"Okay. So . . . blah, blah, blah . . . my name . . . blah, blah, blah . . . identify our feelings. Here we go," he said to himself. "I have asked somebody to read the 'When You . . . I Feel' page." He looked over the group, and I noticed a few groans go up around the room.

"Hi, I'm Paul, and I'm an addict," another guy said as he stood up. "An important part of the recovery process is to shift our thinking away from blame and victimization. One way of doing this is to use 'When you' and 'I feel' statements when we interact with each other. For example, instead of saying 'Mary, I can't stand it when you interrupt me,' we would say, 'Mary, when you interrupt me, I feel unimportant, and that causes me to feel angry.' Does anyone have anything they would like to bring up this morning using 'When you . . . I feel' statements?"

I shifted uncomfortably in my seat. The thought of hearing one of these statements in earnest turned my stomach. I was hoping that we would move on to whatever the next thing was when Doug said, "Yeah, I do. This is for Seth," he said, turning to face him. "Seth. When I say 'I love you' and don't get a response, I feel hurt, rejected, and that my feelings don't matter to you."

I didn't know what was going on, and judging by the uncomfortable silence in the room, neither did anyone else. I was afraid they were going to start fighting or making out. Instead they started laughing and high-fived each other.

"That was a good one, buddy. You had me scared for a minute," Seth said. "Okay everybody," he said, standing up. "We'll now close with the serenity prayer."

After holding hands and reciting the serenity prayer—which we had to do at the end of every group activity—I spotted a scrawny-looking kid who had introduced himself as Josh in the meeting. Nerd wasn't a word I often used to describe people, but this guy was the classic nerd. His shirt was tucked in, his pants were too high, and he wore glasses. He was already losing his hair, and he couldn't have been older than twenty-one. I figured he was a computer programmer. Josh was outside smoking by himself, so I asked him for a light. I felt I had to talk to someone about what just happened.

"Jesus. We have to do that every morning?" I asked him.

"Yeah, but that's the first time I've seen anyone do the 'When you . . . I feel . . . ' thing. Usually the whole meeting takes about ten minutes."

"Where'd those guys come from anyway?"

"You mean the hockey players? This place has a deal with the NHL. That guy Seth, they used to call him Fist. He was one of the most violent players ever. He brought a video of all his fights with him."

"Are you serious?"

"Yeah, it's like two hours long," he answered.

"Shit . . . now it all makes sense." I thought about the story I had heard the other night, and the thing with the teeth.

"How long you been here?"

"About a week."

"For?"

"I'm not even sure. I was told I had to disappear for a while. My boss suggested I come here, or—"

"They were going to fire you?" I finished for him.

"Well, not exactly. It's not really that kind of job."

"Oh. What do you do?" I asked, not so much out of curiosity, but because it seemed like the right thing to do.

"I do various things for the mob. Some money went missing or something, and I had to disappear. But if anyone asks, I'm here for cocaine," Josh said with a totally straight face.

"Uh-huh. So what happens next?" He seemed harmless enough, but in my opinion he should have been across the street. The guy had seen too many movies.

"Oh. Next is group therapy. Who's your counselor?"

"I don't know yet. I guess I should go find out." I put out my cigarette. "I'll see you later," I said, walking away.

G ROUP THERAPY was mostly a chance for the counselor, Bruce, to talk about himself. Invariably one of us would talk for a minute or so before Bruce would interrupt with some story that vaguely might have had some connection to something someone had said. By the end of three hours, I had learned almost nothing about the other clients but knew that Bruce had been the chief of the fire department until he got busted dealing cocaine, was shamed by the local media, went to jail, and completed treatment right here, next door to his old firehouse, where his old subordinates taunted him every day and yelled shit at him any time he went outside. According to him, even that was a blessing, as it got him to quit smoking cigarettes. Bruce also had an AA tattoo on his right foot, always reminding him to take the next right step, and he had a crack-smoking monkey trapped inside a bottle tattooed on his back. This was to remind him that if he kept the lid on the bottle, he could contain the monkey, but if he opened it, who knows what would happen? Tattoo therapy was a unique approach to sobriety, but it didn't seem worth the seventeen thousand dollars they were getting from my insurance company. If a tattoo could keep us clean, this place would be out of business.

T HAT NIGHT, DAWN, whom I still had never seen talking to anyone, approached me after the alumni meeting and asked, "Heroin?"

"What?"

"You're a junkie, right?"

"Uh, yeah. How did you guess that?"

"Me, too. I can spot them from a mile away. It's nice to have another one here. I can't stand these crackheads."

"What crackheads?" I asked.

"Sorry. I call everyone crackheads."

"Oh." I realized I wasn't being too responsive. Although I had been stealing glances at her for the past four days, I hadn't come up with a plan for actually talking to her.

"Well, nice to meet you, Oran," she said, freaking me out even more by using my name.

"You too . . . uh?" *Why was I pretending not to know her name?*

"Dawn," she said, smiling. "See you around."

I smoked two more cigarettes in a row in the hopes of combating my anxiety. It wasn't working.

L UCKILY, I HAD to do group therapy for only one day before the weekend, which, unless we had visitors, was pretty much open for us to do whatever we wanted. Josh found me after lunch and asked if I played chess.

"I'm not that good, but I'll play."

"Don't worry, I suck, too," he said.

We found a bench outside, and he beat me over and over again, but the games were close enough that I kept thinking I had a chance against him.

"You're a fucking chess shark," I accused him after he beat me five times in a row.

"No, I'm not. Honestly. I'm just lucky, I guess. One more?"

"Sure. What the fuck else am I going to do? You don't have anyone visiting today?" I looked around at the parents and spouses scattered on the lawn, all in deep conversation with their loved ones.

"Nobody knows I'm here except my boss. I couldn't even tell my parents," he answered. I was hoping he had forgotten about his little fantasy of working for the mob, or at least come up with a new one.

"Check. Motherfucker."

My competitive side got the best of me. This was the first time I had checked him all day.

"Stalemate," he said.

"What do you mean, stalemate? I got you. You can't move any-where."

"Exactly."

"So I finally won."

"No. It's a stalemate. Nobody won. It's a tie."

"A tie? But I got you trapped. There's nowhere for you to go."

"Another one?"

"Sure. Why not?" I said, setting up my pieces. "But watch out. I'm going to fuck you up this time."

Sunday was the same. Played chess all day, and to make up for lack of skill I started coming up with more and more outlandish intimidation techniques.

"You better move that fucking queen because my bishop is coming after that bitch. I'll teach her to take both my goddamn knights." I was starting to sound like the hockey players.

Josh never reacted, though. He just moved his queen and said, "I believe that's checkmate."

"Fucking son of a bitch!"

"Another?"

"Okay."

"Hey, you know that girl Dawn over there?" he asked, glancing past me. I turned around to see her sitting on the grass.

"Uh-huh?"

"I think she has a crush on me."

"On you?" I suddenly got very jealous. I couldn't concentrate on our game. "Why?"

"Why not?" he asked defensively.

I didn't want to tell him *because you're balding, and despite your claims about being in the mob, you look like a fucking computer programmer.*

"No. I mean, why do you think that?"

"Because in group the other day she said she was distracted because she kept thinking about some guy."

"But still. Why you? There's like fifteen guys here."

"Well, first . . . I'm the only guy even close to her age, and second, I think she brought it up in group because she wanted me to hear it." His logic sounded about right, and it depressed the hell out of me.

"How do you know she didn't bring it up so you would tell me?" I said, joking around.

"I don't," he said in all seriousness. "But I doubt it's you. She's only eighteen."

Jesus. How did these eighteen-year-olds end up in rehab?

"How old are you?" he asked.

"Twenty-five," I said, feeling old, too old for her at least.

"See what I mean? I'm only twenty. So who else could it be? Checkmate."

"Fucking son of a bitch!"

"One more?"

"Okay."

O N SUNDAY NIGHT they loaded all of us who weren't hanging out with our families into a van and drove us to an outside AA meeting. It was like a field trip. People even got dressed up for the occasion. I just assumed we would go to Ventura or something, but we drove to Malibu instead. We got there an hour early, and even before anyone showed up, I could tell that this wasn't going to be a normal meeting. On a picnic table outside the high school gym that held the meeting, there was a huge spread of papaya and mango, smoked salmon, at least ten kinds of cheese, prosciutto, salami, an assortment of freshly baked breads, and on and on. Josh and I lurked around the table, eating as much as we could before people started arriving.

"Wait till you see who shows up for this thing," said Dawn, joining us in our feast.

The first person to show up at the meeting drove a black BMW with tinted windows. There wasn't a single other car in the basketball court, which served as a parking lot, and still it took this guy over ten minutes to park the thing. A few of us were smoking cigarettes and critiquing this guy's parking ability when finally he turned off his car and got out wearing pajamas.

"Holy shit, that's what's-his-name," I said as the guy tried to make a straight line for the entrance. He was weaving all over the place. "Jesus, he's a fucking mess. I always forget that guy's name. Goddamn. Not Gary Busey. You know, the other actor with the low voice."

"You should have seen him last week," Dawn said. "Two guys had to help him walk. He was so cracked out. That guy should not be driving."

"I'd say he seems more drunk than cracked out," I said.

"I meant drunk. I say 'cracked out' about everything," she reminded me.

I had been to a fair amount of these meetings, but this was the first celebrity I had seen, and they didn't seem to be working too well for him either. As the time got closer to the meeting, more and more people showed up whom I recognized, or who were pointed out as being in this or that movie or rock band. Those of us who had dressed up didn't stand out too much, but I was clearly out of my element dressed in the thrift store clothes I had bought before I had lost twenty pounds from my most recent heroin-and-cocaine diet. I hadn't found any reason to shave in the last two weeks either. Rather than avoid me, though, these people, who normally would have to run down the street to escape fans and paparazzi, wouldn't leave me alone. Even that guy wearing the pajamas who had been in that movie—what was his fucking name?—went out of his way to shake my hand. I didn't like it. I got the vibe that everyone was trying to figure out who was who (I know I was), but that once they figured out I was a nobody, that would be the end of it.

"So what do you do? You play music?" some guy covered in tattoos, wearing supertight jeans and pointy boots, asked me.

"Yeah . . ." I answered, keeping it vague, hoping he didn't ask me whom I played with.

"It's hard for us musicians, always on the road. You know, I used to be fine until some hot chick would show up at the hotel with a pile of cocaine. Next thing I know, I'm in the fucking emergency room and the tour's canceled."

I nodded my head to imply that I knew what he was talking about, but the only hotel room I had stayed in on tour was somewhere in the middle of Montana where we had broken down. I had slept on the floor under the bathroom sink.

"Now it's like . . . I don't care where the fuck we are, man, but when I get that urge it's just like . . . I got to go to a meeting, plain and simple. But listen, man, I know what it's like out there, so if you ever need to talk to anyone man, call me." He wrote down his number on a piece of paper but didn't include his name. *Asshole,* I decided. Did he just take it for granted that I knew who he was?

When the meeting started, a British guy got up at the podium and, instead of telling any kind of story, he told us that a documentary had just come out about his band, and if we wanted to know how he ended up in AA we could go see the movie. *Another asshole.*

Because promoting his movie took only five minutes, another guy got up there. He must have been in his seventies.

"I'm Buddy and I'm an alcoholic," he started.

"Hi, Buddy," almost two hundred people said in unison.

"My drink of choice was methadone," he added, which got a laugh out of even me, and I tried hard not to laugh at these meetings. Humor was just another form of recruitment as far as I could tell. You start laughing at their jokes, and pretty soon you start thinking, "Hey, maybe these guys aren't so bad after all. At least they can laugh at themselves." I had good defenses against the more typical recruiting tactics, but humor was the weak spot in my armor. I had to watch out for that.

Buddy made up for the previous guy's poor storytelling. He was a jazz musician in the '50s and '60s and played with all the greats, not because he was that good a musician but because he supplied the drugs. By the time touring groups made it to California, they were often so sick that they would have traded their instruments for a shot of dope. The only thing Buddy asked for in trade was a chance to jam with them. So Buddy got to play with Charlie Parker, Coltrane, Monk . . . the list was endless. Sounded pretty good to me, except he kept finding himself in jail and had to have his heart valve replaced four times.

A T MONDAY'S PEER meeting Fist told Doug, "When you say you love me, I feel conflicted, because as much as I'd like to think I'm special, I know that you say that to all the guys."

There were a few chuckles from the group, but most of us just shook our heads or quietly groaned. It didn't stop them from laughing at their own joke and high-fiving each other again.

I DON'T KNOW how they decided whom to put in which group, but my group was made up of mostly flight attendants. I was the only straight guy aside from Bruce until a police statistician named Peter joined us after my first few weeks.

It turned out this place also had a deal with American Airlines. The flight attendants were an odd lot. Always amicable, they would never get emotional about anything. They always knew exactly when to laugh or shake their heads in disbelief when I told them my stories, but they never had much to say about themselves. While they were always "doing well," "feeling good," or "confident about their sobriety," at least once a week we lost one of them to the facility across the street.

"As some of you already know, Pamela took a whole month's worth of Zoloft last night. We're not sure when she'll be back with us," Bruce started. "Does anyone have feelings about this they want to talk about?"

I just stared at my hands, and no one else seemed to be forthcoming with any feelings.

"How about Kim? You were close to her, weren't you? How are you feeling today?"

"Hmm. It's too bad about Pam. I know she was really feeling good about this process because we talked a lot about how great we've been doing. I'm just grateful that I'm still feeling very strong right now," Kim answered. It was as if American Airlines gave their flight attendants an answer book before sending them here. Knowing the right answers hadn't kept Pam from taking a whole bottle of Zoloft.

"Okay then. Let's move on to Peter." I still felt that Bruce was something of an idiot, but at least he knew when to give up. Getting anything like an honest answer from these flight attendants was like trying to get high smoking Ivory soap, something I had done on more than one occasion.

"So, Peter, do you mind sharing with the group how you ended up here?"

Peter had just checked in the night before.

"Yes, as a matter of fact I do," he answered.

"Okay. Do you mind sharing why you have a problem with it?" Bruce tried.

"Because this is between me and my wife. That's why." He was trying so hard to sound calm, but underneath his calm composure was a rage I had never seen the likes of. Peter's skin was so red it looked like he had a sunburn.

"Can you tell us how you feel about being here, then?" Bruce asked.

"Sure, I feel ashamed."

"Good, now we're getting somewhere. Why?"

"Because I don't belong here. I'm not an alcoholic. I'm here to save my marriage. That's all."

"So can I ask how you ended up in the hospital?"

At this question Peter's skin turned something closer to purple, but his voice still didn't waver.

"You have no business bringing that up in front of other people. That is confidential information, and I will see to it that you are held accountable for this clear abuse of trust."

"Actually it's not. Anything said in this group is confidential by law, so I haven't said anything that can be repeated outside of this room."

"Well, we'll see what my lawyer has to say about that. If you'll excuse me, I'm going to check out now." He stood up to go.

"Okay. We can't stop you from leaving, but we'll have to notify your wife."

Peter paused midstep and turned back to say something. It looked as if his head were about to explode. He couldn't find whatever it was he wanted to say and, much to my relief, continued to the door.

"Okay then. Anyone have any feelings about Peter?" Bruce asked the group.

S ETH, WHEN I SEE you sneaking off with Alex, I feel jealous and confused. I thought that I was the only guy you were sleeping with," Doug said the next morning.

The collective sigh from the group was getting louder every morning as this joke continued on its downward spiral. As much as it annoyed me, I did find myself wondering how far they were going to take it.

I WAS MORBIDLY grateful to see that Peter hadn't checked out. The flight attendants were boring, and Peter actually gave me something to look forward to in group therapy.

"Okay, let's start with you, Peter. Do you want to tell the group why you're still here?" Bruce asked.

"You know damn well why I'm still here," Peter said through his clenched teeth.

"I do, but I think it would be better if you told the group."

"No. Go ahead. Tell these people the preposterous lies you have made up in order to keep me here. I checked in here voluntarily, and you have shamelessly stripped me of my rights as an American citizen, rights I fought for in the Vietnam war, by the way . . . and for your own monetary benefit no less. So go ahead, slander me in front of the group."

"Not for my monetary benefit. I make thirteen dollars an hour." Bruce brought up his wage whenever he had the chance. "Yesterday when Peter tried to check out, the doctors decided to give him a 5150. Peter, you've been on the force for, what, thirty years? You want to tell them what a 5150 is?"

"It's a law that doctors and rehabs use to hold patients against their will, as if they were common criminals. But even worse is that, unlike a common criminal, I have to pay the cost out of my own pocket. Get it? It's a dirty trick to rob me of my money and my dignity at the same time."

"And what reason did they give you for keeping you here 'against your will'?"

"Because my skin is red. Can you believe they can keep me confined here like a criminal because of the color of my skin?" It was a weird statement coming from a middle-aged white guy.

"In psychology, red skin such as yours is usually a sign of inner rage."

"It's all lies to keep me here."

"How many guns do you have at home, Peter?"

"What does that have to do with it? Are you implying . . ." Peter looked for the right words, "that I would use them? How dare you!"

"Why do you have guns at your house?"

"Because I'm a cop."

"But you sit in a cubicle doing statistics. Find much use for firearms in the office, Peter?" Bruce was trying to get a rise out of him. I couldn't tell whether he had gone too far or not far enough, but Peter refused to speak anymore.

The next weekend, instead of the visit Peter had been expecting from his wife, he was handed an envelope containing divorce papers. He wasn't at the morning meeting on Sunday, but a rumor surfaced that he had been picked up on his way back to Sebastopol and was on suicide watch across the street. If I had read the story in a newspaper, I probably would have agreed with Peter, that an evil law had victimized him so that the greedy doctors could make more money, but having seen his red skin with my own eyes, I decided the doctors had made a good call.

D AWN HAD GIVEN up her seat alone on the grass to act as spectator and cheerleader for our chess games. As much as I wanted her company, hanging out with her and Josh together brought out my jealousy, anxiety, paranoia, loneliness, and depression all at once. It was imperative that no one see this side of me, so I channeled those feelings into the increasingly competitive nature of our chess matches. Now that a girl was watching, winning was more important than anything, if not the game itself, then at least the verbal match, which was admittedly a one-sided game. Josh never responded to my insults. So when Dawn started acting as cheerleader for me, I almost started to feel bad for poor Josh. I found myself saying words I had never used before. "Fag," "pussy," "homo," and even "nerd" became a regular part of my vocabulary. I didn't like who I was becoming, but Dawn didn't seem to mind.

"It's hilarious when you call Josh a fag," Dawn said during an after-dinner cigarette one night.

"Why? I'm actually starting to feel bad about it."

"Because he is a little fag."

"I called him a *little* fag? Shit. I've got to calm down. I'm starting to sound like the hockey players."

"It's true, though, he has to be gay," she said.

I didn't know or care, but his interest in Dawn seemed genuine enough.

"Don't you think that's a bit mean? And besides, I thought you had a thing for him," I said.

"You have got to be kidding me. Where'd you hear that?" she asked.

"You know. I hear things," I answered.

"Now I get it. That little homo thought I was talking about him in group. No wonder he started acting different after that."

"You weren't talking about him?"

"Are you kidding? He repulses me. Besides being gay, he's balding, and he's a liar. Can you imagine him in the mob? Where did he come up with that? His parents must have caught him smoking pot while he was playing Dungeons and Dragons or something."

"Jesus. That's harsh. I kind of like him, though." I liked him even more now that Dawn said she didn't like him. As far as I could tell, I was the only one still in the running.

"So if it wasn't Josh, who were you talking about?" I asked.

"I thought it was obvious, but I made a deal with my counselor that I wasn't going to bring it up again until I was out of treatment. By the way, when are they releasing you? Soon, right?"

"I got another week."

"What are you doing when you get out of here?"

"Shit, I don't know. I'll probably go to L.A. or something. Can't go back to San Francisco, and Santa Barbara fucking bums me out."

"You should go into sober living," she said. Sober living here was like a munchkin version of those enclosed communities that were popping up everywhere—the ones where there are four models of houses to choose from, all painted the same color (they even come with silverware and monogrammed towels). It reminded me of the Village in that BBC show *The Prisoner*. It was separated from the rehab by the horseshoe court, a game Josh and I had started playing to supplement chess. At least we both sucked at throwing horseshoes. All the sober-living people ate their meals in the cafeteria, but I could never figure out how they spent the rest of their time. We were in fucking Oxnard. I couldn't see myself staying sane here, and I was itching to get back to playing music and living my life.

"It's just so depressing out here. What would I do?"

"I don't know. Hang out with me and go to meetings."

"Ugh . . . I mean, not the-hanging-out-with-you part . . . but the meetings . . . fuck, it's depressing."

"Well, if you go to L.A., you'll never find out who I have a crush on."

I DIDN'T TELL Josh about my conversation with Dawn during our lunch match the next day, but since he was no longer competition in the other game, I decided to tone down my insults. They didn't help anyway, at least not when it came to playing chess.

Josh was wearing a backpack, which struck me as out of place considering our rooms were twenty feet away. Whatever he was carrying around looked heavy.

"You planning a trip or something? What's with the backpack?"

"Oh, this?" he said, as if he had just noticed it himself. "It's full of rocks." He went silent as he studied the board.

I thought about it for a minute and decided he hadn't given me nearly enough information.

"What the hell are you talking about . . . rocks?"

"Big, heavy rocks. I have to wear it everywhere I go until I start telling the truth. The rocks represent lies, and each time I'm honest they take a rock out of the bag so I can see how life is a lot easier without the weight of my dishonesty."

As usual there wasn't even a hint of cynicism, irony, animosity, victimization, or even any resistance in his voice. I would have been overwhelmed with all those feelings, whether I was carrying around the weight of dishonesty or not.

"Uh . . . so judging by the size of that bag, I take it you're still a bigwig in the mob?"

"I was never a bigwig. Mostly I just drive a car around."

"For the mob . . ." I added, just to make sure he wasn't talking about driving his mom around on errands.

"Yup."

"So what are you going to do about the rocks?"

"I don't know. It's a catch-22. I'll keep telling the truth for now, but if this thing starts hurting my back too much, I may have to pretend to be honest in order get rid the of the rocks, which kind of sends a weird message to myself. It's a strange predicament." He seemed to be approaching it in the same way he approached chess.

"Listen, man. I don't mean to sound like I don't believe your story about working for the Mafia, but I don't. None of us do. If I were you, I would start telling the truth. Not the one you've made up about the mob, but the other one, where your mom caught you smoking banana peels in the basement or whatever it was that actually happened. You're never going to get out of here otherwise. They'll send you across the street . . ."

"We'll see. But I actually kind of like it here. I really don't want to go back to that job anyway," he responded.

There were only two explanations for not minding this place. The first was that Josh lived with his mother and didn't have any friends. The second was Dawn. I had noticed that since yesterday I didn't seem to mind the place that much either.

D OUG. WHEN I had you tied up against the tree last night, I felt frustrated when you clenched your ass muscles and I had to resort to forceful penetration. If you would just relax, it would be easier for both of us."

With hardly any transition, the hockey players' little joke had gone from PG-13 to XXX. One of the flight attendants got up and left the peer group in disgust, and a number of other women followed her.

"Shit. You think I took it too far?" I overheard Seth ask Doug as I was walking out.

Group therapy turned into a three-hour grievance session with the flight attendants bitching about the hockey players.

"They must be stopped. This is supposed to be a supportive and nurturing environment, and this no longer feels like a safe place to talk openly and honestly about my feelings," Kim said. As usual I kept my observations to myself, but this was the first time in three weeks Kim had been open and honest about anything.

"I felt as though I was back in high school. Those are the same guys that used to beat me up and call me a fag. Coming out was probably the hardest thing I've ever done, and this morning I just felt like crawling right back into the closet. I won't feel safe as long as those guys are still here," said John, one of the few male flight attendants.

"John, since you brought it up, why don't you tell us a little bit about high school?" Bruce asked.

"Absolutely not. I said good-bye to that when I was eighteen. There is no reason to revisit that nightmare. I'm here to move on with my life, not relive the past."

"But those feelings are what drive us to drink and—"

"No way, man. I'm here to look toward the future."

Bruce gave up and turned his attention to me.

"Oran, have you decided what you are going to do when you finish here? You're leaving in what? Five more days?"

"Yeah. I was thinking I would go into sober living."

"Really? I'm a little surprised by that, but I think I have a good idea why."

"I have come to terms with the fact that I haven't had any luck out there on my own. I think I need more, uh . . . transition this time."

"Uh-huh. Good . . . very good," he said in a tone that meant he wasn't buying a word of it. "Has anyone told you, by the way, that relationships, aside from practically guaranteeing relapse, are strictly forbidden in sober living?"

"I have no idea what you're talking about, but for three weeks everyone has been urging me to go into sober living. Now that I have a greater understanding of the disease," I said, having learned a thing or two from the flight attendants, . . . "I have reluctantly accepted that it's probably the right thing to do, and now you're telling me . . . Actually, I have no idea what you're telling me, unless you know something I don't. But if you think I would be better off going to L.A., then fine . . ." I threw up my hands in the hopes of conveying the rest of my sentence with body language: *I'll go and relapse and it will be all your fault.*

He stared at me wide-eyed for a few moments and said, "Okay, I'll see you guys tomorrow," but he didn't seem too happy about it. We were a tough fucking crowd.

THE NIGHT OF my release, Dawn and I went to the beach and made out for a few hours. It was gray out, but not the bland monotone gray I had become accustomed to in Oxnard. Dark black clouds sped by overhead, threatening to open up on us, and the wind was blowing sand everywhere. I should have been psyched to be making out with a beautiful girl on the beach in Southern California, but I couldn't tell if the weather was the cause or just a reflection of the ominous feeling I had about the whole thing. *What was I doing here?* Aside from a handful of thrift stores, Oxnard had nothing to offer. There was no music, no culture, and there didn't seem to be any jobs. Dawn wasn't interested in talking, though, so I kept my thoughts to myself. Even while we were making out on the sand, I found myself wondering how long our romance would last before I went stir-crazy.

Dawn and I had to keep our make-out sessions under wraps, and having sex would have been difficult but possible if Dawn had been willing. I had all sorts of creative ideas to work around the rules, but whenever it got to that point, she flat-out refused.

"What's up? What's the problem?" I asked almost daily.

"I'm sorry, I can't. I'm not ready yet."

At eighteen, Dawn had already been through rehab four times, twice for bulimia and once for alcohol, and this time she was in for heroin. Apart from that, I didn't know much about her except that she was a third-degree black belt in karate, her mom worked for a porn magazine, and her refusal to have sex with me was the result of a childhood trauma she was unwilling to discuss. I'd never experienced anything close to this level of sexual frustration, but whenever I brought up the subject of leaving, she would start making out with me and tell me that she would be ready soon.

"I just have to work some stuff out," she said.

SURPRISINGLY, THE ONLY thing saving me from going crazy in Oxnard was a daily 10:00 A.M. AA meeting. Not only did it fulfill my daily meeting requirement from the rehab, but I actually began looking forward to it. I could smoke in it, and I was totally fascinated by the characters who showed up. They were all probably at one time the sorts of people who went around wearing tucked-in shirts and slacks and called themselves consultants, but they'd dropped out of the system even more than I had. None of them were employed, and most of their stories seemed to take place in a nearby trailer park. At first glance, I would have put them in the white trash category and left it at that, but after listening to them, my opinion began to change. Considering their circumstances, they seemed to have a sense of gratitude I would have never thought possible.

"I thought I knew all about desperation until I went to India a few years ago . . . which is why, even though the welfare people are pissing me off with their fucking bullshit, I can still be grateful they haven't thrown me out of my trailer yet. I guess if they do, though, it means I'm not supposed to have a trailer," an older guy said one day. This was the first time I had seen the spiritual tools of sobriety used to not only justify defeat, but seemingly contribute to it. This guy was not going to get a job, *period,* and that being an absolute truth, he didn't seem to mind one bit that he was one step away from being homeless, as a few of the others seemed to be.

"But you know, it's funny. When I was drinking and smoking crack, I had the house, the car, and the career. Shit . . . I even had the wife and the girlfriend at the same time, but I was a miserable piece of shit. I lost all that stuff in sobriety, and I wouldn't trade what I have now to get any of that back."

He was wearing a grayish sweat suit, which had been white once, and I actually believed him . . . that he was happier now. I wasn't sure why, but I did—maybe because he wasn't trying to sell me anything. Not one thing seemed good about his life, yet he appeared to be happier than me. I didn't even know what the welfare office had done to him, but I think I was more pissed off about it than he was.

I never joined in or felt as though I was one of them. It was more like I had become caught up in the drama of a really good TV show and would show up every morning at ten to catch the next episode. While I genuinely liked the characters, I wasn't about to move into the trailer park with them. In the meantime, I had been talking to a few friends who were living in L.A. After three months of unsuccessfully trying to get Dawn to sleep with me, L.A. started sounding like a better option.

twenty-three

In which a no-handed woman learns to
juggle, and a son halfheartedly bats a pillow

I WAS FINISHING UP my junior year in Arizona, discussing with my mom what I was going to do over summer vacation, when she told me that Jack was going to be doing one of his seminars in L.A. and suggested that I could work for him.

"Doing what?" I asked. "Showing his clients what a great job he did on me? Jesus, I don't think I can handle that scene."

"Well, you have to come up with something, and he said he'd give you his old car if you can figure out a way to pick it up. If not, he's going to donate it to charity." I wasn't yet old enough to drive, but I would be sixteen by the time school ended. I did want the car. Badly. I just wasn't sure if I could handle seeing the self-help guru in his own element for a week straight.

"I'll think about it," I said.

"Really? You mean you don't want the car?"

"Okay! I'll give him a fucking call!"

With Mom I always had to have a plan, always had to be doing something. Simply spending my summer at home was out of the question, which was probably part of the reason I liked high school so much. No matter what I did, be it silk-screening huge penises on the girls' volleyball team uniforms or getting into screaming matches with my English teacher about why I thought *On the Road* was the worst book I had ever read, the faculty were all pretty supportive of my efforts to stir things up. Our new headmaster, however, didn't turn out to be a whole lot better than the old one, Bill. Hardly a week went by when I wasn't called into his office for something, but there wasn't much he could do.

"What were you thinking, printing penises on the volleyball uniforms?" the headmaster asked me after a game against our rival school.

"Why? Is there a rule against it?" I asked, using my stock response anytime he called me in.

"What am I supposed to do? Make a rule that you can't put penises on the team uniforms? Then you would probably print a pair of breasts on them."

"That's a pretty good idea." I pretended to contemplate it.

"Come on, man. Work with me. I can't start making up new rules every time you come up with some 'art project.' Just tell me you won't do it again."

"Fine. I won't print any more penises on the volleyball jerseys," I said, standing up.

He wasn't done, though.

"And for God's sakes, would you please get rid of that mustache?"

"Why?" I asked, trying to keep a straight face. I had been waiting a whole week for him to bring it up.

"Don't give me that. What am I going to say if a Jewish family comes here with a prospective student and they see you walking around with that thing on your face? Seriously. Try to put yourself in my position," he pleaded.

"Why would anyone care about a Charlie Chaplin mustache?"

"Very funny," he said sarcastically. "In that case, either start wearing a bowler hat or get rid of it!"

JACK WAS OPEN to the idea of letting me work at the seminar until I brought up money.

"What do you mean, 'how much can I pay you?' I'm giving you a car, for Christ's sake."

"Well, how am I going to get the car back to Berkeley if I don't have any gas money?"

"Okay," he said with a sigh. "How much would you need to get back home?"

"How's three hundred bucks?"

"Three hundred for gas? You've got to be out of your mind."

"No. Three hundred for a week's work. I need the money to visit my friend in San Diego afterward."

"Sheeze! Okay," he said, giving up.

Waiting for Jack at the L.A. airport was like showing up on the first day of a new job after completely lying on the job application. The last time I had seen him I was cranky and coming down from my first acid trip. So, in an effort to make a better impression and fit in with the self-help fanatics, I was wearing a nice button-down shirt, Gap jeans, and a pair of white Reeboks. I had also managed to cultivate a pretty impressive beard for a sixteen-year-old, and I wasn't about to shave it off, even though I had heard him say beards were just another way of hiding from the world. (He had a foot-long one for seventeen years himself, so he was an expert.)

As he pulled up to the curb, I threw the Pall Mall I had been smoking into the gutter and prepared myself for one of his hugs—firm but not uncomfortable, and long but not awkward. If I were into hugs, I'm certain he'd get a ten, but I had always disdained most physical contact. For me, it was just a father-son formality, no different from getting my cheek pinched every time I saw my grandmother.

"Hello, number one son," he said, getting out of the car. I put down my bag and spread my arms for the inevitable hug.

I knew this guy was my dad, but his life of khakis, tucked-in shirts, and self-improvement was much more foreign to me than that of the Mexicans, Central Americans, and Hopis I had spent time with on my field trips—usually poor working people who were trying to just survive. How could anyone with an extra two thousand dollars for a self-help seminar have any real problems? I started having major doubts about whether I was really up to the task of spending a week straight with Jack, when he finally let go of me and we got into his new minivan.

Jack's house in West L.A. was like the set from a TV family. He made the money, while his second wife, Georgia, stayed home all day, cleaned the house, and cooked dinner. They even had the white picket fence. Georgia was always extremely quiet around me. I assumed it was because she felt guilty about stealing Jack from Kyle and me, but maybe she just didn't have anything to say. Spending time at the house just made me nervous and tongue-tied, and I didn't have much to say to them either. I felt so out of place that, when we weren't at the seminar, I drove around L.A. in the Honda looking for record stores, or sat in cafés and drew. Anything not to have to hang out at that house.

Far more unnerving, though, was the seminar itself, which was simultaneously exactly what I expected and scarier than I could imagine. Other than sitting next to strangers on airplanes, I had never really interacted with nicely dressed, normal-looking people, people who had job titles like "consultant," "analyst," and "facilitator." Jobs that sounded so vague that I quickly learned not to ask about them. Even when they gave me a full description, I still couldn't figure out what the hell they did. Of course, the ones at the seminar only looked normal. Underneath the khakis and pastel sweaters, they were seething with self-hatred and memories of fucked-up childhoods. Luckily this was offset by the anticipation that in the next seven days, they were going to work through these traumas and become the perfect beings God intended them to be. They were ready to take back their lives!

The whole thing started with Jack getting onstage and saying, "Okay! Before we do anything, I want to know: Who out there wants a round of applause?" He seemed to catch everyone off guard with that one, because nobody made a move. "Who feels like coming up on stage and getting a round of applause? You're probably saying to yourself, 'I don't deserve a round of applause, I didn't do anything . . . ' But you did do something! You got up today, and took time out of your busy schedules to come here, do some hard work, and improve your lives. If that doesn't deserve a round of applause, I don't know what does! So I'll ask again, who wants a round of applause?"

Very timidly a few people got up and walked to the stage.

"Okay, everyone! Let's really hear it for these folks! They made a decision to turn their lives around. In fact, I think they deserve a standing ovation, don't you?"

It freaked me out see Jack up there striding around the stage, gaining momentum. The last thing I wanted to do was take part in this, but since everyone else was standing up, I felt I had to do the same.

"Who else wants to come up here? You all deserve it . . ." He was relentless. As more and more people started lining up to take the stage, the crowd really started getting into it, even throwing in a few whistles and yells. The more courageous participants did a pirouette or bowed. I was way in the back of the room, but I tried to get a good look at the people onstage so I knew whom to stay away from. As creepy as it all was, I couldn't have asked for a more amazing introduction to the world of self-help. But I was determined to keep my distance, especially from the more zealous types.

Even though I was supposedly there to work, I couldn't find anything to do. The rest of the staff seemed to have everything under control. Officially I was here to teach juggling, but that was a two-hour job. I figured that, in the meantime, I would help out in other areas, but no one seemed to need anything. When the staff kept telling me, "Don't worry about it. Just join in for now," a sense of doom started to set in. I began wondering whether there wasn't more to my being here than I was aware.

Right off the bat, a few of Jack's employees came up to me and said, "Oh, it's so great that you're able to be here for this," before someone else cut in with, "You're so lucky to have Jack as a father. He's such an inspiration, and I can't begin to tell you how much he's helped me. This is going to be an amazing experience for you." I couldn't grasp what was so wonderful about my being here if they didn't have anything for me to do.

One of the staff members, Bob, decided he could relate to me because he'd had a hard life and knew what I was going through. He would say "dude" and "man" a lot, and even throw in some swear words now and again just to let me know I could be comfortable talking to him.

For years, Bob had been a fucked-up speed-freak truck driver, until he met Jack, who essentially saved his life by showing him that he could be more than that. I grew to kind of like Bob when he started telling me some of his trucker stories.

"Man, I would be so high on speed that I would decide not to stop the truck at any cost."

"How did you go to the bathroom?" I asked.

"Well, what I would do was I would piss into a Ziploc bag and throw it out the window. It would get all over me, but I didn't care. I didn't care about anything, man."

I HAD NO CHOICE but to pretend I was taking part, until the time finally came for me to teach the three hundred participants how to juggle. The idea was that if you could learn to juggle, you could do anything you set your mind to. I could juggle seven balls, five clubs, torches, and machetes and ride a unicycle, and I hadn't even managed to lose my virginity. Was I the only one who saw a hole in this theory? What I really wanted to do was tell everyone that they would still be lonely, insecure, unattractive underachievers who knew how to juggle.

Jack called me onstage and gave me a lengthy introduction. "So now, I want you all to meet my eldest son, Oran. At sixteen years old he has already lived all over the world, been in the circus, won a juggling championship, and was just voted student body president of his high school. His juggling has taken him all over the country, and as a result he has a huge 'comfort zone,'" he said. "That means Oran can go anywhere, feel comfortable, and fit right in."

His introduction got big applause, but he couldn't have been more wrong. Looking out at this sea of three hundred people staring at me, I wanted nothing more than to leave and get back to my real comfort zone, the seven-by-ten-foot room on my mom's porch. There was no way out, though. The staff was handing out nine hundred juggling balls, and it was time to do my thing. *Learn to juggle and you can do anything,* I said to myself.

I started off by showing everyone how to throw one ball back and forth, back and forth. As soon as I gave them the go-ahead, the melee began. Balls were flying everywhere, and just as many people were running around trying to catch them, pick them up, or find them in all the confusion.

Braving this mess, I went out into the audience to give tips and correct technique. "You're doing good, but try to keep the ball a little closer to you so you don't have to run after it," or, "Your right-hand toss looks good, but you have to practice throwing from your left hand as well."

Then it was time for two balls.

"Okay, so now when the first ball is just going over its arc, we release the second ball and catch the first ball in the second hand, and the second ball in the first. Everybody got that?"

Six hundred balls flew into the air, and landed all over the place.

It had taken me a week to learn how to juggle, but since I only had a couple hours to teach these people that they could do anything, it was soon time for three balls, whether they were ready or not. Of course most of them were not. After giving a little speech about adding the third ball in order to create a continuous cascade, I went back down amid nine hundred flying juggling balls to give people pointers.

That's when I came across Amanda. She was a burn victim who'd had over 80 percent of her body reconstructed. I felt terrible for her; so much of her face had been grafted that she was truly frightening to look at. She was missing all but her thumb and forefinger on one hand and had only a middle finger on the other. She was completely absorbed in throwing one ball in the air and attempting to bounce it off the hand with one finger and back into the other hand. Seeing what was obviously a lost cause, I tried to get away from her. But she had other plans. She made a beeline straight toward me, demanding to know why she couldn't even juggle just one ball.

I was surprised that she hadn't already figured that out for herself. I hate being the bearer of bad news, so rather than tell her it was because she didn't have hands, I played along and agreed to help her. I felt so guilty about my repulsion toward this woman, who after all was still a human being with feelings like the rest of us, that I was determined to treat her just like anyone else. We spent the next hour, just Amanda and me, attempting to figure out how she might learn to juggle without mentioning or even alluding to her obvious handicap.

It was particularly difficult because she kept asking me, "Why can't I do this? I don't understand why I can't do this."

Christ, what was I supposed to say? Lying seemed like the easiest way out at the time, so taking a cue from my dad, I said, "Sure you can do it. Anyone can. It just takes a little confidence, that's all . . ."

We were getting to the end of our two hours, and I hadn't been able to help anyone else. Jack and one other staff member who knew how to juggle were helping as much as they could, but it wasn't going well. The conference hall was a mess of flying balls and people chasing after them. I didn't know what to do with Amanda. The truth—as uncomfortable as it was—would have gotten me away from this woman, but I couldn't find the courage to tell her. There seemed to be only one way out of this mess. It was going to take all my strength, but Amanda was going to juggle. Facing her, I grabbed on to what was left of her hands. With some effort, we eventually managed to throw the ball back and forth a few times. I held on to her stumps and caught the ball with my fingers wrapped around them. Then together, we made a jerky upward motion to get the ball back to the other hand.

"See? That was great. I told you you could do it!" I felt terrible about lying to this poor woman, but that's what this seminar seemed to be all about: give them some false self-confidence for a week and they'll be sure to come back. I had timed it up perfectly with the end of the exercise, so she couldn't try again on her own, but my hour with Amanda left at least 70 percent of the room still struggling with two balls. The real lesson that day was that *anything* might be a bit out of reach.

I continued to give people pointers on how to juggle as the seminar went on, but mostly I was expected to participate in the workshop and work on my "issues." As far as I could tell, my only issue at the time was that I was being forced to participate in the seminar. I pretended to go along with it by coming up with variations on the writing exercises, or drawing in the workbook to make it look as if I were taking part.

It was easy to fake my way through until we started doing group exercises.

Jack would say, "I want you all to turn to the person on your right and tell them, 'I love you. You're an amazing person.'" Or we would get in a group of six people and he would say, "Now I want you to go around the circle and tell everyone one thing you find special about them. We are so used to people at work telling us what we did wrong, or our spouses and parents telling us, 'if only you were more like so and so . . .' We've heard this so much throughout our lives that we start to believe these things about ourselves . . . that we're ugly, or can't do anything right. This exercise can help us realize that we're all beautiful."

Even with all my acting classes, auditions, and performance experience, this was a stretch. Although I didn't know anything about these people, I managed to compliment Sherry from Reseda on her nice earrings and tell Frank from Occidental what a great smile he had.

The group activities always ended with a hug and a long meaningful look into your exercise partner's eyes. I wasn't into hugs or looking into people's eyes and discovered that the only thing creepier than a fifty-year-old "consultant" telling you he loves you just the way you are is saying, "I love you, too," followed by a hug and thirty seconds of uninterrupted eye contact. I tried to fool them by gazing deeply past their heads or focusing on their mouths, but it didn't help much. I started making myself scarce by sneaking out back of the hotel for a cigarette every time I thought a new group exercise was coming up.

It was during one of these cigarette breaks that Bob, the staff member who could "relate" to me, found me hiding out by the Dumpsters and said it was really important that I come back in. Something special was about to happen. I had a very bad premonition about this.

When I walked back into the conference hall, the staff members were busy passing out hundreds of Wiffleball bats. I had heard of this exercise before. You get a pillow or pad that you designate as your mom, dad, husband, wife, girlfriend, or whomever—and then you proceed to beat the shit out of it with the bat. Rather than Wiffleball bats, my mom had a pair of red Styrofoam clubs called "boffers," which she kept around her office for couples therapy. She didn't see the value of beating up a pillow when you could take your aggression straight to the source. She tried it with Kyle and me a few times when she caught us fighting, but it always ended up with Kyle dropping the boffer and going for the nearest chair or lamp. I don't know how it worked out for her married clients, but we weren't interested in safe-alternative fighting, we wanted to fucking kill each other.

What I wasn't expecting was all the screaming and yelling that was

involved in this exercise: a cacophony of rage. I guess to be truly effective you have to call your mom a fucking bitch for not giving you enough
love or your dad an asshole for telling you you wouldn't amount to shit, all
at the top of your lungs. I hadn't been scared like this since I first heard
people speaking in tongues at the born-again Christian church I had
gone to as a kid. I couldn't help but think about the similarities because,
just as with that experience, I knew that I was expected to take part.
They wanted me to beat the shit out of a pillow, but the real culprit was
right here in the room.

"I know this seems weird, but you obviously have a lot of anger
toward me, and you have every right to be pissed off, but you need to do
this in order to release some of that anger, and move on with your life,"
Jack came over to tell me.

Before he decided to coach me on beating up his stand-in, I mostly
just felt uncomfortable and annoyed by the whole thing. Now I was
pissed. It was as if he were telling me it was my responsibility to get over
the fact that he was a shitty dad. That all I needed to do was hit the pillow and he would be off the hook. I got the sense that, in between outbursts, people were glancing in my direction to see what would happen
when I released my anger toward my dad and cleared the air of my resentment and bad feelings. Reluctantly, and with the most pained expression
I could muster, I hit the pillow halfheartedly and, imitating the shouts I
heard coming from all over the room, muttered, "I hate you, Jack. I hate
you, Jack." I was only able to keep it up for about thirty seconds before I
put down the bat and walked out for another cigarette. I couldn't do it
anymore.

The final event at the seminar had to do with a book Jack was selling.
It hadn't yet been written, and they hadn't found a publisher, but it had
a title. It was going to be called *Chicken Soup for the Soul* and would cost
about twelve dollars in the store, but as a seminar special, you could pre-
order one now for ten. It blew my mind when people started lining up to
hand over money for an unwritten, unpublished book that, as far as I
could tell, wasn't even *about* anything.

A WEEK AT THE Culver City Marriott surrounded by hundreds of
self-help freaks had been tough, but it was the Wiffleball bat exercise that finally pushed me over the edge. I was proud of myself for keeping my feelings locked deep inside for as long as I had, but maybe all the
talk of letting them out finally had some effect on me. Eating lunch at

the Sizzler next door to the hotel, I could no longer control myself. For the first time since this workshop began, I found myself alone with my dad. The rest of the participants were all feeling so happy and full of self-worth that they were all exchanging phone numbers and making plans to consult and facilitate with one another in the future.

Finally getting him alone, I proceeded to very calmly tell him what I thought of his profession as a self-help guru.

"Jack," I started—as far as I could remember I had never called him Dad—"you know that this stuff doesn't actually help anyone, right? Obviously these people are so lonely and desperate that they're willing to pay any price to have someone to fix them. Sure, they're all out there exchanging numbers, having a great time with all their new best friends right now, but tomorrow they have to go back to their shitty little lives. What happens when you're not around to tell them how great they are? Before you know it, they're going to be right back where they were. Lonely and miserable."

Jack seemed to be listening, but he didn't respond. He just nodded his head, so I went on and explained how the self-help industry was like a drug, and that he was essentially a drug dealer peddling temporary relief from a permanent problem.

"For twenty-five hundred dollars, you provide these people with a temporary escape from the pain of being human. All they have to do is give you some money, and they've got three hundred people telling them how great they are, how beautiful they are, giving them standing ovations for no reason . . . *you can do anything* . . . Of course they feel good for a minute! But once they leave this hotel, it's not like that. It's back to their bosses yelling at them, their wives nagging them, until they can't take it anymore and it's time for another seminar. I don't see how that's any different from being a drug dealer."

I went on like this for ten more minutes, eliciting only a few more understanding nods from Jack. I was so sure of myself, I half-expected him to tell me how smart I was for figuring him out.

Without a trace of hurt feelings, he said, "I'm sorry you feel that way," and finished his lunch.

twenty-four

*Shows the disastrous consequences of a
walk to the store*

THE PLAN AFTER leaving Oxnard was to move to L.A., but without any money, credit, or job, finding a place to live was not easy. I made a home base out of my dad's house and couch surfed in L.A., staying mostly with my friend Claudia while I looked for my own place. I also started reconnecting with some other friends of mine who had moved down to L.A. from the Bay Area. We would usually meet up at some bar or another, and having managed to stay sober for almost three months, I decided it was now safe to start drinking again. In a stroke of luck, I ran into a guy whose band, The 400 Blows, I had recorded in my old basement, and he told me about a girl he knew who was looking for someone to help out at her performance space in exchange for a room.

"How much is the rent?" I asked him.

"Free, I think. She just wants someone to help out getting the place set up. I told her about your old space on Mission Street, and she said it sounded perfect." It sounded too good to be true, and I called the number he gave me to find out for myself.

The place was a gigantic first-floor storefront in the heart of downtown. I was surprised to see a thriving urban environment in L.A. I had thought the whole city was an endless one-dimensional sprawl. It was almost as if someone had taken a piece of Manhattan and plopped it down somewhere in Mexico.

The girl's name was Emily. I didn't get a very good read on her in the ten minutes it took before she told me I could move in. The space was amazing, and my room was already built. It seemed that she was dedicated to turning the place into something of a creative hub for the growing "downtown scene," but something gave me the impression that it was not going to be as perfect as it sounded.

I moved in and Emily quickly put me to work building walls, hanging lights, and fixing the floors. I didn't mind, and it helped keep my mind off dope. What had started out as having a few drinks at bars a couple nights a week eventually became more than a few every night, and I was starting to wake up with bad hangovers. It bothered me because I knew I wasn't an alcoholic and that I didn't even like drinking that much, but it kept getting worse.

And then I found myself drinking in the morning. I didn't give it much thought because it would have really bummed me out. It got hard to ignore, though, when this guy Mark, who did all the electrical work on the space, told me he was going to a noon meeting and that I should go with him.

"Oh yeah? What kind of meeting?" I asked. I was bracing the twenty-foot ladder he was standing on with one hand and holding a Tecate in the other.

"An AA meeting. I think you should come with me," he said.

"You mean today? Now? No. I'm not really into that stuff. Thanks, but I got to get these other lights up before tonight," I said.

He climbed down the ladder and tried again. "Dude. It's only for an hour. I think you should check it out."

"It's funny you brought it up. I've actually been before, but my thing was heroin. I'm really not much of a drinker," I said, self-consciously holding the now-empty beer can at eleven thirty in the morning. "But thanks, man. I'll totally let you know if I change my mind."

"Okay. I'll see you in a few hours, then."

A SIDE FROM DRINKING a little too early in the morning, things were going okay. I had managed to join two bands in the short amount of time I had been there, was sort of seeing a girl I had met through living at the space, and still hadn't shot heroin or smoked crack. It all looked good on paper. In reality, though, I didn't like any of the music I was playing, the girl I was sort of seeing thought she could save me, and my hangovers were getting really bad. I did my best not to dwell on the negatives, taking solace in the idea that appearing to do well was all that really mattered. I had never in my life managed anything better than that.

At least my friends back in San Francisco were talking to me again. My birthday was coming up, and I had managed to book a show for the Roofies, on a bill with the two other bands I was in. I couldn't think of a better present or symbolic return to real life than playing with my friends on my twenty-sixth birthday.

But, on my way to buy a sandwich one afternoon, a guy asked me if I was "looking," and I instinctively reached into my pocket and handed him forty bucks. I didn't even know what the fuck he was selling or why he had never asked me on any of my other countless trips to the deli. He spit eight little white things out of his mouth. I pocketed them and went to a liquor store to buy a pipe and a Brillo pad before turning around and going straight home. I had lost my appetite.

The next morning I woke up with the crack pipe still hanging out of my mouth and saw a ten-year-old kid standing by my bed holding out a glass of water to me. I had no idea who he was, or why he was in my room, but what really bothered me the most was that he seemed to know exactly what I needed—as if this wasn't the first time he had seen some-one wake up with a crack pipe in his mouth. I grabbed the pipe, but it had stuck to my lips, and some of my skin came off with it. I couldn't make sense of how sad the whole scene was. It was too sad for me to even cry about. Instead, it caused an almost infinite feeling of emptiness inside me. I reached out and took the water.

"Thanks." I handed the glass back. I still wasn't ready to ask him who he was or why he was there.

"You want another one?" he asked.

I nodded to him and made an attempt to sit upright before he came back. I had passed out leaning against the wall at a weird angle, and my neck was all fucked up, not to mention how crappy I felt from having been seen by this kid.

"What's your name, buddy?" I asked him when he came back.

"I'm Brian," he said.

"Ah. I've heard a lot about you. I'm Oran," I said, reaching out to shake his hand. He was Emily's son, whom she talked about all the time but I had never met. Brian lived with what Emily claimed was his "speed-freak" dad out in Venice Beach or something. Listening to her bitch about her ex-husband always kind of reminded me of my mom going on about Jack. I usually just tuned it out, but it didn't seem like a good sign to me that he was so comfortable hanging around in the room of some crack smoker he had never even met.

I didn't know what to do about any of it. It was too big for me to make any sense of. More immediately, I wasn't sure if Emily knew what had happened or whether I even still had a room here.

"Mom gave me this so we could go get some ice cream," Brian said, pulling some money out of his pocket. Again I didn't know what to do. I felt like a monster who shouldn't be eating ice cream with kids. I even felt guilty about trying to make a good impression on him—it didn't seem like a good idea for him to like me after what he'd seen. He reminded me of myself at that age, as if he'd been through too much shit for such a young kid. I didn't know what I could do to help, but I decided to just go with it. After all, Brian was the one buying *me* ice cream. It was a sad state of affairs.

Two days later, the same shit happened, but this time Emily woke me up holding a glass of water. Again, I took the pipe out of my mouth, taking some more of my lip with it, and drank the water that she offered me.

"I don't want this to sound like I'm kicking you out, but Nora across the street is subletting her place. It's two hundred bucks a month, and I think you should take it," she said.

I nodded.

"Is that a yes? If that nod means yes, I can go upstairs and call her right now," she said.

"Yes," I croaked, and she turned around and left.

A FTER MOVING ACROSS the street, I went downhill quicker than ever. The crack dealer told me that the heroin guys were only two blocks away, and within a few days I was covering all the windows of Nora's converted office space with cardboard and duct tape and ripping out a fair amount of the drywall looking for electronic devices that the cops were using to spy on me. Crossing a new line, I shaved most of my body hair off to get rid of the imaginary bugs that were crawling all over me. It was so goddamned unoriginal, yet I couldn't stop thinking about them and scratching at myself.

That's what I was doing while I was supposed to be playing at that show I had set up down the street. The whole point was to prove to my friends, some of whom had driven down from San Francisco, how well I was doing at my big birthday party. My phone was ringing off the hook, and I could hear my friend Dave yelling up at me from the sidewalk. Turning off my phone and hiding in my apartment with the lights off, I cried, smoked more crack, shot more heroin, and thought about my friends who were only three blocks away. As the days went by, the phone rang less, and Dave's attempts at visiting me became more infrequent. Every once in a while I listened to the messages Jack left every day telling me he didn't care what I was doing, just that I needed to call him, and that he would come and get me.

When I ran out of money, I got my head together enough to get in my van and head back to Jack's house. On my way, though, I passed a Guitar Center and realized I could get a few more days out of this run if I sold my drum set. I had needed more drugs countless times before, but selling my drums had never been an option. When the salesman handed me five hundred bucks, I felt like I had just committed a symbolic form of suicide, and in a way it did put an end to a big part of my life.

I was thinking about suicide all the time by this point, but I was afraid of what people would think when they came and found me in my cockroach-infested, converted office space with the drywall ripped out and the windows covered in cardboard. The place was a disaster, and they were sure to wonder about my mostly hairless dead body. They would undoubtedly find my porn collection, and no one, not even my mother, would show up to the funeral. I had once found a *Penthouse* magazine in Jack's office, so he might understand, but I wasn't so concerned about what he thought. He had pretty much only seen me when I was all fucked up anyway.

The obvious solution was to throw out the magazines first, but the process of collecting them from their various hiding places, putting them in a bag, and then finding a public trash can didn't seem to fit with the hopeless desperation required to take one's life. I couldn't figure out a way around it. Selling my drums was as close as I could get.

I ALMOST CALLED JACK when the five hundred dollars from my drum set ran out, but I remembered a friend doing the "empty envelope trick" at the ATM. All I could think about was that I still had a hundred bucks just waiting to be spent. I wrote a check to myself for a hundred dollars in the hopes of confusing them and went to the ATM. Out came five twenty-dollar bills. I spent it all within a few minutes, went home, and called Jack.

"What's going on? Your mother, Inga, me, your friends . . . we're all worried about you," he said.

I could hear Inga and the kids in the background. "I'm really fucking fucked up. It's really fucking bad. I fucking missed my birthday and I tried to leave but I sold my fucking . . ." I hadn't intended on crying, but it welled up as soon as I opened my mouth.

"Listen." He cut me off. "I don't care what you did. Can you get back here on your own?"

I knew I couldn't. I had already tried that once, and if I said yes, I would have to come up with some magical way to pull more money out of thin air and it would probably involve cops next time.

"I already tried, I'm too fucked up. I can't fucking believe I did . . ."

"Listen to me. Tell me where you are, and I'll come and get you, okay? Are you going to be okay till tomorrow, or should I come now?"

"No. Don't worry about it. I'll be okay. You don't have to do that. I just don't want you guys to worry about me anymore. Really, I'm not worth it. Can you tell everyone for me?" I was sobbing. Even though I had originally called to ask him for help, something had changed my mind. I knew I couldn't kill myself, but what the fuck? These people didn't deserve to have to deal with this shit. I could still sleep in the van or sell it, and then? There was always somewhere to go. The Salvation Army, or maybe one of those refrigerator boxes Starbucks had been passing out with their logo on it. I just wanted everyone to forget about me, and stop worrying. I wasn't worth it anymore.

"We're not going to worry because we're coming to get you, okay? What's the address?"

I gave him the address and told him I would be fine until tomorrow. Otherwise, I was afraid I might do all my dope right then. I had to finish all of it before he got there or I would never leave.

JACK AND INGA CAME TO L.A. the next morning. I hadn't showered in two weeks, and my fingers and lips were burned from smoking crack twenty-four hours a day. I had poked another hole in my belt to keep my pants up. Summer was starting, and I was sweating profusely. I had completely lost track of how long this run had lasted, but I was pretty sure it had been the longest yet.

They drove me back to Oxnard and, aside from my sudden outbursts of crying, we spent the entire drive in silence. What could they say? I was slurring so bad they couldn't understand me anyway. Even though rehab clearly wasn't working, my only success at staying clean in the last two years had been a result of complete isolation from the real world.

I wasn't the only one back at the rehab. Seth, the hockey player, had been flown back a couple of days earlier, as well as a few others I recognized. I was defeated and kept to myself since I wasn't planning on sticking around anyway. The place was bullshit, and I had finally come to the conclusion that I needed real fucking help. Not this sobriety mill shit.

Dawn and Josh heard that I was back, and they both came to the alumni meeting to say hi, offer their support, and fill me in on their lives. Dawn was working at a café in Sherman Oaks and had just had an abortion.

"Wait a second. Doesn't that imply that you had sex with someone?" I asked, before realizing I should have offered my condolences first and then led into that. I was jealous, but at the same time I was glad she had finally worked through whatever demons she was fighting. I had tried so fucking hard with her, though, and I never tried.

"I'm sorry you had to go through that," I told her.

"No, it's great news! I didn't think I could ever have kids."

Josh was wearing an Armani suit and driving a brand-new BMW with tinted windows.

"Looks like you got your old job back," I said. "What happened with that bag of rocks?"

"Those rocks were hurting my back so bad that my boss eventually came down here and spoke to someone." I wasn't a big fan of suits, but he looked pretty good in one. "I don't know what he said to them, but afterward they told me to stop wearing the backpack."

The three of us sat outside smoking cigarettes until they called me in for my meds. It was nice to see that they were doing well, but I had lost faith in myself.

FOLLOWING ANOTHER excruciatingly long and painful night's sleep, I checked out of the rehab, and Jack gave me a ride from Oxnard back to L.A. to get what few belongings I still had out of the apartment. I also needed to get my van before it got towed. Even though Jack had seen the worst of me only a week and a half earlier, I was still too embarrassed to let him see the shithole I had been living in. I could tell him how bad it was, but I couldn't let him see for himself.

I took the cardboard off the windows, threw my dirty clothes into a bunch of trash bags, and cleaned up as best I could. With Jack waiting in the parking lot across the street, I didn't have time to patch up the walls I had ripped apart, and there was nothing I could do to hide the countless cigarette burns I had left on Nora's mattress and carpet. The only thing I could hope for was that I never ran into her or any of her friends ever again. It was unlikely, but I could always hope.

Following Jack back to his house, I felt defeated. I had tried everything I could think of in the past two years to get my shit together, and nothing had worked. I hated all that One-Day-at-a-Time and Easy-Does-It shit with a passion. Although it just didn't make sense that a three-word saying could get me clean, there were a few things that were hard to deny. The one that always struck a chord was when someone would say, "When I was I kid I never dreamed of growing up to be an alcoholic or a junkie. I wanted to be a . . ." Usually a fireman or jet pilot or some shit, which couldn't have been further from the many things I had thought of becoming. But it was true that I had never once entertained the fantasy of growing up to be a crackhead junkie. Having gone through all this shit myself, though, I was way past looking down on drug addicts. Not to say that I thought very highly of myself, but staying high all the time was hard, thankless work, and there were no benefits that I could see. Until I got uncomfortable, of course; then I couldn't see the consequences.

It was all so goddamn tragic and confusing that I decided it was time to go back to square one. Hit the reset button. Go back to where it all started and try to figure out what the hell went wrong. At Jack's house, I did my laundry for the first time in months and got another much-needed night of sleep. The next morning I got in the van and headed back to my first rehab, in Redwood City.

twenty-five

Mostly concerns the uncomfortable topic
of sex

WITH THREE HUNDRED dollars and my first car, I hit the road
to San Diego to hang out with a few of my friends from school
before they went off to college and I returned to Arizona.

When I returned to school, my beard was about four inches long, and
my friends at school thought I looked as if I'd aged at least ten years in
only three months. A few of the new teachers, who looked to be about
twenty-two themselves, asked me what I taught and why I hadn't been
at the faculty orientation.

AS A JOKE, AARON had submitted my name as a candidate for
student body president the previous year. I don't know what the
other kids were thinking, but for some reason they went along with it and
voted me in. Technically I hadn't even run for the position, which may
have had something to do with me winning, because after listening to
the other kids give their speeches, I decided to vote for myself too. My
first order of business as the new president was an attempt to repeal a
new rule that made study hall a requirement for seniors. For as long as I
had been there, seniors were always exempt because our grades wouldn't
affect our college applications at that point. My grades were so bad that,
for three years, I had spent two hours a night sitting silently in the dining

hall pretending to study, and just when I was supposed to get a break from it, they took away the privilege. After a failed attempt at diplomacy, I called for a schoolwide study hall boycott, but I ended up being the only one to participate in it. After only a week, I had racked up almost enough cuts to get suspended. Since my new responsibilities required that I meet with the headmaster once a week anyway, he just waited for me to come to him.

"What's it been? Four days now? I obviously have never had any luck trying to tell you what to do, but in two more days, I'm going to have to suspend you," he told me.

"That's fine. I don't want to be here anyway if you're going to treat *us* like this," I told him, trying mostly to convince myself that I was fighting for a noble cause. In truth, I was pissed because *I* had to go to study hall. There were only thirteen seniors anyway, and out of those, only two other kids had such shitty grades that our studying required adult observation.

"It's just not worth it, Oran. It's like biting off your nose to spite your face."

"I don't get it. What does that mean?"

"You know, you don't like your face, so you bite off your nose," he said, as if it were the most obvious thing in the world. "All I'm saying is, think it through before you do something stupid."

"Okay, but seriously, what does that have to do with my nose?"

"Is there any other business to discuss?" he asked, changing the subject.

"Yeah." I looked at my notes from the senate meeting. As I read off the list of how many liters of soda and bags of chips we needed for the Halloween dance, I realized that a big part of me really didn't give a shit whether they kicked me out. Aside from Aaron and Matt, most of my friends had already graduated, and I felt as though I was just biding my time until I could join them out in the real world.

The boycott was ultimately successful, but I had accumulated so many cuts in the process that I was on very thin ice. If I was late to one class or got caught smoking one cigarette, that would be the end, or so I thought. I did try as hard as I could to start following the rules, but getting through a whole semester without missing a class or being caught smoking one of my twenty cigarettes a day turned out to be impossible. To my surprise, however, my teachers would somehow forget to turn in my cut slips or, when they popped out of the bushes to catch me smoking, would quickly make up some other excuse for why they were sneaking around off campus late at night, once they realized it was me.

"Oh. Hey there. I didn't recognize you. What are you doing out here?" my teacher Gary asked one night.

"Just taking a walk," I answered nervously, hiding my cigarette behind my back.

"Me, too. It's such a beautiful night. Well, I guess I'll be on my way then," he said, heading off to give a group of four other kids smoking violations. Gary was a chronic pot smoker, and it was rumored that he got high with a few of the students. Every once in a while, he had to pretend to be an authoritarian and catch someone. It seemed as though that was the case for all of the teachers, who were mostly fresh out of college and stuck in the middle of the desert watching sixty teenagers run wild.

Once I realized I couldn't really get into trouble, I wasn't nearly so interested in causing it. Aaron and I were taking acid every weekend to use up the sixteen hits I still had left from when I was a freshman, but the headmaster was far less interested in what I did secretly than in my more public troublemaking efforts, such as walking around with a Hitler mustache and calling for strikes. As a result, I found myself on much friendlier terms with the faculty, often spending my evenings at the houses of various teachers who were so lonely they had taken to inviting Aaron, Matt, and me over for dinner.

Holly, one of the administrators, even started including a couple of six-packs of beer every Wednesday night when we went to her house for dinner. We would get buzzed while she would fill us in on all the week's faculty drama. Two teachers were sleeping together, and two others had broken up on bad terms. Curiously there hadn't been any student-teacher relationships so far, at least that we knew about. The year before, I caught one of my teachers, Phillip, red-handed when I went over to his house for a tutoring session. Looking in his desk for a pen, I was shocked to see my pot pipe in the drawer.

"Hey, this is mine," I told him, holding it up so he could see.

"No, it's not," he said, looking as if he had just been electrocuted. I had lent it to a girl a few hours earlier, who, it immediately dawned on me, must have been the robed figure I saw dashing into his bedroom when I had knocked on the door. Phillip rescheduled my lesson, and ten minutes later the girl returned the pipe.

It was virtually impossible to keep anything secret on campus, which was why we were all so surprised when Gary told us, "There's been at least one student-teacher relationship this year." We were hanging out at his house, and he was stoned out of his mind.

"Really?"

"Who is it?" we asked.

"I can't tell you till the end of the year," he said.

I was never very judgmental of these relationships. If anything, I was jealous, because it seemed that everyone was getting laid but me. It wasn't that girls weren't interested in me; it was that I didn't know what the hell I was supposed to do about it when they were. I wouldn't understand why a girl was always trying to wrestle with me until a week later when she'd start wrestling with some other guy and all of a sudden they would be an item.

When I was aware that someone was into me, I would get scared and run away. The closest I had come was when a girl asked me if I wanted a massage and I talked shit about her friends the whole time she rubbed my back. Another time I walked into my room early in the morning after sneaking off campus to hang out with Eli, who was back in Arizona visiting his mom, and I found two freshmen girls asleep on my bed. In a panic I closed the door as quietly as I could and ran away, fully aware that I would never be able to forgive myself for that one.

BACK IN BERKELEY for Christmas, Mom and Kyle staged an intervention. I hated the way Mom always brought this kind of thing up when we were in the car, usually driving fifty miles an hour down the freeway. Even then it was tempting to open the door and get out.

"All we're trying to tell you is it's fine if you're gay. We just want to know," Kyle said.

"Jesus Christ. I swear I'm not gay. Not that it's any of your fucking business!"

"Hey, Ory. You don't need to get so defensive. We're not accusing you of anything. We're just trying to let you know we would still love you."

"For God's sake. Don't you think I know that? But if telling you I'm gay will end this fucking conversation, then fine, I'm gay," I said.

"You're gay? Really?" Mom asked.

"Man! I was being sarcastic, but if I change my mind, I swear to God I'll let you know!"

"Okay. Because Kyle and I will still love you. Right, Kyle?"

I couldn't blame them for asking, but I was annoyed that they thought I would have been ashamed of it. Most of my role models growing up had been gay. The real reason I hated talking about it was because I didn't know why I was so scared of girls. I also had a very real fear that I would never experience sex in my life. I mean, how much easier could it get than finding two girls in your bed?

WHEN I GOT BACK to school, a few new students had enrolled for the second semester. One of them was a junior named Dana. She had long dark hair and wore mostly black clothes with striped red-and-white socks. She even parted her hair down the middle, giving her a distinct Wednesday Addams look. I couldn't help stealing glances at her, and even when I noticed her doing the same, I couldn't bring myself to approach her.

Someone must have told her that if she hoped to have any luck with me, she would have to do all the work and do it quickly, because almost immediately she was sitting next to me during lunch, joining me for cigarettes, and tracking me down after study hall to hang out. The whole situation scared the hell out of me, but I felt like I was running out of time and that it would only get harder once I was out in the real world.

Even so, no matter how much I wanted to, I couldn't bring myself to make the first move. Luckily she didn't have a problem taking charge, and one night, while espousing my views on how utterly fucked up the universe was, she shut me up midsentence with a kiss. My anxiety disappeared instantly, and we made out under the stars for a few minutes until some other kids interrupted us by coming out to get a last cigarette before our in-dorms curfew.

"Let's go to your room," she said.

"Shit, it's already nine thirty," I said, looking at my watch. "We only have half an hour."

"Then we'd better make it quick," she responded, already walking down the path back to campus. I wasn't sure whether she meant what I was hoping she meant, and I was too freaked out to ask her.

She made it very clear when we got to my room, though.

"So, do you have any condoms?"

"Wow . . . Uh . . . No. I mean . . . I've never even done this before," I answered, figuring it was best that she knew in case I screwed the whole thing up.

"Well, you better find one. I'll be right here," she said, sitting down on my bed.

Nervous as hell, I went down the hall and knocked on a few doors to see what I could turn up, but no one was ever around right before curfew. Even if I did find someone, it wasn't certain that they had any more use for condoms than I did. I thought about making a mad dash for the infirmary, where they always left a salad bowl full of condoms on the counter, but there was no way I could make it back in time.

Just when I was about to give up, I heard voices coming from my friend Kazuhiro's room. Kazu was the only Japanese student who made any effort to interact with the American kids. I felt a glimmer of hope because I knew he had a girlfriend. Too impatient to knock, I opened the door to his bedroom, which also served as a clubhouse for all the Japanese exchange students, who would hang out and play video games the rest of America wouldn't see for another year.

"Hey, Kazu. Come here a second," I said, peering in. There were four other Japanese kids, all of them yelling at the TV screen while one of them played *Super Mario Brothers 3*.

"What's up?" he asked, looking up from the game.

"Come here, I need to ask you something." I was freaking out, and it must have shown by the sound of my voice. I only had a twenty-minute window left to lose my virginity.

"Do you have a condom?" I whispered, after getting him to follow me out into the hall.

"Ah," he said, smiling. "I have, but it no work for you."

"What? What are you talking about, it no work? Just give it to me," I pleaded.

"Seriousry. No work. Very embarrassing, but Japanese condom too smar for you."

"Too what? Small? You got to be kidding me," I said. "Just give it to me. It'll be fine. It's not like I have anything to brag about."

"Okay, but I'm terring you. Too smar."

He reappeared a few seconds later with a condom, and I ran upstairs as fast as I could.

"Find one?" Dana asked when I got back to my room. She was already under the covers, and her clothes were on the floor.

"Yeah," I said, locking the door and turning out the light. I didn't remember what was in my tape deck, but I pressed play to cover up any noise that might occur. It was Captain Beefheart's *Trout Mask Replica*—not the most conducive music to lose one's virginity to, but I was running out of time. I took off my clothes, got under the covers, and handed her the condom. Presumably she had more experience with them than I did.

"There's something wrong with it. I can't get it on," she said.

I hadn't even been paying attention to what she was doing for fear of finishing before she even got the damn thing on. Instead I was focusing on the lyrics to the song that was playing.

meaty dream wet meat,

It turned out to be the perfect music.

"Really? He was right then?" I asked, taking the condom from her. Sure enough, the thing was the size of my thumb. I wasn't sure who I felt worse for, myself or Kazu.

"Fuck!" I said. "God fucking damn it!" I had been waiting my whole life for this, and finally, after years of fantasizing, there was a real, live, naked girl in my bed.

"It'll be fine," Dana said. "You just have to promise to pull out."

Squirmin' serum 'n semen 'n syrup 'n semen 'n serum,

Captain Beefheart continued.

Dana barely made it out of my room a few minutes before ten, but it seemed as though the news had already traveled.

"Jesus Christ, man. What happened to you?" Matt asked me out in the hall as everyone was showing up back at that dorm.

"What are you talking about? Nothing," I answered, trying as hard as I could to look normal.

"Oh my fucking God! You finally did it. Congratulations," he said. Then Aaron saw me and figured it out as well. Even my art teacher, Thom, who was more like the crazy uncle I never had than a teacher, did a double take as he checked off our names on his clipboard. When everyone was accounted for, he found me and quietly asked, "So . . . how did it go?"

"What do you mean?" *How could he possibly know already? It had only been three minutes since Dana had left.*

"You know. How long did it last?" It seemed like a weird question, but after hesitating a moment I said, "I don't know. Maybe ten or fifteen minutes."

"Ten minutes? Good job. I don't think I even lasted thirty seconds. Seriously, though, what you just did is a big deal. Congratulations."

"Hey, Thom, how the hell does everyone know already?"

"Are you kidding? Go look at yourself in the mirror, man. You're too young to win the lottery. What else could it be?"

I took his advice and went to the bathroom. It was true. I couldn't stop smiling, no matter how hard I tried, which I actually found rather disturbing. Could getting laid really destroy the cynical, negative, misanthropic self-image I had worked so hard to achieve?

For almost two weeks there was noticeably less bitching and moaning coming from me. Once the thrill of finally having sex wore off though, the old Oran started reemerging, and most of my grumbling was directed at Dana.

"I can't work with you staring at me like that. It's making me nervous," I snapped at her while I was working on a painting in the art studio. For about an hour I had managed to pretend there was nothing unusual about someone staring at me while I stared at a canvas, but that was as long as I could take it.

"Do you want me to leave?" she asked, obviously hurt.

"No, but look around. There are better things to do than watch me. Why don't you make something?" I asked.

"I like watching you," she answered.

Watching me paint? Clearly she's fucking crazy. I didn't like it one bit. Feeling trapped and suffocated, I told her I didn't think it was going to work out between us.

M Y SCHOOL WASN'T big on traditions, but we did have two yearly events that were unique to us. Instead of proms and homecomings, we had Ring Turning and Fire Run.

Ring Turning was a bizarre treasure hunt devised by the seniors, in which the juniors had to solve hundreds of clues, sometimes taking them as far away as Flagstaff or Phoenix. The goal was to find where the seniors had hidden their class rings. There was never any warning for it either. One day a solitary index card with a clue would be pinned to the bulletin board, signaling the start of Ring Turning, and giving the juniors one week to follow the clues and find the rings. Nothing was off-limits: The clue "Fireman Award" led to a spot out in the desert where a kid named Howard had passed out directly on top of a campfire, which the other students had successfully put out by pissing on him. "Sheathed/ Unsheathed" led the clue seeker to the creek, where in a drunken stupor I had given in to peer pressure from fifteen other kids who wanted to see what an uncircumcised penis looked like. As seniors, we were let out of all our obligations in order to take shifts ambushing the juniors with high-pressure fire hoses whenever they tried to go to class, eat in the cafeteria, or make any attempt at walking by one of the many fire hydrants on campus. During Ring Turning the school was turned into a war zone, with the juniors and seniors looking like guerrilla freedom fighters, covered from head to toe in red mud.

Shortly after Ring Turning, the headmaster informed me that Fire Run would happen on the next Wednesday, at 2:30 A.M. I quietly spread the word, and that night, the seniors waited for everyone to go to sleep and watched for the security guard to give us the signal. Armed with flashlights, we snuck out of our dorms and hiked about a half mile off campus to the top of a thousand-foot rock, where we had been amassing a pile of scrap wood over the course of the year for a bonfire. When we lit the fifteen-foot bonfire, the juniors started running through the dorms banging on pots and pans, setting off fire alarms, and yanking everyone else out of bed. We then stood around the top edge of the rock formation holding gigantic flaming torches in the air until we could hear the students cheering us on from campus, at which point we started running down the sheer side of the rock as fast as we could using our torches to light the way. Miraculously, no one had ever been seriously injured during Fire Run, especially considering that a fair number of us were drunk at the time. A couple of kids always got bruised up or sprained their ankles, but even they had so much fun they probably would have gone straight back up and done it again.

I had been antsy as hell all year to go out and make my mark on the world, but running down the side of that mountain made me realize just how lucky I was to have spent four years at this wacky place, doing things most kids would never get to experience, and this was only one of the countless once-in-a-lifetime experiences I had there. How many kids were lucky—or unlucky—enough to get dropped off in Mexico, or the Hopi Reservation, or the middle of Tucson, or Oaxaca for a three-week field trip, virtually unattended?

Mostly I was going to miss my friends and teachers, whose only expectation of me was to be myself. Unfortunately, I didn't fully appreciate what an amazing experience high school had been until I found myself running down the side of a rock at three thirty in the morning, jumping over cacti and trying not to light myself or anything else on fire. I couldn't imagine a more appropriate end to what had been an amazing four years.

O UR GRADUATION CEREMONY took place on the quad, where all thirteen of us seniors sat around while the teachers spoke of their hopes for us and singled some of us out for awards. Despite my shitty grades, I ended up getting the overall achievement award for my creative abilities and duties as the student-body president. I had also managed to get a scholarship to go to the San Francisco Art Institute.

Once we received our diplomas and were shaking hands with our teachers, I found Gary.

"So, who was it?" No one had come up with any ideas about who was involved in the student-teacher relationship he had told us about.

"You haven't figured it out yet? All right. You can't tell anyone, but it was me," he answered.

"You? That's fucked up. I had no idea."

"Of course you didn't."

"Aha. The only reason you told us you knew was to take attention off yourself."

"And it totally worked," he said, gloating.

"Yeah, but you haven't told me who it was with," I said.

"Jesus. I can't tell you that, but I'll give you a hint. She's wearing cutoffs."

"Everyone's wearing cutoffs," I said, looking around. But there was only one girl I could see Gary risking his job over. "Wow" was all I could say when I figured it out.

Jack had come out with his wife, Georgia, and my six-week-old half-brother, Christopher. "I just want to say, I'm really proud of you, son," he told me.

I didn't show it, but it totally pissed me off. I didn't think he had the right to be proud, considering he'd never been involved in my life. True, he paid my way through school, but I wanted to be angry so I chose not to think about that part.

As if he were psychic, he went on to say, "I know I had nothing to do with it, and I'm not taking any credit, but I'm proud of you anyway."

"Well, thanks. And hey, now you have another chance," I said, referring to Christopher, who may have been a cute baby, but it was hard to tell since he was recovering from a rash that completely covered his face. I wanted to feel some kind of connection with him—after all, he was my brother—but babies made me a little uncomfortable. Or maybe it was that I thought I was supposed to act a certain way around babies that made me uncomfortable. Jack seemed genuinely excited about Christopher, though, despite the bags under his eyes.

"And here," he said, pulling an envelope from his pocket. "This is for you."

I looked at the two hundred-dollar bills he gave me, and thanked him, trying to hide my disappointment.

T HE NEXT DAY, hung over from getting drunk with my friends and teachers—another high school tradition I hadn't known about—I set out for my new life in California with Eli, who had come back to see us graduate, Aaron, and two other friends all packed into my tiny Honda. We only got a half mile from campus before the car made a loud noise and died.

When we got it to the shop, the guy told me it was going to cost two hundred bucks and it would be three days before they could get the part. I handed over the envelope Jack had given me, and Eli called his mom to come pick us up and take us to her house.

twenty-six

*In which a learned doctor tells our subject
about the god Iboga, enemy of Chiva*

GOING BACK TO my first rehab in Redwood City was certainly a blow to my ego after all the shit I had told them, but I was fucking beat down, confused, and had lost all hope. I was experiencing incomprehensible demoralization, as they called it in the recovery scene, and I had to admit that it described my situation perfectly. Not a single one of my bright ideas had worked, and I was finally ready to listen to these fucking people. *If they tell me to go to meetings, I'll go to meetings*, I thought to myself. *If they tell me to get a sponsor, I'll get a sponsor. If I have to live in the clean and sober house with four other guys in the same room, I'll live in the fucking clean and sober house.*

"Just have a seat, someone will be with you," the receptionist said when I checked in.

I sat down and looked through the stack of magazines they had sitting on a desk. Although I had been in that room many times, I had never really noticed it before. It was like a waiting room at a dentist's office. They even had one of those *Highlights* magazines I remembered from the last time I had gone to the dentist, when I was twelve. I was looking for the carrot, the starfish, the fork, and the number seven that were supposed to be hidden in one of the drawings when Barry, the head honcho himself, came out. He didn't seem pleased or unhappy to see me. Just unusually official.

"Hi, Oran," he said, without adding any type of "how have you been?" or "good to see you." "The staff is all busy at the moment, so let's get the physical out of the way now."

He led me back to the examination room and told me to take off my clothes. It was weird. Usually he tried to be funny—cracking jokes, making the clients feel at ease. This time, it was all formality. He checked my heart rate, blood pressure, and reflexes, before I noticed him putting on a rubber glove. Grabbing a bottle of KY jelly out of a cabinet, he asked, "Can you drop your drawers and bend over for me, please?"

"Um, I don't think that's necessary. I feel fine, really."

"I'm the doctor, and I think it's necessary. Just bend over. It'll be so quick you won't even know what happened."

"Do you have to? You never did it last time."

"Hey, Oran. Here you are for the third time, and you still think you know more than the professionals? Now bend over!"

He was not fucking around. This wasn't on the list of things I thought they would ask me to do to stay clean, but I turned toward the bed and bent over. *If they tell me to bend over so they can stick their finger in my ass, I'll bend over and. . . .* The whole thing was done before I could even finish my thought, but I still felt violated.

Barry, on the other hand, seemed to lighten up a bit afterward. "All clear, everything's fine. No growths, polyps, or vegetations—you're good to go," he said in a more relaxed tone of voice. I put my clothes back on in silence.

"Hey, man, I don't like doing that any more than you do," he said.

"It didn't seem that way," I responded. "Can I go now?"

"We're done. You can either wait in the lobby or go join the yoga class and Eileen will come get you when she's ready."

"What happened to Jan?"

"Jan's got a full caseload. We're putting you with Eileen for now but will revisit it when Jan has an opening."

It wasn't long before Eileen came to get me. We went to her office, where she told me to start from the last time I was there.

"Well, I jumped out the window and caught the train back to San Francisco," I started.

"Why did you jump out of the window? You could have just walked right out the door. The whole house had to get in the van and drive around looking for you," she interrupted me.

"Because I would have had to deal with twenty people trying to convince me I would be dead within the first ten minutes of leaving," I answered.

"True."

"It was like I was possessed or something. I needed to get high right then."

"Okay, go on."

I told her an abbreviated version of the next two years, but it still took a while.

"So why did you come back here?" she asked me. "You were in what—five, six other rehabs since we last saw you? And in that time you have managed to stay continuously sober for only three months?"

I nodded.

"Seriously, what makes you think it's going to work this time?"

"Well, those other rehabs were bullshit. They were just out to make money, and the counselors only had a couple years sober, and were making ten bucks an hour repeating slogans like a bunch of programmed zombies. I just remembered a much higher quality of treatment here."

"You do know, Oran, that even though we may be more educated, we do use the AA model here because we think it's the only one that works. We may be wrong, but that's what you're going to get here."

"Yeah, I know. I hate it, but I'm ready for it. Honestly, I'll fucking do anything right now. I give up. I'm done. If I knew for a fact I would die out there, I wouldn't have come back, but my big fear is that I'll just keep going somehow and I'm just too much of a fucking wimp to kill myself. I swear, I'm finally ready to do this shit." I was starting to get choked up, so I stopped.

She stared at me for a little while with a sad look. I didn't know what else to say, so I just waited.

"You know, it's kind of funny. The last two times you were here, we would have done anything to get you to say what you just said. But now that you're actually saying it, the whole thing is making me terribly sad. I'm not even sure why. For some reason, I have a picture in my head of a bird with its wings cut off. What happened to that crazy, dope-sick kid who walked in here two years ago? I mean, you hadn't slept in like seven days, you were shitting in your pants, but you were able to stand your ground against thirty people. Do you remember that night?"

"I remember," I said, thinking about what a maniac I must have looked like.

"You were maybe the most stubborn, obnoxious, hardheaded, all-around pain in the ass I have ever seen in my years as a counselor, and . . .

I need to think about this some more, because . . . I don't know where it's coming from, but I think I liked that obnoxious kid who came in here raising hell more than what I'm looking at right now."

"Do you think I'm just saying this shit because I think it's what you want to hear?" I asked, but not in any kind of confrontational way. I was just curious.

"Unfortunately, no. With all the doctors and lawyers that come through here, you think we don't know how to deal with that? That's easy. If I thought you were just trying to say the right thing, then I'd have something to work with."

"Okay," I said, absolutely perplexed. "Then what do you think I should do?"

"That's what's bothering me. The old Oran wouldn't have asked that question. Listen, we talked about you at the staff meeting before you got here, and we had worked out a tentative plan, but apparently we were discussing a different person. I'm going to have to think about this for a while. In the meantime, just jump right in. We'll talk soon. Someone will show you the house you're staying in after the alumni meeting." They decided that, since I had already gone through detox in Oxnard, I could stay at another sober house and do day treatment.

"Thanks, Eileen," I said, getting up to go.

"Oh, here are a couple of books I brought for you. They're both about creativity and addiction. Look them over. It might be totally irrelevant, but we'll talk about it later."

Normally I would have been mortified at the thought of reading a self-help book, but I took them as further proof of how far down I'd come.

When I went back upstairs, it was dinnertime. Not feeling at all like jumping right in, I used my freedom as a day patient to walk down the street and get a sandwich. I sat down with my food and mulled over what Eileen had said. I couldn't make any sense out of it. Was there an angle? If there was, what the hell could it have been? I didn't like it at all, but something had resonated and not in a good way. I was still lost in thought on my way back for the alumni meeting. She was right, though. The old Oran wouldn't have said any of that shit. In fact, the old Oran might have committed suicide for me had he seen a glimpse of his hollow shell walking down the street two years in the future, actually looking forward to an AA meeting. Goddamn, that would have made things easier.

I took a seat in the back. It was an anniversary meeting, meaning that those who had celebrated a milestone in sobriety would go up and ramble on about how the rehab and AA changed their lives, and everything was amazing now, and all we have to do is not drink, and go to meetings, and get a sponsor, and do the steps, and help a newcomer, and read the book, and keep it simple, and on, and fucking on, and life will be fantastic.

Even though I had said I would do anything to stay sober, there was still a big difference between me and these people. I was resigned to this AA sentence because I simply had nowhere else to go. These people were so psyched to tell the world how awesome AA was that I couldn't tell whom they were trying to convince. Themselves? Me? Their wives? It all looked like a big charade. *If I just act all excited and stuff, then maybe I can convince myself everything will be okay.* Oh well, I didn't come back here to make friends.

Toward the end of the meeting, a guy who had been a client the last time I was there walked up to the front of the room to get his two-year anniversary coin.

"Hey, I'm Frank, and I'm an alcoholic," he said to the crowd. "I want to thank everyone for this. When I came in here, I'd been smoking pot every day since I was twelve, you know. But at some point it stopped working, and it just started making me angry, and, well . . ." The same old shit. I did remember him as being extremely angry, though. I started zoning out and thinking about the last time I had been here and we were in group therapy together. He was the only guy I had ever met who was in rehab for pot. It just wasn't that common. He would go on and on about how addictive pot was, as if he had to prove something to us. I remembered hating the guy. Not so much because he was a pothead, but because he just seemed like a fucking idiot and said the stupidest shit, like, "You know how people think pot's not addictive, man? Well, I'm here to tell you it is. What about the shakes, man? What about the cold sweats, huh? What about the wanting to jump out of your fucking skin, man?"

I didn't get it. The guy looked like a real estate broker, but he talked like a cross between a hippie and an ex-con trying to scare the kids away from a life of crime. "You guys have no idea what it's like to wake up from these nightmares, and they don't go away just 'cause you wake up, man. Oh no . . ."

"Um. Excuse me? Am I allowed to say something?" I had asked Jan at the time, cutting the guy off from his after-school-special pot rant. I hadn't yet learned how this group therapy thing worked, but I couldn't take this anymore.

"Well, normally we like to wait for people to finish with their turn, but sure. Go ahead." I think Jan was giving me special treatment because it was the first time I had opened my mouth voluntarily. The pothead looked as if he wanted to rip my head off for interrupting, but that seemed preferable to having to listen to any more of his bullshit.

"Hey. Would you shut the fuck up? Look around you, man. We're all going through this shit. Please . . . do you think any of us wants to be here? Jesus fucking Christ! It's pathetic, man." I didn't know where it came from, because the last thing anyone would have called me was a tough guy. Instead of lunging at me, though, he just kind of collapsed back in his chair looking stunned.

"Well, Oran," Jan said with a hint of amusement. "That is not usually how we do it here, but . . ."

"I'm sorry," I said, a bit stunned myself.

"Frank. Did you hear what Oran just said?" Jan went on without missing a beat.

"Yes."

"And how did it make you feel?"

As my mind came back to the alumni meeting, Frank was up at the podium saying, "I don't think he meant it this way, but when that junkie kid told me to shut the fuck up . . . . . . that I wasn't the only one going through this . . . well, for the first time in my life I realized I wasn't alone. All of us have been through hell, and that's what gives us the ability to understand and help one another."

I couldn't believe what I was hearing.

"That kid saved my life, but I'm pretty sure he just wanted me to shut the fuck up. Thanks."

I found him after the meeting and congratulated him for his two years. "Hey listen, man. I'm assuming that story was about me. I need to apologize for telling you to shut up. I was out of my mind back then."

"I know you were out of your mind. We all were, but until you said that I really thought I was the only person who had ever felt that way. I mean, Jesus . . . you were sitting there kicking heroin and you had to listen to a pothead bitch about withdrawal symptoms? Seriously, man, you saved my life. I tell that story at almost every meeting I go to."

I had to admit that he did seem a hell of a lot calmer now. That whole tough, hippie, real-estate-broker persona had vanished.

"It's pretty ironic that I was able to unintentionally save your life, and here I am back at this fucking place."

"Oh. You're back as a patient? I assumed you were here for the meeting. I just thought I should come back and show the new people that it works," he said.

"Well, I'm a 'new people,' and it seems to have helped you," I said, trying to be funny. God, I had even lost my sense of humor.

"At least you don't look as bad as you did last time. I'm sorry you're still struggling, but it's good to see you, man. Good luck," he said, shaking my hand.

I STAYED THERE for another four months, slowly trying to make connections and set up a safety net back in San Francisco. I did whatever they told me to do. Underneath it all, I was as anxious and uncomfortable as ever, and I wanted to get high so fucking bad.

My weekly meetings with Eileen were depressing. She had told me they had been expecting a challenge, and instead they got a piece of silly putty they didn't know what to do with.

"So are you talking to your sponsor?" she asked.

I had asked this musician from San Francisco to be my sponsor, and I was calling him every day.

"I can see that you're going to meetings," she said, glancing over my attendance card. "Are you making any progress with the steps?"

"I'm working on them," I answered.

"Honestly, I don't know what to do with you. We've tried everything, and no matter what we come up with, you just do what you're told."

"Isn't that a good thing? Isn't that what I'm supposed to do?"

"Yes and no. Sure, it makes our job easy if you just say yes to everything, but . . . I don't even know how to say this. . . . We're concerned that this person who is going around following suggestions and doing all the right things is not really you. I would expect you to change a little after what you've been through, but you're almost unrecognizable. We want to work with that hardheaded, stubborn, obnoxious, charming, charismatic Oran because—and both Barry and Jan agree with me on this—that's the guy who's going to keep you clean. If we can't bring that part of you out, we have nothing to work with."

"I don't know what to do about that. Believe me, I wish I could."

"Hey, are you still doing that *Artist's Way* book I gave you?" One of the books she had given me was a workbook with different exercises designed to trigger creativity. Eileen and the whole staff, including Jan, had changed their minds since the last time I was there. They had decided that the key to my staying sober involved getting back into music and reconnecting with my old friends. She hoped the book would help.

"Yeah. I'm writing every morning, and going to the city to see music on the weekends." One of the exercises was to experience some kind of culture, art, or nature once a week. I had even started sitting in on a film-making class back at the Art Institute.

"Good. What about the affirmations?"

I was hoping she wouldn't bring those up. "Um, I can't do the affirmations," I said, waiting for her to tell me how important they were.

"Why not?"

"Honestly, because I think they're bullshit."

"I'd like to hear more about why you think affirmations are bullshit, Oran. I mean, they seem to work for an awful lot of people, including myself. But for some reason, you think they're bullshit?" she said.

I should have just lied. I didn't want to argue about it, but since she asked, I answered, "Yeah, I do think they're bullshit, and here's why. They're based in fantasy. Standing in front of the mirror and saying 'I'm pretty and people like me' doesn't make someone pretty or likable. If it affirms anything, it's that they're ugly and people hate them. I mean, who else would say something like that? I'm sorry, but I can't do the affirmations. I refuse to look at myself in the mirror and tell lies. I already hate myself enough as it is." I got a little worked up.

"Okay, Oran. The next staff meeting is tomorrow, and I'm going to recommend that we start working on an exit plan," she said.

"You're going to kick me out because I won't do those fucking affirmations?" This was bullshit.

"No, no, no. I'm going to recommend we release you soon. This is what we've been waiting for. I finally got a glimpse of the old Oran."

What the fuck? I didn't understand what had just happened. "I have to admit, I cannot figure you guys out for the life of me," I said.

"That's a good thing, because if you could, we wouldn't be able to do our job," she said with a grin. "Listen, that was good work today. I'll let you know what happens at the meeting. And one more thing, Oran . . ."

"Yeah?" I asked.

"Promise me you won't do those affirmations."

AFTER MY RELEASE, I stayed on at the sober house, did outpatient treatment three nights a week, and had even started a band called Dig That Body Up, It's Alive, with a guy named John Dwyer. I had met him at a place called Adobe Books, in the Mission, where a lot of my old friends congregated.

I wasn't having any luck finding a place to live, though. As much as my friends were starting to warm up to me, no one seemed ready to give me a set of keys. It was still going to be a few more weeks before I was released from outpatient anyway. The rehab still wanted to see my relapse prevention plan, and I could tell they were watching to make sure my outburst wasn't just a onetime thing.

I didn't go crazy, but I allowed myself some room for what I was hoping would be interpreted as a bit of healthy cynicism. Not just to convince them the old Oran was coming back, but because it also made me feel better. I had been clean now for a record of four months, but nothing seemed to help with my anxiety. The best I could do was to try hiding it.

Unable to find a room in San Francisco, I ended up moving in with a trombone player named Chad I knew out in West Oakland. I didn't know him that well, but I told him what I had been going through, and he didn't seem to care too much, probably because his place was a shithole and there was nothing to steal anyway. Nothing. No TV, no pots and pans, no stereo, and aside from the food and water bowl for his cat, there weren't even any dishes. I even had to buy a spoon at the thrift store, when unable to stand the anxiety for one more fucking minute, I found myself in the Mission buying heroin again. When the euphoria faded, I found myself in my bare room, sitting on the piece of foam I used as a mattress, once again wondering how the fuck I had let myself relapse again. I had no idea what led up to it, and my despair and self-loathing was beyond anything I had experienced in the past. Once I started, though, there seemed to be nothing I could do to stop, and a few hours later I was back in the Mission buying more.

It didn't help that it was Christmas, my least favorite time of year, and even though Mom was only a couple of miles away, I hadn't spoken to her since those orderlies tackled me in Santa Barbara over a year ago. Kyle, who was caught in the middle of our relationship, was hanging out with her. I spent Christmas Eve and Christmas day alone at the house— more depressed than I thought humanly possible—shooting speedballs and cuddling with Chad's cat. I knew intellectually that there was a window of opportunity to stop before I got physically addicted, but as always I pushed through that window and rode out the binge for as long as I could.

Because I had sold my drum set, Dig That Body Up, It's Alive had to rehearse at a studio that rented out drums by the hour. I still had my cymbals, though, and Dwyer figured out exactly what was going on when I showed up to rehearsal without them.

"Fuck. I must have left them in Oakland. You got a few extra bucks so I can rent some?" We always split the cost right down the middle, but this time he had already paid for the whole thing. I had been doing such a good job at staying clean that my trust managers had agreed to help out by sending me a thousand dollars a month until I got back on my feet, but I was still always broke.

"You mean you left them at the pawnshop?" he asked me. "Let's go," he said before I had a chance to respond. While driving to the pawnshop, he asked me what I planned to do.

"I love playing with you, man, but it's not going to work out if you keep selling your cymbals for dope." It was funny coming from him, because I wasn't so sure he didn't have a problem with drugs himself. Unlike me, though, his "problem" always seemed to result in having fun and getting laid. My problem led me to hiding out by myself on Christmas Eve trying to figure out how I had become such a miserable piece of shit. Although I didn't know what the hell I expected them to do for me, Dwyer convinced me to go back to Redwood City.

I MEAN, REALLY," Barry said to me in his office a few days later. "What the hell do you expect us to do for you?"

I didn't say anything. All my focus was going into not letting the floodgates burst. A few tears came out anyway despite my valiant attempt. It hadn't even been close to my worst relapse, but given a few more days, I'm sure it would have been.

"I'm sorry, Oran. I'm not saying this to be condescending or patronizing," he continued. "I've been there, and I know how hard it is, but I just don't think there's anything we can do. If you can think of anything, I'm all ears."

I couldn't think of anything. I had tried it all so many times that I figured the best thing I could do now was just try to accept that I was doomed to failure.

"Thanks anyway," I said, getting up to leave.

"Sit down a minute," he directed me. "I want you to call this woman, Dr. Mash, in Miami. She's running a program out on a Caribbean island with an experimental hallucinogen called ibogaine. Her work appears to be having positive results."

He handed me a number copied out of his Rolodex.

"Give her a call and find out when the next session is. In the meantime, try to take it easy on yourself and let us know if there's anything we can do to help."

I gave the woman a call. Her secretary said they had a session coming up in three weeks and gave me a list of things I needed to do if I wanted to take part. First I had to convince my trust administrators to pay twelve thousand dollars for the treatment and fly me to the Caribbean so I could take this highly illegal drug. I also had to go through another physical and get my heart checked out because there had been a couple of deaths related to this drug. On the off chance that I could get all that shit together, I needed a passport. Last but not least, I knew I wouldn't be able to get any of this done if I was dope sick. That's what I told the rehab psychiatrist anyway, and he gave me a prescription for a month's supply of methadone. I took it straight to the pharmacy, where my co-pay was a shocking eleven dollars. I'd been going about this whole thing wrong from the start.

A S IF TO AFFIRM what a complete fuckup I was, I waited till the day before I was supposed to leave for the Caribbean to go to the passport office. I stood at the counter, stunned, as the passport clerk told me there was no way she could verify my information that quickly.

"Listen, lady. I'm in a whole lot of trouble, and I need to get on that plane," I said as calmly as I could.

I had given them all the paperwork, which included a letter from Dr. Mash explaining that I was going to be a test subject in a drug rehabilitation experiment. Even without the paperwork, one look at me should have conveyed a lot. I was sweating profusely, smelled awful, and was back to my regular active-addiction weight of a hundred and twenty-five pounds.

The clerk looked at me, then looked at the paperwork and said, "Come back tomorrow at 9:00 A.M. You should still be able to make your plane."

twenty-seven

In which the boy sets out to become a man,
but does a terrible job of it

COLLEGE DIDN'T REALLY agree with me. I picked what was possibly the worst school at which to be a controversial artist. It was hard to get attention at the San Francisco Art Institute, without either threatening your own life or someone else's.

Even getting naked had lost its shock value and was considered a legitimate genre. I saw naked people yelling at their parents. Naked people rubbing themselves with meat. Naked people sewing their fingers together. Naked people laughing . . . crying . . . masturbating . . . giving birth to Hello Kitty dolls . . . Anything you could do while naked that hadn't been done before. At first it made me uncomfortable, but when that wore off, I found myself annoyed at how predictable it all was.

Because I had zero interest in getting naked or threatening people, I decided the next best thing might be to actually learn how to draw and paint. My technical skills were extremely limited, but when I asked for help, my teachers were hesitant to offer it.

"Is there a trick to drawing hands I don't know about?" I asked my drawing teacher while I struggled with a sketch of what appeared to be the offspring of a squid and a lobster claw, coming out of a shirt cuff.

"There are techniques, but if I showed them to you, your hands would look like everyone else's. Now, what makes your drawing so amazing is that I can guarantee you will never see another hand like that. I could show you how to draw a hand, but I think it would be more valuable to keep following your own path," he said, moving on to the next student.

Fucking lazy bastard, I thought to myself.

With few exceptions, I encountered the same attitude among most of the teachers.

"What I find most intriguing about these paintings is that none of the subjects are showing their hands," my painting teacher said to me during a critique. "All of them are hiding them in their pockets, behind their back, or off the canvas, which raises an intriguing question. What are they trying to hide?"

"That I can't paint hands," I answered.

"Perfect. Does everyone see how Oran was able to use his limitations to make an otherwise uninteresting portrait a work of art?" she asked. As far as I could tell, the only thing they were teaching us was the art of the underhanded compliment.

FOR THE FIRST couple of years, I lived in Berkeley with Eli and some other friends, and commuted to San Francisco at six in the morning to sweep up the school halls for ten dollars a day. At night I delivered pizza, or drove a limousine, often not making it back home till two or three to get a few hours of sleep, then waking up to do it again. Jack was helping me out with eight hundred bucks a month, but tired of the painting instructors, I had switched over to photography and film, which used up all of the money he sent me.

What little free time I had between work and school was spent messing around on a drum set that one of Eli's coworkers had donated to the house along with an electric bass. On the occasion that Eli and I were home at the same time, we would attempt to make something resembling music. Playing the drums was the only respite I got from the endless running back and forth between work and school.

At school, I mostly kept to myself, talking only to Aaron and only if there wasn't anyone else within earshot. I would have liked to make some new friends, but I had no idea how to go about it. I had been hanging out with the same group of people for so long that we almost had our own language.

Aaron wasn't very good at this business of meeting people either, but he was better than me. Through his efforts, we collectively made one new friend, Sam. According to Sam, who was from Baltimore, he had been a full-blown alcoholic since he was twelve. We met him when he was trying to cut down on his drinking by taking acid every day. He was basically an eighteen-year-old white version of Redd Foxx, and, like me, he didn't need to use big words when critiquing art.

"That shit is wack," he'd say, looking at yet another self-portrait of some kid glamorously shooting heroin.

"Yup, that shit sucks," I agreed. Sam and I understood each other just fine without using *didactic, juxtaposition, tension, balance, referential, color temperature.* . . . Like Sam said, the shit was fucking wack.

After getting into an irreparable argument with one of my roommates in Berkeley over my inability to do the dishes, Sam and I started living together in San Francisco. If Sam was Redd Foxx, then I was an eighteen-year-old Walter Matthau, and our apartment was like a spinoff show of *The Odd Couple* and *Sanford and Son.* Sam hung a couple of pieces of cardboard from the ceiling of the living room to give himself the feel of having some personal space, and I took the room in back with no windows.

Living with Sam, who was far more of a mess than I ever was, turned me into more of the Jack Lemmon character. I was constantly nagging at Sam to do the dishes, clean his room, stop drinking so much, and eat something besides ramen and Cheetos. I'd never seen real alcoholism before, and I hadn't read much into the fact that Sam had turned down three much nicer apartments because the corner stores had carded him.

Partly to set an example for Sam, and partly because I was so broke I was eating oatmeal three times a day, I rarely drank. The limousine company I was working for was shut down by the city for operating illegally, and I was lucky I hadn't been arrested myself. The boss rented out the cars for seventy dollars a night, and we would drive around the city trying to lure customers by offering them a bottle of wine, or by undercutting the cabs. The penalty if caught was a two-thousand-dollar fine, and two months in jail. Eli found the job first and warned me of the possible consequences, but when I made three hundred and fifty bucks my first night on the job, I decided it was worth the risk. Unfortunately, that night had been a fluke, and afterward I rarely came away with more than forty or fifty dollars. When that ended, I was so exhausted from hustling all the time that I decided to stop working and went down to the welfare office and got on food stamps. To cut down on art supplies, I invested in a pair of bolt cutters and started breaking into the Fotomat Dumpsters, where I found far stranger pictures than I could have ever come up with on my own.

At this point, Jack had just bought a three-million-dollar mansion. I took a perverse pride in the fact that I was now technically a welfare recipient, and I relished the irony that my dad's books were not only on the bestseller list for almost two years running, but that they were in the self-help category.

Chronic destitution didn't agree with me, and I became a depressed hermit, spending days at a time in my windowless room. My only human interactions were nagging Sam to get his shit together.

The hermit's life came to an abrupt end when summer came and I was cut off from Jack's money. Instead of looking for work, I usually let Eli do the job hunting and then I would use him as a reference. This time I followed him to a little building downtown where they handed me a walkie-talkie, a bright orange helmet, and a moped, and sent me around the city delivering packages. It was demeaning work since we got shit on by everyone, from the doormen to the mail clerks to our dispatchers, even the bike messengers treated us with disdain. The moped they assigned to me was so loud that it set off every car alarm I passed, and at least two times a week I would get pulled over and handed tickets for noise pollution.

The bike messengers did seem a lot cooler than us, and after a few months I bought an old Schwinn cruiser, which wasn't very functional as a means of taking packages around the city, but it was hipper than the moped. For the first six weeks I rode my bike nine hours a day, slept for twelve, and woke up so sore I could barely move. After getting through that, I found that I had more than enough energy to work, practice my drums afterward, and go out drinking till two in the morning, which I could now afford. I hadn't done anything in the way of physical exercise since I was thirteen and was amazed at how much it helped my mood.

Eli was now living in a gigantic loft space in the Mission District with a bunch of artists and musicians who didn't mind if we played music there. We picked up where we had left off with our funk jams, and a couple of his roommates decided to join in. Before I had any business performing for an audience, these guys set up a show at a café and I found myself playing in front of a few hundred people. The show was much more fun than any art opening I had been to, and I met twice as many people as I had in the, by now, two years I'd attended art school.

That band ended after only one more show, but Eli and I found two guitar players and started doing a weekly Sunday-afternoon gig at a bar called the Chameleon. The two other guys were virtuosos, and Eli was a quick learner, but I was out of my league and began losing interest in school, as my focus shifted to practicing drums. We went by a different band name every week until settling on Sparkle Cock. Our shows were always hit or miss, since the concept was that we didn't write songs or rehearse. We also asked other musicians to sit in with us, including my mom, who had no idea what she was in for when she came to check us out. Mom, who had started playing piano again, was enrolled in classes at a community college in Oakland with Pharoah Sanders, who had played with John Coltrane back in the day.

"You mean he's teaching the class?" I asked her when she told me about it on the phone.

"No. He's a student. You've got to get down here, man. I mean, how often do you get to see your mom play with Pharoah Sanders?"

When I went to her next class, I was surprised to see that the drummer was a kid named Tre Cool, whom I had gone to hippie camp with. He was now playing in stadiums with his band Green Day. It was pretty impressive watching my mom keep up with those guys, so I knew she wouldn't have a problem keeping up with us.

"Are you kidding? What do you expect me to do up there?" she asked when I told her she was going to join us for the second set.

"You know. Do that Cecil Taylor shit. Go nuts," I told her.

"But I hate that stuff. Anyone can do it," she responded.

"Then do it," I said, grabbing her by the hand and leading her up to the stage.

Before we even had a chance to start, she began banging on the Chameleon's decrepit, upright piano as hard as she could with her fists. When we joined in, she moved on to using her forearms and knees, and by the end of the set, she had climbed up on the piano and was jumping up and down on the keyboard.

D EPENDING ON HOW one looked at it, I either had amazing or terrible luck with girls. Considering I never approached them and ran away whenever they tried to talk to me, it was something of a miracle that I got laid at all. Of course, it had only happened once in the three years since I'd been in high school. Just like the first time, the girl took all the initiative, and I had been drinking enough to go along with it. That ended after our second date, when she locked herself in my bathroom and was screaming at the top of her lungs that she was going to slit her wrists. I had just worked my first day as a bike messenger and, exhausted, kept falling asleep while we were messing around in my room.

The next thing I knew, Sam was shaking me awake, and she was yelling and crying from the bathroom. We had moved from our basement apartment to a second-floor flat in the Mission. After failing to reason with her, I climbed out on the fire escape and scaled the side of the building to see if I needed to call 911, but she had apparently just done the whole thing to get my attention. If anything, that experience only made me more afraid of women, and I continued avoiding them for a while after that.

There were, however, two girls I was able to talk to. Joan, whom I had been roommates with in Berkeley, was nonthreatening because she had a boyfriend. The other was Joan's friend Jibz, the first girl I had ever had a crush on, when I was at summer camp. The first time I saw Jibz again I recognized her immediately. She looked almost exactly the same as she had when we were kids, except that she was two and a half feet taller. I had tagged along with Joan, who was going to meet her for coffee. I had barely managed to introduce myself when she said, "I remember you! You were that amazing juggler kid who was too cool to talk to anyone else."

I didn't know what to say to that. Just seeing her again made me so anxious I couldn't think straight, so I just nodded dumbly and asked her if she still kept in touch with any of our old camp mates. It was amazing to see how little I had changed since I was nine, at least when it came to interacting with girls. I was still attracted to the same one, and I was still hiding my nervousness by acting too cool and aloof to talk to her. My side of the conversation was so forced and awkward that I assumed she must have thought I was an idiot, and probably hated me.

"Well. Hey, it's good to run into you," I said as we were leaving.

"Yeah. It's really great to see you again. We should hang out again soon," she said.

"Sure" was all I managed.

Unfortunately, I was only able to get over my fear of talking to her after she started dating Eli, at which point she no longer seemed as scary. When she broke up with Eli a year or so later, I got nervous again, until she started seeing another guy. By that time I had convinced her she should go to the Art Institute, so we were hanging out almost every day. When she broke up with that boyfriend, I decided that for the first time in my life, I was going to take some initiative.

I just didn't know what taking initiative meant. I had been told as a kid that opening doors for women was sexist. That pulling out chairs, waiting for them to get out of elevators, and paying for dinner were all sexist customs. From these lessons I inferred that asking a girl on a date or even having sexual thoughts was sexist, and I believed that if I so much as touched a girl, let alone leaned in for a kiss, she would produce a whistle out of nowhere and I would be branded as a predator for the rest of my life. It was a tricky situation, and the only option I could think of was to win her over with reason.

"You know, we both have a similar sense of humor, and we're interested in the same stuff," I told her awkwardly after class one day. "And, well, I've been into you ever since I first met you, and just the fact that I'm still into you . . . well, it feels like it's meant to be," I continued before realizing that what I was saying was a thousand times creepier than simply asking her to go to the movies. "Uh, what I mean is that . . . after ten years, it's amazing that we both ended up doing the same kinds of things, you know?"

Remarkably, after all that, she agreed to give it a try. I was ecstatic. She was the one thing missing in my life, and now everything would be perfect. That was my thinking anyway. I didn't realize that, without some kind of hopeless desperation over a girl, I had no idea who I was. And when I started dating Jibz, a central part of my identity just disappeared.

By now, I had moved out of my apartment with Sam, and into a much nicer place down the street with a guy I knew from school, and his friend Suzy. Whenever Jibz came over to hang out, I found that I was just as nervous around her as I ever had been before, and I couldn't come up with anything to talk about. Jibz seemed nervous, too, which was rare, and her visits were always extremely awkward until I pressed the play button on my VCR, giving us an hour and a half of relief.

That didn't stop me from being devastated when I didn't hear from her for three days. God forbid I call her and possibly give the impression that I was obsessed. When I saw her walking down the street at two thirty in the morning while on my way home from a bar, I was instantly struck sober. I noticed an almost imperceptible pause when she saw me, like she'd been caught. I knew in that moment that it was over, that it probably had been for three days.

I didn't want to talk to her, and she didn't seem too excited to see me, but one of us would have had to cross the street to avoid the situation.

"Hey," I said.

"Hi."

"How have you been?"

"Fine," she answered. I was hoping she would voluntarily tell me what she was doing walking in the opposite direction of her house so late at night, but she just stood there.

"What are you up to?" I asked before I could stop myself. I already knew the answer was going to be bad, because she certainly wasn't headed to my place.

"Oh. I'm just going to a friend's house." She was nervous; I was nervous; neither of us knew what to say.

"Okay, I'll see you later then," I responded to get out of the situation. But the situation came with me. I went from being angry for a few days into a full-blown depression for months. We shared almost all of the same friends, so it was impossible to avoid her, and seeing her amplified my feelings a thousand percent.

I F THERE WERE anyone whom I would never talk to about anything important, it would be my grandma. We spoke to each other once a month, but I always limited it to talking about the weather or the latest show at the museum. I never brought up my personal life, figuring she wouldn't understand what I was going through. I was so consumed with thinking about Jibz, though, that I couldn't even make small talk.

"Why do you think I keep myself so busy?" she asked me after I told her I was heartbroken. I knew she wouldn't understand.

"I said, why do you think I run around all the time, going to book clubs, throwing cocktail parties, painting. . . . Why do you think I do more now that I'm retired than I ever did?"

Grandma did do an incredible amount of stuff for an old woman. She had recently sent me pictures of herself hanging off a cliff in Italy, cutting her own piece of marble out of the mountain.

"I don't know," I said, annoyed. "I figured it was because you liked all that stuff. I thought that's what people did when they got old."

"It's because if I don't keep myself busy, my head starts saying terrible things to me."

"Really? Mine, too." I had thought she was just a ditsy old social butterfly, immune to bad feelings.

"I started sculpting marble because I needed the sound of the drill to overpower the nonsense in my head. You'll get through this, but you have to keep yourself busy."

It wasn't much, but it felt like the first real connection I'd ever made with her. She had fooled us all into thinking she was just a vapid, shallow old woman. A week later Mom called me to tell me she had been found dead on her kitchen floor.

"What?" I'd heard what my mom had said, but the shocking part to me was not that she died. That's what old people did. The shocking part was that I didn't feel anything. I had never experienced anyone dying, but I had seen others go through it and I had always thought there was a way you were supposed to feel.

"Kyle and I are flying to Florida. Do you want to come?"

"Uh. Should I come?" I had never been to a funeral.

"Grandma expressly said in her will that she didn't want a funeral. That she wanted to be remembered as full of life, but her friends are having one anyway. I want to respect her wishes, but it won't look too good if I don't show up. I'll just tell them you couldn't get out of school, okay?"

"Okay," I said.

I wasn't aware how much time passed when I was startled by my roommate Suzy's voice. Even then, it took a moment to realize she was talking to me.

"Hey, are you okay?" Suzy asked.

"Yeah, I'm fine," I said, getting my bearings.

"Because you've just been standing there, holding the phone for like ten minutes."

"I have? No, I'm fine. I was just thinking," I said, hanging up the phone. I wasn't thinking though, I was waiting. Waiting to feel the thing you're supposed to feel when your grandma dies.

"Are you sure? 'Cause you don't look fine," she said.

"Seriously. Everything's all right," I said, deciding in that moment to take a walk before going to class.

Unaware of how I got there, I found myself seven miles from home, standing on a cliff overlooking the Pacific Ocean and what used to be the Sutro Bath House. I sat there for a while before walking through the Presidio to the Golden Gate Bridge. I could have used a drink, but by the time I got back to the Mission it was late and all the bars had closed. I had been gone some twelve hours, aimlessly walking around, thinking about my grandma. I still hadn't figured out why I wasn't feeling anything.

JUST BECAUSE I wasn't feeling sad about my grandma's death didn't mean I wasn't going to use her as an excuse. School had become even more of a drag since I was always afraid that I was going to run into Jibz, and I was having trouble making art anyway. I also found out that Grandma had left a will and that Kyle and I had inherited two hundred and fifty thousand dollars each. Even though I was still collecting food stamps, and we wouldn't see the money until we were forty, I was now the thing I despised more than anything in the whole world: a trust-fund kid.

I didn't plan on dropping out of college but somehow, whenever I left the house to go to school, I would end up at my practice space instead. Eventually I gave up any pretense of going to class and spent my days playing the drums.

Though Kyle and I didn't have access to the trust, ten thousand dollars in interest showed up in the mail, and I decided then that I needed to take a semester off. I spent sixteen hundred dollars on a beautiful drum set and hid away in my rehearsal studio. Like my grandmother, I needed something louder than oil paints to stop the fucking racket in my head.

twenty-eight

*Chronicles the journey to a faraway isle in
search of the mystical god Iboga, who reveals
the identity of our subject's true nemesis to
be none other than himself*

WAITING FOR MY connecting flight in Puerto Rico, I went outside to smoke a cigarette and realized that they might search me
on my way back in to the terminal and find my remaining supply of
methadone. I couldn't bring myself to throw the pills out, or see them get
confiscated, so I decided to take all six pills at once.

When the flight attendants finally managed to wake me up in St.
Kitts, the plane was empty and they were already halfway through cleaning it. I was so out of it that two of them had to help me walk to the
customs booth.

The people in Miami had given me specific instructions to tell the
customs officials about exactly where I was going and why I was there,
but the piece of paper I had written the information on had doubled as a
page marker for the eleven-hundred-page book I brought with me and
subsequently left on the plane when the attendants dragged me out. It
was bittersweet losing that book. On the one hand, it wasn't looking like
I could get past these guys without it. On the other hand, I had been carrying around that five-pound monstrosity for the last six months and I
was only around page eight hundred, and at least a hundred of those
pages had been footnotes. Even the footnotes had footnotes. It was one
of those things you don't realize is such a pain in the ass until it's gone. I
should have lost that thing a long time ago.

I really didn't want to walk back to the plane to get it since I wasn't sure I could make it that far without lying down and taking a nap on the marble floor, but the customs guy was serious.

"Please esplain to me again how it is dat ya come all da way here, and know not where ya going?" the officer asked, speaking a little slower this time. I thought this was an English-speaking island, but I could barely understand him.

"Because I've never been here before," I answered. "How would I know where I'm going if I've never been there?" This explanation sounded logical to me, but he just shook his head and called a few more guards over to help figure it out.

It was all too confusing. I just wanted to lie down, when a guy showed up and asked me if I was Oran and said something to the customs guards that got them to let me through. I think he tried to talk to me as we drove to the place I would be staying the next ten days, but I couldn't understand him either, and once I sat down in the car I started nodding out again. Luckily I was the last to arrive, so I didn't have to meet or talk to anyone. The driver showed me to my room and I passed out with my clothes on, only to be woken up a few minutes later by a woman holding a vial of blue liquid.

"Hello. I'm Dr. Mash, and you must be Oran." I couldn't remember ever being this high in my life without having some cocaine to keep me awake, but I managed to sit up and say hello to her.

"Now we don't want you getting sick before your treatment, so we need you to drink this. Judging by what you told us, this should be enough liquid morphine to tide you through the night," she said, handing me the vial.

"I actually think I'm all right for the moment. Can we wait and see how I feel tomorrow?" I asked, without explaining that I was on six days' worth of methadone.

"Actually, no. I don't want you waking up in a few hours going through withdrawal. So drink this now, and we can talk about it tomorrow after you've gotten some rest."

I drank it just to get her to leave.

It was late in the afternoon when I woke up and wandered out of the little cabin I was in. I was still way too high to be engaging with other people, and I instinctively resorted to my teenage stay-the-fuck-away-from-me tactic of walking around hunched over while looking at the ground with a pained facial expression. It wasn't all feigned; I really did feel terrible, and it wasn't just the drowsy, nauseated feeling of having way too many opiates in my system.

As far as I could tell, this was my last chance. If this shit didn't fix me, I didn't think anything could. My Internet research on ibogaine beforehand looked positive, but so did much of the research on AA, NA, rapid opiate detox, rational recovery, harm reduction, and every other fucking thing I had tried. I had looked into all that shit, and all of it claimed to be the thing that worked.

The first four days we were there were for . . . I don't know what exactly. It all seemed kind of thrown together, but they gave us a bunch of literature to look through about the history of ibogaine. We learned that it was first discovered by the Pygmies of West Africa. The Pygmies then gave it to a few local tribes who went on to start an offshoot of Christianity based on their experiences with the drug. Since their experiences were always different, the Bible had become an amorphous, ever-changing, and constantly amended text to reflect new experiences and insights from village to village. One anthropologist who studied this phenomenon described his experience, which involved lying on a dirt floor while a priest alternately fed him the drug and punctured holes in his skin with a meat hook. The priest knew he had given the anthropologist enough ibogaine when he stopped flinching. He brought his story and the drug back to Europe with him, and by the early 1980s, a junkie in New Jersey got ahold of some and took it for no other reason than to experience a new high. When he came down from it, he realized that he wasn't experiencing any withdrawal symptoms from heroin. The heroin withdrawal never came, and he never used dope again. He then gave it to seven more junkies, five of whom also quit doing heroin after taking the ibogaine. *But what about the other two?* I wondered.

So far there was documentation of only a few hundred people taking this stuff to combat addiction. My official identity as a participant in this round of treatment was Ibogaine Human Test Subject #121. It sounded like science fiction, but Dr. Mash used this numbering to differentiate us from her Simian Test Subjects back in her lab at the University of Miami.

We were also told to get rid of any expectations we might have about our "journey," as we were told to call it. A number of people had been unsuccessfully lobbying the FDA for approval to use this drug in the United States, but the government was afraid it might instigate another 1960s-type movement like acid had done, so Dr. Mash and her crew of counselors were very adamant about distancing ibogaine from the word *trip* or anything else that might suggest a relationship to LSD.

In my free time, I sat outside chain-smoking and drinking this unbelievable grapefruit soda called Ting. Someone needed to start importing this shit to America. There were eleven of us, plus a few staff members, and I just wasn't in the mood to talk to any of them. Other than one of the counselors, no one seemed too interested in talking to me either. I had been under the impression that this stuff was used to treat heroin addicts, but there was only one other opiate addict there. They were mostly alcoholics, two of whom were back for a second try, and there was even one woman there who was hoping this would treat her codependency issues. I made a minor attempt to reach out in solidarity to the other opiate addict, but he was a Republican doctor from Texas who had become addicted to pain pills and saw no connection whatsoever between his addiction to morphine and mine to heroin.

One thing was for sure; we were all antsy as hell to get this fucking "journey" going. None of us had come up with twelve thousand dollars to fly over here and talk. We came to get cured, and the sooner the better. Dr. Mash had been lowering my dose of liquid morphine, and although I wasn't in full-blown withdrawal, I was a long way from being comfortable. Unfortunately, only four of us could go on our journeys at a time.

For whatever reason, I was in the last group to go in, so for two days I watched with nervous anticipation as the other clients came prancing out of their "journeys." They weren't supposed to talk about it, but they were so jazzed up about having hung out with their dead grandfathers or finding out that the person who molested them was actually a human being with feelings just like the rest of us that the staff couldn't shut them up.

On day two, though, I watched as the doctor from Texas came out shaking and white as a ghost. He went straight to his room, and we didn't see him for a couple of days. The other three in his group were acting as if they had all won a game show.

I wasn't allowed to eat that night, which wasn't much of an issue since I was hardly able to eat anyway. I couldn't sleep either. I just tossed and turned till the sun came up and sat on the porch and smoked cigarettes. Around 7:00 A.M., the door to the clinic opened, and someone tentatively walked out and bent down to touch the grass. He was followed by a woman, who walked over to a flowerbed and stared at it for a while before puking up a small amount of white paste and returning to the clinic. Two others came out and just wandered around kind of checking things out. Then I watched and smoked as one of the staff members started to bring the next batch in one at a time. He came to get me last.

I WAS NERVOUS walking into the clinic. It was a cabin just like the others, but black plastic covered all the windows, and the lighting had been reduced to near total darkness. I was led to a room with three side-by-side hospital beds. Next to each bed was an EKG and an IV rack. Two other clients were already attached to their machines and were lying on their backs wearing sleeping masks and listening to headphones. Another thing we had learned while waiting to get our cure was that no one was very excited about being hooked up to machines while they went through their "journey."

"Thank you for calling it a 'journey,' but you're still thinking about ibogaine as if it were LSD. It's not. I promise you. Not one person has ever had an issue with it," Dr. Mash said. As much as they told us it wasn't going to be like LSD, it still seemed like a sterile fucking environment to be going through something like this.

In total silence, so as not to disturb the others, I was directed to lie down while the nurse hooked me up to everything. I stared into the darkness above, waiting for Dr. Mash to administer this drug, which I was suddenly having second thoughts about. All I could think about was that Republican doctor, who was still, a day later, in his room crying. The guy couldn't have been more different from me, and the general consensus was that his "hard journey" had more to do with him being an asshole than anything else, but I began wondering if it couldn't have something to do with him being an opiate addict like me. Then Dr. Mash came out holding a tray with six enormous capsules.

I had to take them one at a time, following each with a big gulp of water. The nurse then put a mask on me, placed a pair of headphones over my ears, and pressed play on the CD player. While I waited for the "journey" to come on, I was expecting Kenny G or Muzak or something. Instead, they played a song I vaguely remembered from high school, when the Goth kids decided to listen to something other than The Cure or The Smiths. It featured a bagpipe, what sounded like a Native American drum, an African shaker-type instrument, a Middle Eastern dumbek, and thank God, no lyrics. The next song had a similar world-music vibe.

The "journey" didn't exactly "come on." No matter how much the doctors insisted we let go of our preconceived notions of psychedelics, my high school acid trips were all I had to go on. I was expecting some kind of gradual transition from reality into whatever was in store, but when the third song started, the shit hit me like a baseball bat to the head, in perfect unison with the first note. Again the drums sounded Native American, but the music didn't seem to have a source, as though it were omnipresent. I imagined it could be heard at the same thunderous volume throughout the universe, and each note hit me like a ten-foot wave. I remembered bodysurfing on a particularly rough day at the beach; massive waves slammed me to the ground continuously. Getting sucked under for the fiftieth time, I made a split-second decision not to fight it and let my body go completely limp. I was tossed head over heels every which way, but I didn't get slammed onto the floor as I had before. This was a similar feeling, but I felt more like a pinball getting knocked around in space at unbelievable speeds every time the universe played another note on its bagpipe, pan flute, French horn, or koto.

I tried to cast aside my cynicism about this ethnic hodgepodge of world music made by "enlightened" white folks and attempted to relax and enjoy the interaction between the harpsichord and didgeridoo. As soon as I did that, I found I was able to navigate a little better or at least trick myself into thinking that I had some control over this bizarre free fall through space and time.

That song ended, and I was still floating in space, but there was an almost deafening hum that rose and fell at a slow but steady rate. When the next song started, I could no longer hear individual instruments or see the specific shapes, patterns, and colors they formed. Instead the colors and sounds coalesced into a visual scene.

I found myself standing in a desert wilderness. Possibly the Southwest, maybe Australia or Africa? It didn't matter. Something told me that this was long before there was an America, or Australia, or any concept of progress, or borders, or time. I stood there forever, waiting for someone or something to come along and tell me the secret or give me the message I was supposed to get. The sun came and went, but time didn't move forward. It just went around in a circle.

I had to take a piss.

I'm not sure why I didn't whip it out right there and piss on the ground. Maybe out of consideration? In any case, I began walking toward a nearby bush. Halfway there, I noticed that the desert landscape was beginning to fade, until it looked as if it were going to disappear altogether. I didn't give it too much thought. I needed to get to that bush quickly so I wouldn't piss in the loincloth I was wearing. As I got closer, the bush transformed into a hospital bed floating in the middle of space. I climbed in it and reached up to take off my sleeping mask.

The light in the room was blinding. I had to squint as I threw my legs over the side of the bed. My sight adjusted quickly, and I could see the two other figures in their beds. God only knew what was really going on with them. We were told to never try to get out of bed without the nurse, but she was slumped over in a chair. I just wanted to take my piss and get back to the desert scene as soon as possible. I was worried I would miss the person who was supposed to bring me the message while I was in the bathroom. I disconnected myself from the EKG machine, rolled the IV stand around so the cord wouldn't get caught on the bed, and stood up to walk to the bathroom.

My leg didn't do what it was told, though. It came up when I leaned forward to take a step, but for some reason it didn't go back down to catch me. I reached out to grab the IV stand and catch my balance, but my arms weren't following directions either. I fell down and knocked over the IV stand, waking the nurse, who quickly ran over to help and, with some effort, got me back on the bed. She kept shushing me as I tried unsuccessfully to apologize. My mouth was doing the same thing as the rest of my body. My brain was sending it very clear signals, but I could hear my voice coming out like mush. The nurse got me one of those old-person walkers, and, with her help, I was able to get to the bathroom, where she insisted that I sit down on the toilet since she didn't want to have to pick me up again.

I didn't like it in there. It was way too bright, and staring at my hairy ivory-white legs made me sick to my stomach. But I could tell that there was a vital message here in the bathroom that I desperately needed to find. My pale legs, the jet-black hairs sticking out of them, the sterile bathroom, the window covered in dark plastic, the bottle of liquid disinfectant hand soap, the plunger. Every object in the bathroom was vibrating at its own frequency, but coming together as a whole to create an overwhelming hum that was coming from everywhere and nowhere. The key I was looking for was somehow hidden in all these things, but I couldn't find it. Sitting on the toilet to take a piss seemed extremely symbolic of something, but I couldn't for the life of me figure out of what. I needed to get back to the desert and try to get some more information.

With the help of the walker I was able to stand and pull up my sweatpants all by myself, and was even doing a slow but okay job of making my way to the door, when I caught my reflection in the mirror, and stopped dead in my tracks. Staring back at me was an ashy-looking dead person. I could make it move, but there was no sign of life behind it, just gray flesh with a week's worth of stubble sticking out of it. I wasn't so much shocked as fascinated that every inanimate object in the room was vibrantly pulsing with some kind of inner life, while the face looking back at me—the only living thing in the room—appeared dead. I leaned in real close to see if there was anything in my eyes . . . a spark . . . a message . . . a hidden meaning. . . . All I saw was nothing.

The nurse came in before I had a chance to get too deep into thinking about the mirror. She was clearly alive, colors and vibrations flying off her like a sprinkler system.

"Now, whach you lookin fo in dat mirra?" she chuckled. "Come now, and hush yo'self, fo you bother dem othas." I barely understood the nurse through her heavy Caribbean accent, but I had a pretty good idea what that chuckle meant. Our housekeeper, Laurel, had made the same sound whenever she laid eyes on me. *You white folks sho is crazy* was how I translated it, and I couldn't have agreed more.

When she put the headphones back on and I closed my eyes, I expected to be back in the desert, but the desert was gone. I would never get to meet whomever was supposed to give me the message. Instead I'm in a basement at the Art Institute watching what appears to be a student art film. It's a loop of a fast zoom-in on a five-year-old kid sitting on a set of stairs staring vacantly at the camera. The film loops over, and over, and over, and over, and the kid looks so sad, incomprehensibly sad. I can feel the sadness, and I know what he feels like because it's me. No big revelation there. We were told we would probably confront scenes from the past, but why is he so fucking sad?

I get up and walk toward the screen. I want to see the kid's eyes, but the closer I get, the more I can feel the sadness coming from him. I realize too late that, instead of looking at the kid's eyes, I should get the fuck out of there and go looking for some ancient Celts, or wise elders, or wood nymphs . . . or whomever else I'm supposed to meet in a psychedelic journey. It's too late, however. His gaze controls me, and I can't escape. I get closer, hoping my shadow will block out the image coming from the projector, along with incredible sadness that's coming from him, but this movie doesn't work that way. It just keeps looping, and, as I expect, the kid's eyes are the same ones I just saw in the bathroom mirror.

The eyes suck me in, and now I'm sitting on the stairs watching, trying to figure it all out, as new scenes loop before me. They're no longer film loops, though, and I can't connect any of it. A mushroom cloud, then me landing on my bloody knees while attempting to ride my new unicycle. All I can do is watch as my knees get bloodier every time the loop repeats. Then a new scene starts creeping: a mass grave with hundreds of rotting bodies in it. Small dark bodies with huge bellies, and the deafening sound of buzzing flies. Then I'm in a car with my mom trying to pronounce the word XING underneath the two kids on the street sign that we've now passed at least fifty times. I can't figure it out for the life of me, no matter how many chances I get when the loop starts again, and again, and again . . . but she was so proud of me when I figured out YIELD. Then a stranger is handing me a twenty-dollar bill in the bathroom airport and telling me I am a good whistler. Then I'm trying to pop a zit on my back. I get the zit, and it pops over and over, zooming in, leading into more weird nonsense. *What the fuck is this shit? What's the fucking relationship? Why don't I get it? The answer has to be here,* I'm thinking.

I'm now desperately trying to figure it out. It's becoming unbearable. A neglected Big Wheel . . . stepping on a cockroach . . . husking corn . . . none of it makes any sense, but the more I try to figure it out, the darker it becomes. Rows of carcasses hanging from meat hooks . . . open wounds . . . pork rinds . . . unrecognizable gelatinous ooze, rotting fish . . . all of it looping . . . all of it throbbing. I no longer possess a physical form, but have become free-floating anxiety without a body to absorb it or a brain to rationalize it. And it occurs to me that there could be a way out.

People had died on this shit before, so it could happen again, I reasoned. I could stand anything for a certain period of time, but there was no time here. None. I couldn't count the moments of eternity I had already been through or the moments that passed so quickly as to almost go unnoticed. I knew that the "journey" lasted twenty-four hours, but I didn't have a clue if it had been two hours or twenty-two. I start looking for a way out and . . .

. . . I find myself on a beach. An ugly-ass beach covered with lumps of tar. A bunch of tankers and off-shore oil wells dot the horizon. I look down to see a pair of scrawny nine-year-old legs sticking out of a pair of cutoff jeans. One of my feet is covered in a glob of tar. Turning my head, I see the school bus parked on the highway shoulder while cars and trucks whizz past it. Then, with no warning, I'm suddenly way out in the ocean, gasping for breath. I cut back to the beach, where I'm hopping around on one leg, trying to scrape the chunk of tar from my foot. It seems like a weird thing to do for someone who wants to kill himself, and then I'm back in the water trying to keep my head up. And then I'm back on the beach, this time trying to get the tar off my hands. The loops are unending, each one slightly different or displaced in time from the one before, and I realize it might take an eternity for me to die this way. Could I die in one loop and still be alive in the other? Fuck. Fuck. Fuck.

I start to sink. It feels good to stop struggling, and when I can no longer hold my breath, I exhale and watch the bubbles shoot up toward a distorted image of the sun. Just as quickly, I'm back on the beach looking for a rock to try to scrape off this nasty tar shit, which is now all over both my hands. I sink even further, keeping my eyes on the sun, before I rub my feet on a patch of sea grass, still unable to get the tar off. I'm just about to inhale when a shadow blocks the sun and an arm reaches down and grabs my hair. Then I'm back on the beach using a stick to try to clean my foot. Then the hand violently yanks me upward, and it fucking hurts as it rips out a bunch of my hair. It hurts just as much in the second loop, and then in the third, and then I surface, and gasp, and try not to inhale water.

It's Denis. He's trying to get his arm around me, but he's not being very gentle about it. He's squeezing me so fucking hard.

"Fuck, man. It hurts," I try to tell him between breaths.

"It's going to be okay," he says, but it's not Denis, it's my old dance teacher, Roger.

"It's not okay," I tell him, but I'm talking to Anna, who saved my life in high school.

"It's going to be okay, Oran" is all she says before turning into my old heroin dealer, who turns into the woman who gave Kyle and me a ride home after we washed ashore in our little blow-up raft. Then my mom . . . Jake . . . Dr. Mash . . . Dawn . . . Inga . . . Eli . . . Mr. Lutkenhouse . . . Andy from The Farm turns into Andrew from the Pickle Family Circus . . . Heather . . . Eileen . . . All of them holding on to me so tightly it hurts, and then telling me it will be okay.

There is no sense or order to any of it. One moment, I'm almost at the shore; the next moment, I'm so far away it looks as though I'll never get back. There's always someone holding me, telling me I'm going to be okay. Some people I vaguely recognize (Dan Millman, my old trampoline teacher), some whom I fucking hate (Fred), some whom I don't know how I feel about (my dad), and some who have always been there and will always be there (Kyle, Aaron, Grandma). I just wish they would loosen their grip a little. Thom . . . Carroll Ono . . . Miguel . . . Mario and Snoo . . . Akbar Bey . . . Claudia and Helen . . . And there are people I've never even met getting thrown into the mix . . . Eric Dolphy . . . Ronald Reagan . . . Captain Beefheart . . . My

grandfather Arthur . . . Jay DeFeo . . . Al Jolson . . . Zora Neale Hurston
. . . Stu Martin . . . Diane Arbus . . . George Clinton . . . Dubuffet . . .
Eartha Kitt . . . Anton LaVey . . . Gibby Haynes . . . Lucille Ball . . . St.
Francis . . . Paul Bowles . . . Woody Allen . . . Malcolm X . . . and Audrey
Hepburn, whom I definitely don't want to let go of, until she turns into
Hitler.

"It's going to be okay," Hitler tells me, before morphing into Wavy
Gravy, who says the same thing.

I'm getting my breath back, and I'm not struggling so much anymore,
but I'm still trying to figure it all out. Hitler? Eartha Kitt? What the fuck?
The distance still varies back and forth without any rhyme or reason, but
I'm getting closer, and more people keep appearing to tell me it's going
to be okay. It's fucking endless, but they're finally starting to loosen their
grip on me.

And I'm real close, almost there, and Jibz says, "It's going to be okay,"
before letting go of me. I don't want her to let go, and I turn my head to
see her, but it's not her anymore. I'm looking at me, but bigger, older,
hairier. One of my eyebrows is higher than the other, and I've got three
distinct creases on my forehead.

"It's going to be okay," the older Oran tells me. "But you've got to do
this last part by yourself, little buddy. We're all waiting for you."

For some reason, I trust him. That it's going to be okay. I take a
couple of strokes toward the shore, and I feel my feet graze the sand on
the ocean floor. Everyone I've ever seen, or will see, is waiting for me on
the beach. Alive, dead, past, present. Even though I have reached the
shore, I still have to battle the fierce undertow from knocking me off my
feet and sucking me back out, until I eventually collapse exhausted on
the beach, the surf rocking me back and forth.

I'm watching the scene from above now, and I'm getting farther and
farther away, and I can see that everything on earth is in an impossibly
intricate balance, and the solar system is in balance, and the universe is
in balance. I don't know how it works, and I don't need to know, but I
know that it is.

And I can see myself, just as important and just as insignificant as
anything else, lying in the fetal position on a hospital bed, attached to an
EKG, an IV, and now I've got a catheter attached to my dick, which I
have no recollection of anyone putting there.

I open my eyes . . . squint . . . look around . . . pull the catheter out of
my sweatpants, which makes a loud suction pop, and I know with absolute certainty that I am exactly where I'm supposed to be.

epilogue

In which our speaker brings his audience
up to date

S O, ANYWAY, the ibogaine didn't end up being a cure exactly," I'm
saying to the crowd of nearly a hundred people who are staring at me
in the church basement. My anxiety is starting to fade, since I'm getting
so close to the end. "Because within half an hour of getting back to San
Francisco, I found myself in the bathroom of a Mexican restaurant getting high again. But what was weird was that the heroin didn't really work
anymore, and for the first time, I was able to put it down without being
locked up in a rehab. It was funny, because I had traveled halfway around
the world hoping to get some sort of cosmic message, but the message I
ended up with was the same shit people had been telling me for years:
that I needed to go to these meetings, and try to stay out of my head.

"So I started going to meetings. And, well, a lot has happened in the
last seven years. I moved to New York, which I always wanted to do. I got
back into playing music, which is still a huge part of my life. I've got a
relationship with my dad, and my mom and brother were just out here
visiting, and . . .

"Anyway, I recently started writing a more detailed version of my
story, and well . . . it's been fucking intense because it has meant going
back inside my head and reliving all that shit." I avoid looking up for fear
of being overwhelmed, but I hear a collective sigh fill the room.

"Yeah," I agree with them, as it had been a particularly tough week remembering some of the darker moments in my life. "But the weird thing is that I'm now seeing all these stories from a totally different perspective, and . . . you know, I've spent so much of my life blaming my parents for everything I went through, and for the first time—I think from writing about this stuff—I'm actually able to see that they really were doing the best they could, and—" Out of nowhere, an image comes into my head of my mom, and dad, and Kyle, frantically trying to lock the car doors on me when I'd walked out of that first rehab so long ago. I see the look on their faces, and I can't imagine what they must have been feeling as they drove away from me. Before I can stop it, something wells up in my chest, and I choke up right as I'm completing the second half of my sentence. "—that I'm sick of hating them. That I actually love these fucking people."

By now my face is contorted, and I'm unsuccessfully trying to hold back my tears in front of all these people (my worst nightmare come true). But even more frightening was hearing myself use the L-word in reference to my family. I have never said that in my life, and it freaks me out. It takes me a while to say anything after that, and the audience is totally silent while they wait for me to go on. I wipe my face off with my sleeve and say, "Holy shit! Where did that come from?"

I'm relieved to hear the crowd burst into laughter, and slowly I start to regain my composure.

"Man, I don't know where the fuck to go from there," I say, taking a moment to think. "I had this profound thing I wanted to say at the end, but I can't remember it . . . Oh yeah. A few weeks ago I heard this woman speaking—from this same chair actually—and she didn't know what to say, so she just started rattling off every twelve-step slogan she had ever heard. I've always kind of hated the slogans, and I was sitting in the back of the room, bored, and twitching in my seat, when she said one I had never heard before. Anyway, I think it describes my experience perfectly.

"She said, 'The only way out is through.' "

gratitude list

A LOT OF FOLKS WERE involved in helping me put these memories on paper, but none more than Beth Lisick. Without Beth's inspiration and guidance from the very beginning, this book would still just be a title floating around in my head.

To my editors Cassie Jones and Johnathan Wilber at William Morrow, I owe a tremendous amount of thanks for their tireless and enthusiastic involvement in turning my initial drafts into a readable manuscript. I would also like to thank my editor Charlotte Cole at Ebury Press, both for her insights and for making sure I stayed on track.

Without my agents Loretta Barrett and Nick Mollendor at LBB, I wouldn't be thanking anyone, and I am extremely grateful to them for taking on this project.

Writing a memoir wasn't exactly the easiest thing I have ever done, but it was a lot easier knowing I had the love and support of my parents.

Countless others helped me through various stages of this process, whether to listen to me moan or to offer me their feedback, but of special note are J. C. Morrison, Josh Korda, Inga Canfield, Luke Calzonetti, and Tim Dahl.

Finally, I want to thank all the people who made appearances in this book, and those I was unable to include. It goes without saying (but I'm going to say it anyway) that this would have been a very different story without all of you.